Dracula as
Absolute Other

ALSO OF INTEREST

EDITED BY SIMON BACON
AND KATARZYNA BRONK

*Growing Up with Vampires:
Essays on the Undead in Children's Media*
(McFarland, 2018)

Dracula as Absolute Other

The Troubling and Distracting Specter of Stoker's Vampire on Screen

SIMON BACON

McFarland & Company, Inc., Publishers
Jefferson, North Carolina

ISBN (print) 978-1-4766-7538-1
ISBN (ebook) 978-1-4766-3712-9

LIBRARY OF CONGRESS AND BRITISH LIBRARY
CATALOGUING DATA ARE AVAILABLE

Library of Congress Control Number 2019943403

© 2019 Simon Bacon. All rights reserved

No part of this book may be reproduced or transmitted in any form or by any means, electronic or mechanical, including photocopying or recording, or by any information storage and retrieval system, without permission in writing from the publisher.

On the cover: *clockwise from top* Christopher Lee in *Dracula AD*, 1972 (Warner Bros./Photofest); *30 Days Night*, 2007 (Lionsgate/Columbia); *Daybreakers*, 2009 (Lionsgate)

Printed in the United States of America

*McFarland & Company, Inc., Publishers
Box 611, Jefferson, North Carolina 28640
www.mcfarlandpub.com*

Acknowledgments

My deepest thanks to my two partners-in-crime for this project: Andy Boylan, who has probably watched and read more vampire texts than is healthy for one human being (see his blog on all things vampire film and books here: https://taliesinttlg.blogspot.com), and Teresa Cutler-Broyles, a truly Renaissance soul with an interest (and expertise) in everything, who is always ready to help (see https://www.cutler-broyles-editing.com). A million thanks to the always fabulous Mrs. Mine, without whose continual encouragement, help and patience nothing would get written, and to Seba and Majki for being … themselves. And finally, to Mam i Tata Bronk for your ongoing and much appreciated support.

Table of Contents

Acknowledgments — v

Introduction — 1

One. Undead Memories and Troubling Histories — 15

Two. The Land Beyond the Forest — 48

Three. The Trouble with Money — 80

Four. Violent Distractions — 111

Five. Distracting Technologies — 143

Filmography — 175

Chapter Notes — 179

Bibliography — 195

Index — 203

Introduction

This book is based on the idea that the Count in Bram Stokers *Dracula* embodies the absolute other of the late-Victorian society from which he emerged. This otherness is made up of many different aspects that encapsulate particular anxieties of that milieu which, due to their inherent nature as being socially abhorrent or abject in some way, trouble or distract those who come into contact with him. "Trouble" and "distract" are used here as they not only capture the uncertain psychic and physical effects produced on those in the vicinity of the fictional Dracula in the late 19th century but are also valid in relation to the rise in populism and the shift in global power in the real world in the early 21st century.

This idea of Dracula troubling and distracting those around him due to his absolute otherness is taken forward to examine what his continued re-creation in film says about Western society and the subsequent generations that recreate him. To this end we look at a number of films and television series, spanning the time from F.W. Murnau's *Nosferatu* (1922) to del Toro and Hogan's *The Strain* (2014–2017).[1] Ultimately this book is a timely examination of the ways in which anxieties around the declining British Empire in the 19th century mirror those in the orbit of the troubled American Empire in the early 21st, and their respective constructions of otherness.

Dracula as Absolute Other

Dracula's absolute otherness is made up of various forms of unacceptable difference which are felt to have the most damaging effects on the British Empire and its colonial endeavors, many of which would consequently be deemed to be also ungodly and/or against nature. Simultaneously, as seen in Stoker's novel, these kinds of otherness are often represented as being transgressively irresistible and tempting, as most graphically seen in the "voluptuous lips" of Dracula's "brides" (Stoker 1996, 41). These aspects of otherness, which this book explores, are all interrelated so that when taken together they resonate and affirm each other far more strongly than if they were represented individually. Unsurprisingly, the characteristics highlighted in certain films mentioned herein contain other aspects of otherness as well. The most obvious signifier of Dracula's difference is that he lives outside the Empire in an old, savage, and superstitious land—"beyond the forest"[2] (Stoker 1996, 259)—suggesting he is uncivilized, a heathen just like the many immigrants who swarmed to London in the 19th century. These immigrants were often seen to come from both the real and metaphorical East and were members of ethnic groups such as Jews (see Malchow 1996), Irish (see Valente 2002), reverse colonialists (see Arata 1996, Gibson 2006), or direct threats such as Russia (see Cain 2006). Contained within this is Dracula's distinctive foreignness in his dress, accent, and manners but also the way in which he quickly sheds his outward signs of otherness to be assimilated and pass unnoticed in the modern metropolis of London and beyond.

His construction as a monster from history, or as being the embodiment of a monstrous past, is equally important, and Stoker's novel makes much of his links to barbaric, uncivilized times. As such he is also the absolute other to modernity and civilization and all they infer, i.e., as expressions of British Imperial expansionism. In the novel, modernity, as the ongoing project of capitalism and industrialization, is very much seen in terms of science, technology, and communications and is symbolized through the use of transport, telegrams, photographs, and stenographs, to name but a few examples. Dracula is denied access to these platforms of communication even though his solicitor Jonathan Harker finds books in the Count's library to suggest he is aware of them.[3] Van Helsing claims this lack of sophistication is due to the vampire's "child-brain" (Stoker 1996, 348) and that his intelligence and cunning are more on the instinctual level rather than due to intellectual development. This also helps to distinguish the evolved and enlightened Victorian society, based on the idea of superior reason and intelligence, from the devolved "dark ages" of ignorance and superstition that preceded it—and which can also be seen to signify the original inhabitants of the colonies.[4] Dracula's means of communication are therefore created oppositionally, utilizing methods such as mesmerism,[5] mental telepathy and even bodily transformation, that are subsequently constructed as being supernatural and even demonic. In many ways, in fact, these methods are far more effective than the scientific methods used by his hunters but are inevitably tainted by their association with the vampire's inherent evil.

Alongside this, Count Dracula is constructed as the embodiment of a monstrous past. While Stoker does not make the connection between Vlad Țepeș, also known as Vlad the Impaler (1428/31–1476/77), and Dracula explicit, it is inferred that Dracula lived through and took part in the savage history and bloodletting that happened on the borders of Europe hundreds of years before the setting of the book. In many ways he is the traumatic memory of Europe's barbaric past come back to haunt the civilized 19th century and to return the continent to chaos under the rule of a bloodthirsty despot, as well as suggesting that the decline of the Empire will see it degenerating back into its feudal past. The vampire's immortality further intimates that it is a past that will never die, and if ignored and denied will constantly return to plague the present.

As an Old World Count, Dracula also represented the passing of the aristocracy in Britain who were predominantly seen as decadent and lazy and feeding off the youth and vigor of the Empire, and so were being replaced by the middle and professional classes.[6] These privileged and selfish vampires also held onto their wealth, keeping their old, dead money stored away and removed from the living and expansionist capitalist system (see Moretti 1988). The new social hierarchies which allowed men to strive for greater social recognition, however, had equally transgressive consequences, as seen in the New Women who saw themselves entitled to the same rights as men (see Senf 1988). Of course, such power in the hands of soft-bodied and weak-minded women was not allowable, and Stoker shows in his female characters Mina and Lucy that such females provide easy access points to the heart of the Empire, unable to resist the influence of Count Dracula who will inevitably turn them into his "bountiful wine-press" (Stoker 1996, 318) and even inside agents to his cause. The author of *Dracula* might specify females as particularly susceptible, but the vampire's excessive and transgressive sexuality brings both men and women under its spell. The Count sexually and physically possesses Jonathan Harker, which he later reinforces by doing the same to the young solicitor's wife, Mina. As such, even though represented as male and heterosexual, the vampire's sexuality, as an expression of his otherness, exceeds these normative bounds to embrace many other positions. Christopher Craft sees the Count as embodying uncontrollable homosexual desire (see Craft, 1994), while Sue Ellen Case sees him as performatively female (see Case 2000) which is taken further by Elaine Showalter who describes Dracula as a third thing (Showalter, 1992), neither male or female but something else; queer in both sexuality and nature. Over time of course this absolute otherness is constructed of many different qualities but even with that, the vampire Count still retains a "oneness" or singularity of identity that inevitably affects those around him/her/it/them.

Troubles and Distractions

Dracula manages to trouble and distract virtually all the other major characters in Stoker's novel. His nature as an absolute other makes his very presence in London inherently troubling to all those he comes into contact with, and his manner of insinuating himself into Harker's life and the circle of friends around his wife and Lucy Westenra is the essence of distraction as he makes everyone look elsewhere until it is too late.

In many ways, trouble and distract are quite similar in that people who are "troubled" can also be described as "distracted" and vice versa, though perhaps more recently the words are used with less gravity than they once were. This similarity and seriousness grow out of the early modern period, as noted by Carol Thomas Neely, who quotes Roy Porter:

> "Distract" was a common symptom of and name for extreme cases of mental disorder. The widely term used meant "Deranged in mind; crazy, mad, insane" (OED 4), ... The term emphasizes that sufferers of mental distress were viewed as divided, diverted, disassembled—beside themselves—*temporarily*. Like the many other overlapping adjectives that label disordered states—"love-sick," "troubled-in-mind," "idea-headed," "melancholic," "lunatic," "frenzied," "mad"—"distract" (or "distraught" or "distrait") is an adjective denoting not permanent attributes, but temporary behaviors [Neely 2004, 3].

Here both words have serious implications, though the notion of "disordered states" is one worth keeping in mind as it denotes a level of confusion over one's own identity, a common theme throughout this volume. With regard to Count Dracula and this study, this might be taken further to say that a disordered state intimates a loss of identity or a divided self, if only temporarily. Troubled/troubling and distracted/distracting can then be terms used to describe the state when one's identity is disordered, or one is no longer oneself.

Returning to Stoker's novel, "trouble," "troubles," and "troubled" occur 61 times and largely in the context expected today, indicating either a physical or psychological problem to be overcome. One instance, though, describes it as more serious in nature and helps to inform how the preceding and proceeding instances should be read. This is in relation to Lucy's drastically waning health and her associated troubling dreams (Stoker 1996, 97) which are, in fact, the phantasmic visits of Dracula himself. Troubled in this instance becomes a state when one is not oneself or is even possessed by another. In Lucy's case this sees her normal, rather carefree identity being replaced by one which is at turns weary and tired, then excessively lascivious. Indeed, one could suggest that she has more than one troubled self. As such, troubled is used to describe the state when someone is induced to, or unable to prevent, having their normal self/identity change into another one; potentially this can apply to a group or community as is discussed in later chapters. This, of course, changes over time in the films to be examined, and more recently it can be seen to imply a shifting identity where one's sense of self is constantly changing. Zygmunt Baumann calls this shifting sense of self a liquid identity and sees it as integral to the experience of modernity, but also one that, because it is never settled, is never at home with itself (Baumann, 2000).

Distraction, or distracted identities, charts a slightly different course, though it can equally be, as seen from Neely's quote, applied to those who quite literally have lost their minds, or sense of self. Stoker mentions the word once in this context when Arthur Holmwood is talking to Dr. Seward about his fiancée Lucy's recent decline in health and says, "I am almost distracted when I think of her" (Stoker 1996, 118). Arthur's own father is suffering from ill health at this point, so the comment infers that it is more than just a drifting of attention; it is also a loss of mental focus, or a loss of one's normally focused self. Further mentions of the word, of which there are three, concentrate on the distracting aspect of the term in regard to one's intellectual focus and realworld situations. This latter use remains strongly related to its more recent use and maybe even more so to those who live in increasingly intelligent and/or informationally dense environments where constant interaction with smart devices/interfaces, etc., is impossible to avoid. It then becomes related to issues around attention span and focus but also to the ways in which one is able to relate to or engage with the world and those in close proximity. However, it has not totally lost the earlier implication of a loss of self, particularly if one sees individual identity as a full or partial product of one's social milieu and/or environmental interactions. Therefore, as mentioned in relation to Holmwood above, one can be distracted from being one's normal self, by one's surroundings.

It is worth returning to Count Dracula himself as the source of these effects and while it is very particular aspects of his otherness that distract and trouble the various characters in the novel, and indeed later adaptations, he actually remains extremely undisturbed himself. In Stoker's novel the vampire knows exactly who and what he is, and this does not change throughout the course of the narrative. Consequently, this gives him a sense of oneness or completeness that is absent from most of the other characters in that his identity does not change and is not affected by those around him—he quite literally possesses himself. It is this very self-possession that allows the vampire to possess, or trouble, the identities of those around him. This is most obviously seen in the novel where the Count uses mind control, hypnotism, glamoring, and mental telepathy to, quite literally, possess people.[7]

Troubling Distractions

These are the main aspects of Count Dracula's otherness seen in Stoker's novel, and the present volume focuses on five parts of this in particular with each one dealt in a separate chapter: (1) history/undead memory; (2)

foreignness; (3) money/consumerism; (4) violence[8]; and (5) technology, to show just how characters in the novel and subsequent cinematic adaptations are affected by this otherness, and to ask how the vampire's difference in regard to them has evolved or not, and if so, how. The development in each of these areas is shown by examining five films per section, spanning as wide a time period as possible while illustrating some of the more extreme ways in which either Count Dracula or the manifestation of otherness has changed. This includes films which at first glance do not appear to fit into the accepted canon of *Dracula* adaptations but which, as is shown, contain sufficient details, characters, and themes in common with the original to be considered as such.

The first chapter in this book is "Undead Memories and Troubling Histories," and looks at the ways in which Count Dracula is portrayed as a monster from the past, a carrier of traumatic or repressed (undead) memories that refuse to die. More often than not the present into which he erupts is totally unprepared either for him or what he represents, usually with troubling results on both the people and places around him. However, the King Vampire does not always represent the same traumatic memories or even manifest in the same body, as is shown in the films examined.

Dracula (Browning: 1931) features Bela Lugosi's seminal performance as the Count and in particular his thick Eastern European drawl which manifests his otherness in the film more strongly than any other aspect of his character. His voice not only separates him from those around him but also from the very fabric of the modern world he has entered; this is as much 20th century America as it is 19th century Britain.[9] Lugosi's Count embodies not just a superstitious and dangerous, Old World past but also more recent traumatic memories of conflict and death in Europe during World War I.[10] Interestingly, at the end of the narrative, unlike the original novel, the vampire is killed while still in the land he has invaded, hinting that though he may have been put to rest, the troubles he represents might emerge again. *Blacula* (Crain, 1972) sees Dracula as 18th century African royalty created in the image of white European aristocratic colonialists but reawakened in 1970s Los Angeles. The mirror image mimicry of Blacula/Dracula purposely complicates the notion of agency and identity, and is a troubling reminder of what African Americans have lost in modern America, demonstrating how unprepared they are for the intrusion of their own past.[11] Although Blacula manages to reignite some memories from the past, namely those of his resurrected wife Tina/Tuva, his otherness is again repressed, though again not forever. *Nadja* (Almereyder, 1994) is a very different film from the previous ones. It seems to be a story about Dracula's daughter but is more about the Count's undead identity living on in a female body. Set in 1990s New York, the narrative itself becomes a traumatic repetition of history featuring many of the same characters—Van Helsing, Renfield and Lucy—and dynamics similar to Stoker's original, but rather than enacting national trauma it focuses more on the individual and the possibility of one's past. The vampire's spirit, as an eruption of memory, tries to lose itself in the distractions of modern life but soon realizes the impossibility of assimilation. The vampire hunters think chasing the vampire home and killing it without recognizing the history it represents will dispel the monsters of the past forever. They are, however, mistaken. Unbeknown to them, Dracula's soul migrates to one of their party, intimating that the present will not remain untroubled for long. In a similar vein, *Let the Right One In* (Alfredson, 2008) appears to be about two preadolescent children in Stockholm in the 1980s but again the resonance of its characters and tropes with those in *Dracula* reveal it to be about a present that is totally unprepared for the monster of the past about to erupt in its midst. Here it represents the traumatic past of Sweden's large immigrant communities that, left unaddressed and uncared for, will infect the hearts and minds of their youth. *The Strain* (del Toro and Hogan, 2014–2017) returns to a more traditional representation of Dracula and is both "new, and very, very old" (del Toro and Hogan 2009, 164). It shows the Master Vampire landing in present day New York, the beating heart of the Empire, to complete the reverse-colonial work begun in Stoker's London at the end of the 19th century. This last example shows an America so distracted by its consumerist imperative that it forgets the lessons learned from its traumatic recent past; these inevitably erupt into the present. The Master here conflates the undead memories of 9/11, wartime Nazism, and a resurgence of alt-right nationalism to reveal the ongoing inability of the nation to recognize and address its troubling past to the extent that it literally loses its present.

A vital part of Count Dracula's otherness lies in the fact that he comes from a land beyond the civilized world of the Empire; more than that, he is both distinctly other and able to blend in. Unsurprisingly, maybe, as the original narrative has been adapted it is the latter part of this anxiety that has come to the fore. While obvious foreignness still forms the basis of much prejudice, it is the other who can walk unnoticed in the "crowded streets of your mighty London, to be in the midst of the whirl and rush of humanity" (Stoker 1996, 22) that fuels the terror of possible religious extremists and mass murderers. The book's second chapter, "The Land Beyond the Forest," focuses on this and how the figure of Count Dracula is used to embody various ethnic groups that have been seen to "trouble" Western society, from early 20th century anti–Semitism to the War on Terror and Islamic/religious extremism.

Nosferatu (Murnau, 1922) displays its anti–Semitism even more openly than Stoker's novel. Writers such as Harold L. Malchow and Tabish Khair have noted that many of the Count's characteristics embody late–Victorian racial prejudice against the large Jewish community that inhabited it, and post–World War I Germany did something of the same. *Nosferatu*'s Count Orlok is troublingly feral and his grasping fingers and lust for the blood of German youth and womanhood—the nation's future—mark him as a Jewish monster who is a plague on the land that needs to be destroyed. *Love at First Bite* (Dragoti, 1979) is a very different film and the Count, played by the extremely suave George Hamilton, is actually a refugee from Communist Romania who has been evicted from his castle by the local workers' cooperative. Dracula is only distinguishable from the New York socialites he mingles with because of his thick Eastern European accent—more a spoof on Lugosi— which is accepted as an interesting quirk in a nation of immigrants.[12] Yet it is this Eastern otherness that constructs his romancing and eventual departure, with socialite and actress Cindy Sondheim, as representative of a Cold War anxiety over the loss of the hearts and minds of America's youth. Dracula's good looks and comedic style are but a distraction to this Communist émigré's hidden agenda of ideological vampirism. Troubling discrimination continues in *Modern Vampires* (Elfman, 1998) where Dracula is something of a gangland boss from the Old World who lives in modern day Hollywood. The human characters from Stoker are replaced by vampires who are American and proud of it. Unsurprisingly, it is not long before the New World undead are, presciently, spouting rhetoric that is strikingly similar to that of President Donald Trump, as heard when Nico (a vampiric Lucy) shouts at Dracula "I'm an American citizen, no foreign bag of shit is gonna run me out of my own goddamn country."

In many ways *Hannibal* (Fuller, 2013–2015) gives form to the nationalistic fears expressed in *Modern Vampires*. Here Dr. Hannibal Lecter, "the stranger in a strange land" (Stoker 1996, 22) perfectly embodies Stoker's Count, a sophisticated other who is obviously foreign, but his quick assimilation hides his hidden and nefarious intentions.[13] Lecter is a vampiric serial killer who literally consumes his host nation. Assimilation has troublingly allowed him to mimic the culture around him so that he can better hide in plain sight and conduct his deadly agenda under the noses of law enforcement and even the FBI. *The Witch* (Eggers, 2015) continues this theme and affirms the troubling idea of the hidden agent within looking to destabilize the society around him. Although set in 17th century New England—60 years before the Salem witch trials—it speaks of the religious extremism that founded America and which, even today, is fertile ground for subversion, prejudice, and violence. Dracula here is in his guise of the Dark Lord (Satan) and has transformed into a large black goat to infiltrate a family homestead. Once there he uses his brides (witches) to create terror within the family so that he can groom the children into his ideology. The foreignness he embodies is so excessive that it is constructed as being beyond human, even supernatural, which makes detecting him and his cohorts almost impossible, resulting in a continuous, and troubling, sense of constant suspicion and impending violence.

"The Trouble with Money" is the third chapter and considers the ways in which Count Dracula's association with money and/or consumerism troubles the world around him. Franco Moretti describes the vampire as the ultimate capitalist in that he is driven to own/consume everything. Indeed, the act of vampirism has often been correlated to the exploitation of others and to the acquisition of wealth. This situation has only been exacerbated at the start of the 21st century where globalization, consumerism, and technological innovation appear to commodify almost every aspect of one's life and environment. It is not surprising, then, that Count Dracula thrives in such surroundings and reveals the more troubling truths that beat at its heart.

The Son of Dracula (Siodmak, 1943) does not immediately appear to be about money or the acquisition of wealth, though Dracula's (Alucard's) consumerist credentials are stated explicitly in the film when his hunters claim he has come to America to "fasten on it and drain it dry." He moves to the New World and takes up residence in an estate, a former plantation and a living memory of slavery and exploitation. This further correlates to the film being set during World War II, a time when America made huge amounts of money and established itself as a world power, positioning both the vampire and the woman, Kay Caldwell, who knowingly invited him to her estate, as traitors both to the nation and its capitalist agenda. Caldwell wants all the Count's power for herself, a situation that is too troubling for a wartime regime and so, inevitably, she is destroyed. However, her actions release the troubling spirit of the vampire into the U.S., inferring that the troubling spirit of the plantation will rise again.[14]

The Satanic Rites of Dracula (Gibson, 1973) brings Count Dracula back to London in the 1970s and sees him as the head of a development company, one linked to all the systems of power in the UK—the government and the aristocracy. He then becomes the troubling heart of corporate development and the infrastructure of the future of the metropolis, turning London into a vampiric city. More troubling still, the vampire plans to release a plague that will destroy all humans across the world—consumerism literally consuming itself. The alternate reality of *Daybreakers* (Spierig Brothers, 2008) sees Count Dracula's nefarious plan succeed, and he rules over an empire of vampires but in true capitalist spirit he continues the daily exploitation of (undead) labor to maintain his authority. However, he cannot produce enough of the one commodity his workforce requires, human blood. His attempts to perfect this ultimate consumerist society produce troubling revelations that ultimately doom it to failure; consumerism eats itself back into humanity.

Twilight: Breaking Dawn Part 1 (Condon, 2011) shows that Dracula's undead money is now well and truly alive in the 21st century. The hierarchies of the film's vampire family, the Cullens, make naming a central "Dracula" figure problematic but Edward and his New Woman, Bella, form a convincing Count and his Mina—as intimated in the film *Dracula* (Badham, 1979) among others.[15] Here, though, rather than troubling the characters around them, they affect the watching audience who lose themselves to vampiric consumerism. The contemporary vampire franchise and in-film product placement see *Twilight*'s Dracula suck the money out of his audience via fashionable consumables and cross-platform branding, so that all that he wears, drives, and eats, as well as where he lives are troublingly available to buy in the real world. *Jupiter Ascending* (Wachowskis, 2015) completes the cycle, with an unwitting vessel/human avatar carrying the undead spirit of Dracula within her. Space vampires in this film literally consume the living energy of planets and have their sights set on Earth. Jupiter, the human who contains the dormant undead memory of the vampire, claims the Earth for herself so that it will remain safe. But, as the films ends, there lingers the troubling threat that the past will awaken and the Earth will once again become nothing more than a commodity to be consumed.

Stoker's novel is full of violence, much of it against women—the vampire's performative identity as feminine can be seen to place it within this category as well. Largely this gendered violence is excused in the book by the fact that the women in question are being "saved" or "redeemed" in terms of the late–Victorian heteronormative society, but as discussed in the fourth chapter, "Violent Distractions," this abuse of female characters is curiously something that has not really changed over time. As such the violence enacted upon the body of the vampire—largely seen as female—no matter how recently they were still considered human, becomes a distraction allowing systemic violence to continue against those considered other.

Nearly all films about Count Dracula involve staking at some point—*Nosferatu* being an exception as he is decimated, somewhat poetically, by sunlight.[16] *Dracula* (Fisher, 1958) is the first of these; while the Count himself is killed by an inventive combination of crossed silver candlesticks and then sunlight, his "bride," a vampiric Jonathan Harker, and Harker's fiancée Lucy Holmwood are all murdered with a large wooden stake. Mina, Lucy's mother, is severely burned with a silver cross to prove her earlier transgression with the vampiric outsider. Curiously, while the setting is nominally given as "Austria or thereabouts," apart from the Count's mountain castle it all feels extremely English, making his otherness seem less about race than it is about his sexuality. All go to affirm, in the typically excessive manner of Hammer films in general and Fisher's *Dracula* in particular, that extreme violence against all those seen as feminine, feminized or other is perfectly acceptable.

The Last Man on Earth (Ragona and Salkow, 1964) does not make an easy fit with *Dracula* but if one sees the human protagonist, Nèville, as a Van Helsing character, then the Count could be the unseen leader of the ultimately triumphing vampire-humans.[17] In this reading, Nèville becomes something of a maniacal serial killer who justifies the indiscriminate murder of almost everyone he meets because they are not the kind of "human" that he sees himself as—this includes brainless zampires (zombie/vampires) and mutated human/vampires alike. Violence here is not just acceptable but a way of maintaining one's identity. The violence in *Blade* (Norrington, 1998) is a little more focused in that it largely targets vampires—though Blade himself (a dhamphir)[18] is the recipient of much violence, too. The distracting part of *Blade* is that excessive violence and graphic torture on the body of the other is shown as totally justifiable. The Count here is somewhat dispersed in that something of him is embodied in the outdated King Vampire, Dragonetti,[19] but also in the rebel vampire Deacon Frost, though maybe most strongly in Blade himself who has a "Renfield" sidekick and, in this film at least, a "Mina" character alongside him. Torture is the most distracting aspect here as Blade's own otherness implies that he does not break any kind of moral code in performing such acts on our behalf—fighting fire with fire as it were.[20]

This notion of the "just" vampire comes to the fore in *Dracula Untold* (Shore, 2014). While the violence in it is more computer generated than actual, its most prominent point is that it cites Count Dracula as the monster the world needs, particularly when the Christian world is being invaded by heathen armies from the Middle East. Here the Ottoman horde, that the actual Vlad III fought in defense of Christian Europe in the 15th century, become radical extremists that can only be defeated by one who is even more monstrous than they. The acceptability of torture finds its apotheosis in the series *The Vampire Diaries* (Plec and Williamson, 2009–2017)—which again is not an easy fit for *Dracula*, not least as it ran for eight seasons—and contains many of Stoker's tropes, plots, and characters. The troubling violence it displays occurs around the series' Salvatore brothers, but other characters too, who regularly inflict extreme pain and extended periods of torture on each other, often for little reason. As a result, it loses all meaning, and excessive violence troublingly becomes a natural part of everyday life and the only distraction is reasonable behavior.

In Stoker's novel, Count Dracula was constructed as oppositional to all forms of modern science, both biological and technological. The last chapter, "Distracting Technologies," examines the ways in which he in later adaptations has not only mastered such devices but has become an inherent part, or the ghost in the machine, of 21st century technology and its ideological intent (see Wicke 1992). Equally important is the effect of technology on the other characters in the novel. The more the vampire hunters interact with technology, the more fractured their identities become, and the tools utilized to capture the vampire are just as likely to distract them from this goal. This final chapter, then, studies the ways in which Dracula's increasing incorporation with science and technology becomes more and more distracting to those around him.

Abbott and Costello Meet Frankenstein's Monster (Barton, 1948) is an odd film, and Lugosi's second and last performance as Count Dracula. Here, though, he is a very different vampire than in Browning's film and is no longer afraid of science but embraces it as he attempts to bring Frankenstein's monster back to life. The film sees the Count swap his usual evening wear for the medical garb of the mad scientist, and it foreshadows many later movies such as *Mother Riley Meets the Vampire* (Gilling, 1952), *Blood of the Vampire* (Cass, 1958), and *Atom Age Vampire* (Majano, 1960). While Dracula himself lost much of his power to frighten audiences directly after World War II, the unknown and almost supernatural powers attributed to atomic weapons and radiation seemed to give credence to the vampire's supernatural abilities and powers of distraction when applied to science. *Rabid* (Cronenberg, 1977) carries on very much in this vein of an undead biological science but the physical embodiment of Dracula himself is unnecessary; his vampiric energy lives on in the cutting-edge biological experimentation and transplant methods employed by a cosmetic surgery clinic. A young girl involved in a motorbike accident is grafted experimentally treated skin with catastrophic results. Just as in Stoker's novel, the mediation of the vampire creates suddenly sexual and eroticized subjects—the girl infects her victims through the bite of a penis/vagina in her armpit—that distract their victims from her true intent of total contamination.

The focus moves away from the medical to the communication sciences in *Dracula III: Legacy* (Lussier, 2005) and the notion of the almost supernatural qualities of media platforms and broadcast signals become entwined with the spectral essence of the vampire. Here Count Dracula connects himself to a battery of television sets and antennae so that his blood can infect the signal—combining and perverting the main two technologies, blood transfusion and communications, shown in Stoker. Vampirism could then be broadcast across the world to contaminate all those distracted by their televisions and radios. *Dracula* (Haddon and Knauff, 2013–14), like *The Strain*, is both old and new, showing the Count returned to an alternative Victorian Britain but with pioneering technology that does not exist even in the 21st century. He builds a machine/turbine to produce and transmit free wireless electrical energy across London, a benevolent act that is of course a distraction to undermine the powers that control the city and its wealth,[21] and who were also responsible for killing the vampire's wife.[22] As the wronged party, Dracula's ultimate intentions behind his mastery of technology are ambivalent at best but the distracting qualities of it are definitive, and the vampire only ever gives so that it can receive.

This ambivalence of intent, and the moral high ground being distinctly vampiric, continue in the final example *Ex Machina* (Garland, 2014). As in Stoker's novel, Dracula distracts those around him/her so that his/her identity is not revealed until late in the narrative. Unlike the original, in this adaptation Dracula *is* the technology and is shown as being the first ever humanoid artificial intelligence, or AI. Following the narrative arc of the first part of *Dracula*, the story concludes with the vampire escaping from its lair "beyond the forest" into the heart of civilization, though it has already connected to the internet and exists both materially and virtually. The film, as with earlier examples here, explicitly makes the connection to the supernatural powers of atomic weapons and radiation, leaving an open-ended question of whether this vampire of the future, as a spirit-fueled cyborg entity, is also the end of humanity.

ONE

Undead Memories and Troubling Histories

In which the absolute otherness of Count Dracula is portrayed as a monster from the past, a carrier of traumatic or repressed (undead) memories that refuse to die.

Dracula, Tod Browning, 1931

Bela Lugosi's voice is central to Count Dracula's absolute otherness in the film, and the actor's East European drawl is still a common identifier for the vampire in popular culture. He was by no means the first choice for such an important part, even though he, along with Edward Van Sloan who plays Van Helsing, had performed their respective roles for some time in the American theatrical production. In fact, Universal studios felt that Lugosi was "'too foreign' for the part" (Lennig 2003, 95) but the casting proved to be an inspired one. Even though critics remain divided over the actor's performance, his voice and accent get almost universal approval, as Robert Spadoni observes:

Low-pitched and thickly accented, Lugosi's voice exuded a sensuous strangeness that commentators since 1931 have taken pleasure in describing. From the "mellifluously thick Hungarian accent," to the "liquid, if sepulchral, voice," to the "stately, slightly over-ripe readings," to the "succulently foreign intonations," writers have suggested that Lugosi's voice constitutes within the film an entity with a material weight and density, one that even has its own smell and taste (Spadoni 2007, 63).

The importance of this should always be weighed against *Dracula*'s place in film history as the first talking horror movie. The introduction of sound made voices, and Count Dracula's in particular, central to the narrative and its meanings, and so the casting of Lugosi is important. In the original novel the Count speaks almost perfect English, as noted by Harker on his first evening in the castle, "But, Count ... you know and speak English thoroughly! Indeed, ... you speak excellently" (Stoker 1996, 22). In large part this is because Stoker did not construct the vampire's otherness through its being obviously foreign but because it was almost indistinguishable from Harker and his associates. For Browning, though, Count Dracula's European-ness was of tantamount importance.

The 1920s and 30s saw a period of growing isolationism in America. Due in part to World War I where the United States lost 116,516 soldiers with 320,000 ill or wounded of the 4.7 million men who served.[1] While this was quite light compared to the main countries involved, it still left much anti–European feeling at home as the deaths were largely viewed as unnecessary—America even refused to join the League of Nations created the year after the conflict had ended. This occurred alongside what was seen as a worrying number of European immigrants coming to the U.S. The same flux of Jewish and Catholic immigrants from Russia and Southern Europe respectively that had formed part of the anti–Semitic/anti-immigrant impulse of Stoker's novel at the end of the 19th century also affected America in the early years of the 20th century. So much so that the Emergency Quota Act (1921) and the Immigration Act (1924) were created to restrict the number of immigrants from any one country allowed into America; Lugosi himself fled the revolution in Hungary in 1919 to arrive in New York the following year. Then came the Great Depression in the 1930s which naturally led to a greater focus on internal affairs and reconstruction, and a less welcoming stance in relation to outsiders.

Of course, Stoker's novel is largely set in England where the threat is of an older, more superstitious world infecting the modern, civilized British Empire. Browning uses this idea to construct, through Lugosi's voice, a European vampire who has travelled across the ocean—as most immigrants did—to suck the life out of the New World. The director supplemented the vampire's otherness with the now iconic cape and evening dress, though much of this was taken from the stage play, which reinforces the aural cues of the Count's otherness with Old World aristocracy, an aristocracy that the Americans had purposely distanced themselves from when gaining independence. Subsequently, everything about Count Dracula marks him as different, a dangerous other that is a reminder of the recent violent history of World War I that sees one's undead "relatives" as vampires sucking the life out of the present—the Count might flatter and charm, but his ultimate goal is to bring to life the memories of the traumatic past.

The Count's effects on those around him are equally as strong here as in the novel but far more focused, largely due to the smaller cast of main characters—the stage and film versions lose Arthur Holmwood and Quincey

Morris altogether leaving just an elderly Dr. Seward (Herbert Bunston), his daughter Mina (Helen Chandler), her fiancé John Harker (David Manners), and Mina's friend Lucy Weston (Francis Dade) who is first to come under the vampire's spell. Arguably, though, the people most troubled by Count Dracula's absolute otherness are Mina and Renfield; the latter becomes a major character in this film version and it is to him that we shall turn first.

For expediency and dramatic effect the Balderstone/Deane stage version sees Renfield rather than Harker make the fateful journey to Castle Dracula to get his foreign client's signature on a real estate transaction, although it is not performed in the play as such but only mentioned as backstory to the rather strange inmate at Dr. Seward's asylum.[2] The film, however, makes much of Renfield's arrival at the excessively Gothic Castle Dracula and subsequent stay with the vampire, making the otherworldly nature of these scenes jar with the rather mundane nature of the later episodes. The swapping of Renfield for Harker makes sense within the internal logic of the film, even though it relegates the latter to an insignificant role.[3] More importantly it changes the focus of the main relationship of the narrative, that between Count Dracula and Harker, making the story less to do with passion, transgressive sexuality, and blood, and more about the invasion of the New World by the Old.

Browning's film begins with Renfield (Dwight Frye) already sitting in a full coach heading toward the Carpathian Mountains, eliding Harker's geographical transition from civilization to the dreamlike land beyond the forest. As the coach speeds into an open courtyard, a crowd rushes out to greet them and hurry the new arrivals to the inn before the sun goes down. However, Renfield, who is dressed rather dapperly, tells the driver to leave his bags where they are as he needs to be at the Borgo Pass by midnight. The people around him remonstrate but the young man cannot be dissuaded and the coach speeds away. The scene cuts to the Castle, and as if aware of his approaching victim the Count and his brides are shown rising from their coffins in preparation for their guest's arrival. Meanwhile Renfield's coach has dropped him at the Pass and a small coach awaits where, unbeknownst to the young man, its driver is none other than the Count himself. Renfield boards and the vehicle speeds away across a wild and rugged landscape—the painted scenery makes the location seem dreamlike and otherworldly. This is reinforced when Renfield leans out of the window to see a large bat flying above the horses pulling the carriage at breakneck speed.

Upon arrival, he gets out and enters the dilapidated Castle—made to look unrealistically decayed and old and so becomes more of a signifier of the dissipation and corruption of the aristocratic vampire himself[4]—and walks into the hallway where a dark shape descends the large staircase at one end and intones one of the most famous first lines by any character: "I am Dracula." Renfield's response is peculiar, but maybe typical of the young, modern person he was before being "troubled" by the vampire: "Oh, it's really good to see you. I don't know what happened to the driver and my luggage and.... Well, and with all this, I thought I was in the wrong place" (Browning, 1931). He is off balance in a very strange situation, but he can also be read as needing to complete a deal with a very idiosyncratic client. In the end it is his drive for money that impels him to continue, despite all the warnings he has received. And as the naive young man walks further into the vampire's lair his host declares, "The spider spinning his web for the unwary fly. The blood is the life, Mr. Renfield" (Browning, 1931).

The Count is keen to scrutinize the documents Renfield has brought, but as the young man is putting the papers away he cuts his finger, arousing the vampire's interest and sealing the estate agent's fate. The final scene in which we see Renfield as his untroubled self closes with him collapsing in front of a huge window outside of which flies a large bat. The bat transforms into Dracula who then fends off his three brides so that he has the young man for himself, with the vampire's "kiss" represented as Renfield being enveloped by the Count's black silk cloak.

The next scene opens with a storm at sea and a ship, the Vesta,[5] being tossed side to side, buffeted by the wind and waves. In the hold is Renfield talking to a large box. As he lifts the lid, a claw-like hand snakes out revealing a dark figure who is none other than the Count himself. Suddenly the vampire is out of the crate and standing imperiously, his eyes glowing in the darkness as he stares at his newly-made assistant who cowers and scrapes before his Master. Renfield is a changed person, no longer a dapper, smartly-dressed salesman brimming with confidence; now his suit is disheveled and his button shirt open with no tie, his hair is scruffy, and his face appears permanently distorted.

On reaching Whitby, Renfield is the only survivor on the Vesta and is discovered in the hold, standing at the bottom of the stairs with his face turned upward to the opening, fixed in a gargoyle-like grimace while a menacing, throaty laugh resonates in the air around him. Renfield is obviously deeply troubled by Count Dracula, and though bitten by the vampire he has not become one. In part his quest for small lives and small amounts of blood manifests his earlier commercial-self—someone willing to travel miles to clinch a deal for a single property; a small drop of blood in capitalist terms.

For Renfield one of the troubling aspects of the Count is his extreme wealth; as described in Stoker's novel he literally bleeds money when Harker slashes him with a knife "making a wide gap whence a bundle of bank-notes and a stream of gold fell out" (Stoker 1996, 332). The capitalist Renfield, too, wants to consume large amounts of financial "life." Alongside this one can also read the vampire as manifesting the recent traumatic past of World War I—and the "undead" memory of the slain youth of America. In this way Ren-

One. Undead Memories and Troubling Histories

A troubled Renfield (Dwight Frye, left) troubles Professor Van Helsing (Edward Van Sloan) in *Dracula*, dir. Tod Browning (Universal, 1931).

field's troubled self sees him become a delayed victim of that conflict, infected by a delayed cultural trauma carried by the vampire. In fact, it is possible to interpret the young man's behavior as being that of someone suffering from shell shock, or post-traumatic stress disorder (PTSD).

In the aftermath of World War I, the effects of shell shock were beginning to be investigated and understood.[6] While sufferers of the condition were often portrayed as weak, cowardly, or deserters and treated accordingly, continuing research intimated that it was an actual psychological condition with physical manifestations, many of which were likened to female hysteria.[7] Photographs from the period show sufferers with facial expressions not dissimilar to that of Renfield, with the patients often being diagnosed as mentally insane. As seen in Browning's film the condition worsens without proper treatment or recognition of what malady Renfield is suffering from and culminates in an internal battle between his former (untroubled) and present (troubled) selves. His troubled self feels the vampire as a constant presence whom he must convince of his loyalty, even when the Count is seemingly not present. These "conversations" culminate with him being fooled into disclosing Dracula's location to Van Helsing: "I'm loyal to you, Master, I am your slave, I didn't betray you! Oh, no, don't! Don't kill me! Let me live, please! Punish me, torture me, but let me live! I can't die with all those lives on my conscience! All that blood on my hands!" (Browning, 1931). The last part is particularly interesting as it could relate to the little lives of insects he has taken while locked up and the guilt of being the one that helped the vampire travel to civilization, or to the traumatic memory of conflict in Europe that the vampire has troubled him with.

The correlation between hysteria and shell shock, where the former was configured as being a predominantly female malady, is important here. Renfield as a male hysteric is feminized within the context of the film so that he needs to be protected and fought for/over by the men, which indeed happens. Dr. Seward takes even more care protecting Renfield than he does of his own daughter and her friend, and in later scenes Van Helsing and Count Dracula are seen, often psychically, fighting over who controls the troubled mind of the former estate agent. His feminization highlights the patriarchal anxiety over of the weakness of the female body and mind, making them easy targets for corruption and contamination which is even more strongly seen in Mina Seward.

It would be more obvious to choose Lucy as the troubled figure, being what Mina calls a "romantic," or being of a "morbid" disposition. This reading features in the two sequels to Browning's film, *Dracula's Daughter* (Hillyer, 1936) and *Son of Dracula* (Siodmak, 1943) both of which feature female protagonists—Countess Zeleska[8] and Kay Caldwell respectively—who are depicted as dangerous because they are overly morbid and pre-occupied with death and/or the occult.[9] Lucy then is marked from the start, but Mina is shown to be less enamored of such musings and is important to the group of men—even Renfield refuses to harm her when ordered to by his Master.

Dracula only begins to trouble Mina once he has already made Lucy a vampire, and as the "final girl"[10] alive she becomes representative of America itself—not quite the motherland, but as a prospective bride and future mother she is the bearer of the next generation and is treated as such by the men. Of note here is that the vampire begins feeding on Mina before the men even realize that there is something untoward taking place, as though America is already being infected by the undead corruption of Europe.

The morning after Mina has been bitten, she is lethargic and distant, and tells her fiancé of her unsettled night which ended with "a white livid face" (Browning, 1931) that appeared from a red mist that filled her room. Harker dismisses it as a bad dream, but Van Helsing questions her further and discovers two bite marks on her neck. At this point the Count appears and distracts the men by suggesting that Mina's bad dreams are due to his "grim tales of my far off country" (Browning, 1931). Once she leaves the room

Van Helsing realizes that Dracula is in fact the vampire they have been searching for. Despite their best efforts Mina's troubles worsen and, not unlike Renfield, she now has something of a divided identity, or is at least aware that her troubled self is now in control of her. In this state she tells Harker that they are no longer together: "No, John, you mustn't touch me, and you mustn't kiss me ever again.... It's all over, John, our love, our life together" (Browning, 1931). The trauma of World War I manifests in the Count, and the prospect of being drawn into another conflict not only separates Mina and Harker but threatens to quite literally destroy the next generation of Americans. Mina appears lost as the Count vanishes with her but, as mentioned earlier, Renfield is tricked into revealing their location.[11] As in Stoker's novel the apparent death of the vampire releases his victims. After Van Helsing announces that "There's nothing more to fear, Miss Mina. Dracula is dead forever" (Browning, 1931), Mina appears to return to her normal untroubled self, though curiously it is only after saying this that the vampire hunter disappears off screen to drive a stake into the Count's heart.

Van Helsing plays a curious role in the film and one that in many ways is very different from the Dutch Professor in Stoker's narrative. In the novel he is represented as a foreigner, his accented English is at times almost comical,[12] and his nationality is largely interpreted as colonial/postcolonial European which situates him in a similar categorization as the British members of the crew of light. However, along with Quincey Morris, his otherness also marks him as possibly being vampiric himself. In Browning's narrative, Van Helsing is very much part of the same nation and heritage as the other vampire hunters—his name might indicate European roots, but he is undoubtedly American. What is curious is how easily distracted he is at the start of the movie. He ascertains very quickly that the deaths are the work of a vampire but not that it is the mysterious new stranger in the area. Even with the extreme, almost comic moment when Mina is describing her unsettled nights and her fiancé turns and asks Van Helsing "What could have caused them, Professor?" and a split second later a maid appears and announces, "Count Dracula!" (Browning, 1931), Van Helsing only realizes the vampire's identity by chance later on. Van Helsing happens to see a reflection of Mina talking to the Count in a small mirror in the top of a cigarette box, or rather he does *not* see the reflection as vampires do not have one. The Professor confronts Dracula with this phenomenon and it is only through the Count's extreme reaction that Van Helsing's suspicions are confirmed. Equally curious, it is only after this occurrence that the Professor realizes that Renfield's condition is directly due to the vampire. Van Helsing's distraction serves as a warning that even experts can be fooled, and the most charming and sophisticated Europeans may hide mischief and murder. Van Helsing seems to save America's next generation by killing the vampire, but unlike in the novel his body remains in the land it invaded, leaving a taint that will forever be undead and ready to rise again.

This taint of otherness, of a past that will never die, features in all the films chosen in this chapter. They each see the vampire as a manifestation of a monstrous historical trauma invited in to the homeland from overseas—the past represented as a foreign land—and in this next example it is Africa via Transylvania.

Blacula, William Crain, 1972

Crain's film sees the vampire's absolute otherness as directly related to the undead historical trauma of African Americans—undead as in past events that cannot, or will not, be laid to rest. Therefore, *Blacula* is unsurprisingly a very different film than Browning's, not least in that it is part of the "Blaxploitation" era of films that found huge popular success in the 1970s that featured "Black themes" or as Jan-Christopher Horak further qualifies "films that featured violent and sexualized Black images" (Field, Horak and Stewart 2015, 119). As with the early sound horror films they were seen by Hollywood studios as a cheap way to make money and curiously, for this study at least, Crain's film also begins in Transylvania at Castle Dracula, though a very different one to that seen housing Lugosi and his undead brides.

The film begins with a prologue which sees an African Prince, Mamuwalde (William Marshall), and his wife Luva (Vonetta McGee) visit Count Dracula (Charles Macaulay) in his Castle in 1790 to petition for an end to slavery in Europe. Understandably, the Count does not agree with this and turns Mamuwalde into a vampire, renames him Blacula, locks him in a coffin, and seals it in a room along with his wife Luva. Fast forward almost two hundred years and the contents of the castle are bought in the 1970s by two interior designers who send all the furniture back to Los Angeles, including the box containing Blacula. The vampire escapes and finds a woman, Tina (also Vonetta McGee), who he thinks is the reincarnation of his wife Luva, and turns her into a vampire.[13] Unfortunately, she is killed and, in his despair, Blacula takes his own life by walking into the sunlight. As such the beginning of the film describes the nature of the violent past that will inevitably come back to plague the present. Implicit within this is the construction of slavery as a historical trauma that irrevocably others all those complicit, actively or otherwise, with its continuation.[14]

As noted, this Castle Dracula is a very different building than that seen in Browning's film; no decaying ruin of a building here but a bright, opulent interior with manservants in attendance—more reminiscent of the light, contemporary feel of *Hammer's Horror of Dracula* (Fisher, 1958). Consequently, the interior makes the castle seem very modern, leaving the dating of the opening scenes to the dress and language of the vampire. Mamuwalde wears evening dress more reminiscent of the late–Victorian period, not unlike that worn by Lugosi, rather than the late 18th century, and speaks like a 20th century Shakespearean actor as indeed Marshall, the actor playing the role, was. This incongruity becomes even more extreme in regard to the dress and language of the interior designers who buy the contents of the castle 180 years later as the furniture seems very in tune with them, exemplifying a kitsch Hollywood Gothic, though the vampire is old fashioned and out of place.

These early scenes construct the African American vampire as an immortal creature outside of time who remains unchanged and othered; by extension, so do the violence and oppression of white patriarchy that imprisoned and cursed him, making him the undead and undying creature he is. As such, Mamuwalde already bears the marks of his future trauma even as we see him meeting the vampire; one is marked as soon as one enters the vampire's lair, as was Renfield before him. In a sense then the prologue contains two "Draculas," one who actually represents the patriarchal/imperialist system and one who is that system's absolute other—the black, African savage. Ironically, of course, Mamuwalde is as civilized if not more so than his host but the racial othering inflicted upon him by his skin color can only see him categorized as less-than, or non-human: "It is you that comes from the jungle" (Crain, 1972). This otherness becomes absolute when the Prince hands the Count a letter laying out his plans for the abolishment of slavery, something which causes Dracula to finally reveal his true self and dispose of his guests.

Consequently, Count Dracula is framed as being representative of the white 18th century oppression/exploitation of Africa and the undead/undying violence of slavery.[15] This point is further made when the vampire becomes Mamuwalde's Master by turning him into a vampire and giving him his slave name, Blacula.[16] As noted by Stacy Abbott, "This backstory reinterprets the vampire myth through the discourses of racial oppression and slavery, relevant to the 1970s civil rights movement, as the prince is effectively enslaved by Count Dracula through his transformation into a vampire" (Abbott 2007, 83). Yet Blacula's reawakening in the 1970s does not see him resuming his earlier form of otherness, which would cast him as a heroic figure. Rather he becomes the thing he originally hated, an oppressor of his own kind. In fact, just as white slavers looked down on him and his race so now, he looks down on humans as inferior (O'Brien 2017, 166). Leerom Medovoi observes this change in otherness in the African Prince: "The legacy of the slave trade is figured not only by the vampire's victims, of course, but also by the vampire himself, in the transition from Mamuwalde, a wise, noble and humane African leader, to Blacula, a creature cursed with a violent desire for human blood" (Medovoi 1999, 8). As noted by both Medovoi and Robin R. Means

Coleman (2011), Blacula's birth into the 20th century also sees him turn from altruistic leader to a self-interested and violent individual—something emphasized by his obsession with perusing the woman he feels is the reincarnation of Luva.[17]

Blacula's otherness here becomes somewhat complicated as on one hand he embodies (carries the curse of) and reenacts the violence of slavery and as such fulfills the role of white patriarchy, reinforced by his strict heteronormativity and homophobia. But on the other hand, as Medovoi further comments, Blacula's rage can be seen as an effort "to undo the damage wrought by the enslavement depicted in the opening scene … expressed in his struggle to regain his past wife, Luva, in the present through Tina, and thus to recuperate the nobility of African culture" (Medovoi 1999, 8). The issue with this recuperation is that, as Medovoi notes, it centers on Mamuwalde's/Blacula's sense of humiliation at the hands of Dracula. It is because of the perceived loss of nobility as "embodied in homosexuality, miscegenation and black women's insubordination—that in turn leads them [Blacula] to a violent, sadistic rage against that humiliation" (Medovoi 1999, 8). However, it is possible to read this in light of the slightly later Blaxploitation film *Ganja & Hess* (Gunn, 1973) which is also set in America of the 1970s and equally sees the interruption of a traumatic past disrupting the present.[18] Briefly, the film sees Dr. Hess Green (Duane Jones) as a respected member of white society who owns a large house full of antiques, due in part to his position of influence at a museum. However, he takes home a sacrificial dagger, an item from a current exhibition on ancient Myrthian culture from Nigeria and is cut/bitten by it. Not only does the knife contaminate his blood so that he becomes a vampire, but it also "infects" him with his ancient African heritage. While this ancestry is portrayed as being violent it is also represented as being organic and connected to nature and, more importantly, one's own traditions. This is in stark contrast to the life of refinement and sterility imposed by the white hierarchy that Hess has been "vampirized" by—sucking out his own traditions and culture. If *Blacula* is read in a similar way, and one of Mamuwalde's comments to Count Dracula regarding his own culture, "my people are eager to bring our ancient culture into the community of nations," suggests that it is plausible, then his actions in modern day L.A. become a manifestation of the loss, or repression of, one's own heritage, and indicate that the black vampire's violence expresses the cost of distancing oneself from one's past. As such, Blacula's absolute otherness is that he is too connected to his traumatic past; he has too much memory in a time that requires one to forget. In part this also explains why Blacula does not fit in with either the white or the black residents of Los Angeles. He looks with barely hidden disdain at the clientele of the black clubs where he pursues Tina. This is also evident when he attacks Bobby McCoy, a gay black man who is one of the interior designers who brought him to L.A.,[19] and a "promiscuous," black, female cab driver, both of whom can be seen as disgracing or forgetting their ancestry.

In this reading, Mamuwalde in 1790 can be seen as being othered because he embodies the future while in 1970 the same happens because he manifests the past. Given that the majority of the film addresses the effects of the traumatic past in the present of 70s L.A., it is not surprising that it is here that Blacula troubles and distracts those around him the most, with the most troubled being Tina/Luva (the Mina role) and the distracted Dr. Gordon Thomas (the Van Helsing role). Before looking at Tina it is worthwhile discussing her possibly former self, Luva.

When Mamuwalde and Luva are first seen at Castle Dracula they are constructed as the perfect couple, though she rarely speaks other than to praise her husband as the "crystallization of our people's pride" (Crain, 1972). Her adoration of her spouse is fully in keeping with heteronormative and patriarchal expectations, and her colorful dress and scarf intimate her respectfulness to her Abani heritage.[20] In fact it is Count Dracula's verbal abuse of the African Princes' wife—suggesting the "benefits of slavery" while leering at Luva—rather than the vampire's other racist remarks, that spark the fight between Mamuwalde and his host's henchmen. It is because of this altercation that Dracula locks the newly turned black vampire in a coffin—he thinks for eternity—and seals Luva in the same room so that she can hear the screams of her husband until she herself dies.

In 1970s L.A., after Blacula kills Bobby McCoy, Tina, her sister Michelle, and Michelle's boyfriend, Dr. Thomas (Thalmus Rasulala) attend Bobby's funeral. This places Tina very much in line with African American culture of the day, as is further seen when she goes out to local clubs where she appears to be known by the regulars. It is only with the appearance of Blacula at the funeral that she begins to question this; at the same time, the vampire spots her and begins his pursuit. The more Tina sees of Mamuwalde the more troubled she becomes with her life.

As Medovoi observes, she "transforms *Blacula* into the story of a woman who must decide between her fidelity to a compromised, contemporary black community and her longing for an idealized African civilization of the past, embodied by Mamuwalde" (Medovoi 1999, 15). However, as seen in *Ganja & Hess* (1973) this troubling past is already out of reach and seems to destroy most of those who try to embrace it—in the 1973 film only the woman Ganja Meda (Marlene Clark) survives. Her two previous husbands, Hess Green and George Meda, both die largely because they cannot come to terms with what their African past turns them in to. Similarly, in *Blacula* as Tina becomes more and more convinced/troubled by Mamuwalde's belief that she is his reincarnated wife, she falls more and more in love with him (Duda 2008, 38).

Tina (Vonetta McGee) being troubled by Blacula (William Marshall) in *Blacula*, dir. William Crain (American International, 1972).

Medovoi sees their love affair as a stand in "for a grander romance with Africanist blackness," but one that contemporary society sees as simultaneously "monstrous and terrifying," so that when Mamuwalde finally turns Tina into a vampire she "becomes a screaming, ghastly creature" (Medovoi 1999, 15).

The film has a rather normative ending, particularly when compared to *Ganja & Hess*. In Gunn's film, Hess turns his new wife Ganja into a vampire so that they can be together forever while embracing their shared heritage, but he cannot come to terms with the continual violence that will entail and so commits suicide. Ganja on the other hand has no problem at all and fully embraces her new life and the agency it offers, as the past allows her to be truly herself. *Blacula* should have had a similar ending, as Tina now accepts her connection to the past and sees herself as the reincarnation of Luva—her untroubled self no longer exists, and the immortal couple only want to be left alone—though the inevitable murders this will involve in the future are largely ignored. However, Dr. Thomas, who is the Van Helsing character here and consequently acts as guardian of the present, cannot allow such anomalies to exist and so kills Luva/Tina for the "monster" he sees her as. Mamuwalde cannot cope with the trauma of losing his wife twice, nor the one chance he felt he had in returning to, or making reparation with, the past, and kills himself by walking into the sunlight—symbolically severing his connection to the past.[21] This makes *Blacula* safe once again and much like the figure of Dr. Thomas, who is not so much troubled by the sudden emergence of the monstrous past—he does not "lose" who he is as Tina does—but is distracted by it.

Thomas works as a pathologist for the L.A.P.D. and appears to have a good working relationship with the department's white chief, Lt. Jack Peters, which places him in a rather curious position in relation to the black community he comes from. Only a few years before *Blacula* was made the Watts area of Los Angeles was the scene of violent race riots after an altercation between a young black man and the police department over a traffic violation. While Crain's film never explicitly mentions this, as Abbott observes "the memory of the Watts race riots circulates throughout the film through references to police corruption, institutional racism, and the eventual invasion of Watts by the white police force in search of the black vampire" (Abbott 2007, 83). Thomas then would seem to have to negotiate his position with the specter of collaborating with the enemy never too far away. Similarly, his assistant Michelle, who is also his girlfriend, is the only other African American at his job place which likewise marks him out as different and other—she only ever seems to work closely with her boyfriend and no others in the department.

In many ways this sense of Thomas's otherness, or liminality—not being quite one thing or its other—is what makes him the only one prepared to believe that the recent murder victims drained of blood might be linked to vampirism, and it is this which distracts him, though interestingly not by the traumas of his own cultural past. To prove his thesis on vampirism, he secretly takes his assistant with him to a graveyard at night to dig up the coffin of Bobby's partner, Billy, to see if the body is still there. As he opens the box Billy lunges, baring his fangs, but the doctor manages to jab a stake into the vampire's chest and kill it. Not long after he also happens upon a photograph of Tina and Mamuwalde, except where the stranger should be there is nothing—not unlike Van Helsing and the mirror in the cigarette box. Following a bizarre incident at the morgue where one of the victims, the female cab driver, comes back to life and attacks an orderly, he follows the trail of dead bodies to the warehouse Bobby and Billy used to store their antiques. He persuades Lt. Peters to go with him and they stumble into a nest of the undead who they begin to kill, but Mamuwalde escapes.[22] Thomas and some police officers follow him and in the ensuing scuffle in his new hideout, Tina is shot. Blacula then turns Tina into a vampire to save her life and they both hide. Peters and Thomas find a coffin thinking Blacula is in it and stake the vampire inside, but it turns out to be Tina/Luva. The two men corner the now forlorn vampire but rather than arrest him, Thomas allows him to walk into the sun and take his own life.

Unlike Van Helsing before him Dr. Thomas has no extensive knowledge in the lore or beliefs associated with vampires. His profession marks him as a man of reason and science, indeed as Medovoi observes, in some measure he serves as a mirror to Blacula, offering an alternate and contemporary version of a response to the traumas of slavery by embodying a "masculine hero, a scientific investigator who is straight, stands up to the white man when he should, and is respected by his lover" (Medovoi 1999, 8) and in some measure a return to Mamuwalde himself. He is no vampire hunter, but is distracted into it. This is partly due to his liminal status where as a member of the black community he is the only one interested in the strange deaths happening within it, yet he is largely able to do anything about it only because he is affiliated with the, essentially, white police force. Heather L. Duda sees Thomas as a rather peripheral character and unnecessary monster hunter who is "always just a few steps behind the two lovers," and "has nothing to do with Blacula's death" (Duda 2004, 38). Arguably this is not the case, as although he does spend most of his time trying to discover the vampire, ultimately, he forces the narrative to a climax; without him the police force would not have gotten involved. What he also manages, and which probably categorizes him as a *bad* monster hunter, is to go beyond the distraction of the vampire to identify its significance in the cultural/historical moment. Thomas has realized that treating Blacula simply as a vampire ignores the historical trauma of slavery that he represents, and the link between African Americans and their African heritage.[23] But as seen in the figure of Tina this past is too violent to directly connect with; not only does it ignore the complexities of contemporary life but is not compatible with it and recreates further rage. Thomas remembers his former undistracted self, and liminal position between the two communities, and restores the possibility for Blacula to regain some of the nobility of his former self, Mamuwalde, and to break the traumatic connection he has created between the past and the present.

Of course, as a "relative" of the undead Count, Blacula does not stay dead for long and *Scream Blacula Scream* (Kelljan: 1973) saw him rise once again. While that film is not part of the present study, the persistence of the undead aristocrat's spirit definitely is, which brings us to the next movie, *Nadja* by Michael Almereyder.

Nadja, Michael Almereyda, 1994

Nadja is different again from the previous films, not least in that it is a story about Count Dracula's daughter. It functions as something of a remake of *Dracula's Daughter* by Lambert Hillyer from 1936, which was itself a sequel to Browning's film. Almereyder's narrative moves the story from England to America and sees Nadja (Elina Löwensohn) attempting to forget her heritage in the hustle and bustle of New York City.[24] Countess Zeleska (Gloria Holden) from Hillyer's film attempted the same in London but the city just proved she was incapable of escaping her destiny.[25] In contrast, Nadja enjoys roaming the city as a space within which she can *lose* herself in the mass of humanity, as opposed to her father who wanted to *be* himself "in the midst of the whirl and rush of humanity" (Stoker 22).

The beginning of *Nadja* sees the female vampire cut loose from her heritage, almost floating around the dark streets of nighttime New York, seemingly without any fears or concerns—she is truly a creature of the night. And yet even as she does this her hooded cape/coat moves like large wings around her, as though her very essence, or way of being, is bat-like.[26] Even at this early stage in the narrative it would seem that her chances of escaping her past are slight, and this feeling only increases as the plot unfolds and begins to resonate with characters and details from Stoker's novel. We discover that her "assistant" is called Renfield; she meets a young girl, Lucy (Galaxy Craze), in a bar and they end up having a relationship; and Lucy's husband Jim (Martin Donovan) is the nephew of Van Helsing, the man who killed Nadja's father. After various plot turns Nadja, just like Stoker's Count, runs back to Castle Dracula in Transylvania, where she is killed.

Even more than in Hillyer's film there is a sense here that Nadja is doomed from the start and that her hopes of changing her life, and her destiny, were never attainable. However, unlike Zeleska before her she does not go gently into the night. Before revealing her end we should first look at what defines Nadja's absolute otherness in this narrative.

What sets this film apart from most other vampire films is the equating of the female vampire with the city—in this case New York—and more specifically, with possession of the city itself; possession is an important term in relation to this film and is strongly aligned to the idea of troubling. Stacy Abbott describes this relationship to New York in the opening scenes of the movie when Nadja still has possession of herself: "The dreaminess of the opening montage of urban images overlain by her haunting voice establishes the atmosphere for the late-night reverie of the urban vampire and the use of superimposition and seamless dissolves equates Nadja with the city itself" (Abbott 2007, 146–147)[27] This fusion with the space of the city is further described by her freedom to move through and around it—something which is specifically read as feminist and as a "taking back" or "reclaiming" of environments that were not considered either safe or suitable for women. As such Nadja's dreamlike possession of the spaces she moves through—the city here is constructed as a phantasmagoric space, seeing possession as both ownership but also a kind of haunting—configure a form of othering to environments largely controlled by men. Subsequently, much of Nadja's abjectness is constructed through her self-assurance and ability to be herself. This is not just psychological but relies as well on her greater than human strength, which increases her abject nature and constructs her as gender-ambivalent, a strong, masculine female. Further, Nadja is so strongly self-possessed and able to possess all those around her that she repels almost everyone she meets, except those she wants to feed on. This is noted by Paige A. Wilson, Melissa Goldsmith, and Anthony J. Fonseca in terms of her obvious difference to those around her: "[the film] literally stresses the foreigners of its main character, her intense feelings of alienation not being *normal*" (emphasis in original, Wilson, Goldsmith and Fonseca 2013, 50).[28] Consequently she feels most at home in a space where she is most alienated from the people around her, in many ways a perfect description of city life. Unfortunately for Nadja, while she might be able to lose her old self during short periods of metropolitan reverie, her bodily history inevitably returns to remind her of her past. It is this that Almereyder's narrative chooses to focus on.

All seems well until Nadja has cremated her father's body and goes to tell her twin brother Edgar (Jared Harris) what has happened. Not surprisingly, such an event stirs up many memories, so much so that she not only becomes possessed by her past but also by her father, and hence why the traumatic cycle of repetition begins from this point.[29]

She takes to the streets on one of her hallucinatory trips around the city and in a bar encounters a young girl called Lucy who is very quickly "troubled" by her new acquaintance. It is not long before they are back at the girl's apartment having sex. Much of this echoes Le Fanu's *Carmilla*, with the lesbian love affair beyond/outside of patriarchal control. Lucy keeps this secret from her husband Jim (Van Helsing's nephew). This also increases the need to read Nadja's otherness as that of an anti-patriarchal feminist, though this is not necessarily as clear-cut if she actually is driven by her father's spirit.

Later in the film we are shown a short flashback to Nadja's mother being observed by a distant figure we assume to be the vampire.

Van Helsing, in a voice over, describes this woman as the one that Dracula truly loved, one with whom he dreamed of a new life—just as Nadja has attempted to create in the city. After his wife died giving birth to twins, Nadja and her brother Edgar, the vampire lost all hope of change. Oddly in the clip the woman, who is in the foreground, is never shown as being close to the vampire, who always remains as a dark, cloaked figure in the background, more a predator watching its prey rather than a lover. This clip is close enough to Nadja and Lucy meeting—it is between their conversation in the bar and their love scene in Lucy's apartment—to be considered as adding significance to their encounter. Either the vampire is looking for love to change her or, in failing to truly find this love, she will repeat the violence of her father's undead life. Equally it is worth viewing in relation to the similarities between this and scenes in *Dracula* and *Dracula's Daughter*, both being important source material for Almereyda's film. In these earlier films, the vampire preys

The distant and troubling presence of Nadja's father (Peter Fonda) in *Nadja*, dir. Michael Almereyda (October Films, 1994).

on a girl it meets while out walking at night—Dracula and Zeleska each kill a street girl in London in their respective films. Consequently, Nadja meeting Lucy takes on a more ominous air. Also, in regard to genre history, which plays a significant part in virtually all vampire films (see Gelder, 2012 and Weinstein, 2012), Lucy is the name of the vampire's victim in Stoker's *Dracula* and spurs on the actions of the vampire hunters. It is almost as if Nadja's destiny were laying traps for her, that like her father before her she would be drawn to a dreamy young girl, who would inevitably be called Lucy and is related by marriage to her father's nemesis. There is a sense here of psychological or hereditary trauma that can never be resolved and will be re-enacted over and over again, and that Nadja too will be forced to perform the same violent story that her father did. And in many ways, this is what occurs.

Lucy becomes part vampire, not unlike Mina in *Dracula*, which only increases the urgency with which Jim and Van Helsing try to track the vampire. Nadja's meeting with Edgar goes badly as she tries to turn him into a blood-drinking vampire like herself—up until this point he has refused to drink blood—and so she kidnaps his nurse/fiancée, causing him to join forces with the other two men. Now that her life in the New World has unraveled, she is forced to return home where her self-possession and otherness is taken over by the spirit/memory of her father, reigniting the cycle of violent trauma from the past that previously destroyed him. Indeed, it can be read here that sees the environment she inhabits as implicit in that historical trauma, seeing the violence of her father toward women as a synecdoche of wider male society, and it is the "world of men" that creates her destiny.

However, as observed by Abbott, Nadja might not be as passive a victim of her past as she appears, as she "manoeuvres the men into staking her in order to facilitate the transference of her spirit" (Abbott 2015, 51), potentially finding a way to re-possess herself and the control of her own otherness. Before describing the final scene, it is worth discussing the troubled self of Lucy.

When we first see Lucy, she is blurry and out of focus. It transpires that we are looking at her through the eyes of her husband Jim, who has just been knocked out at a sparring fight in a boxing gym. And although she slowly gains clarity, this initial view establishes her as a miasmic figure, without form or identity. Indeed, it is something of this that brings her and Nadja together as they both seem adrift when they meet in the bar. Once they go back to Lucy's empty apartment—Jim is with Van Helsing, who he has just bailed out of jail—Nadja seduces her and drinks her blood, a graphically visual scene as she licks Lucy's menstrual blood. This has the effect of possessing her, making Lucy even more distant than before. It can be argued that it is the traumatic repetition embodied in Nadja, the spirit of her dead father, that troubles Lucy, making her even more lost than she was but also in thrall to the vampire. It's almost as if the spirit of Dracula within Nadja provides Lucy with the authoritative voice of a "father" that her husband Jim seems to lack, which will be discussed further later on.

Jim's ineffectual presence is shown later when Lucy leaves him to go to the vampire. They are in a bar talking, and Jim feels as though he is successfully reasoning with her to stay with him when she suddenly throws him across the room, her partial vampirism giving her increased strength. This effectively emasculates him, the man who boxes to prove his manhood being thrown across the bar by a woman half his size.

Unsurprisingly, Lucy escapes to be reunited with Nadja, her new troubled self actually more assured and focused—mentally and physically stronger—than her former self. It is possible that Lucy was more like this before the city took hold of her, and that the hallucinatory nature of the lights, signs, and crowds which help Nadja to forget her past and "find" herself, has the opposite effect on the younger girl. In this way the trauma of the past/spirit of Dracula that now possesses Nadja gives Lucy the past she has lost by living in the city.

On arriving home in Transylvania Nadja seems to fully accept the traumas of her family history and any resistance to her father's influence is gone; she even sees the city as a fleeting distraction, a costume that one might wear then cast off. Reassured of the eternal nature of her heritage she allows herself to be killed so that like her father she can be reborn; something of this is seen in the way that Nadja's eyes are shown floating over the scenes of the vampire hunters entering the castle, resonating with an earlier close up of Count Dracula's eyes (Bela Lugosi) in the film that suggested the continuing influence of the past. Her rebirth is partially facilitated by her performing a blood transfusion with Cassandra (Suzy Amis), Edgar's fiancée, and in a curious scene just as the vampire hunters enter Castle Dracula, Nadja's blood is shown moving under its own volition through tubes connecting the two women, as if her blood/life/spirit has its own intelligence and sense of purpose. Once Nadja is dead we see that she has somehow possessed Cassandra, not unlike Dracula's spirit had previously possessed her. As such, although her body is dead, the spirit of the traumatic family heritage lives on in the body of the woman who becomes Edgar's wife. This is simultaneously incestuous and an ominous sign that the surviving twin will not escape his family's undead past. Family history is what distracts the final character to be looked at here: Jim, Lucy's husband.

Jim seems equally as lost as Lucy in being cut adrift from his past by life in the city, but in particular he exemplifies a kind of masculinity that is lost in the face of strong-minded femininity, though much of this is due to how distracted he becomes as the narrative progresses. We first see him boxing and getting knocked out—even his attempts at hyper-masculinity fail—and being brought round by his wife. Their relationship seems as rocky and as undefined as his vision is, and in an attempt to create the impression of focus he tells Lucy he wants to be with her forever; this is potentially rather prescient given they are about to cross paths with a vampire. Lucy tells him that his uncle, Van Helsing, has been arrested for suspected murder and is in jail. This begins to unsettle Jim, and the conversation he has with his uncle after getting him released from prison causes even greater amounts of distraction. Van Helsing tells him about vampires and how he has been hunting Count Dracula for years, and that the person he killed was not human but one of the undead. He further tells Jim the story of the Count's twin children and the vampire's failed attempt to change.[30] Van Helsing looks not unlike an aged hippy, giving the impression that he might be deluded in his narrative. Jim treats him accordingly but leaves the meeting rather bewildered.

Jim returns home to find their apartment trashed and Lucy huddled in the corner of the bedroom looking extremely unwell, even more distant than usual and with dark circles around her eyes; she has just been with Nadja. As he tries to comfort her, her nose starts to bleed and she has a large discharge of menstrual blood. Disconcerted by this he leaves Lucy and meets with his uncle again, telling him about Lucy's condition and that she was with someone. His uncle reiterates the very real threat of vampires and that he will need Jim's help in finding Dracula's body to ensure it has been disposed of properly—Nadja had earlier stolen it from the morgue. Van Helsing goes to Jim's apartment with him, where Lucy leaves for work despite her husband's halfhearted attempts to stop her. Once they are alone, Van Helsing tells Jim that he is in fact his father and while the younger man is processing this, they find photographs of Lucy with a woman neither of them know. As in Browning's film, the vampire hunter notices that the woman does not have a reflection in a mirror in the background and realizes that she must be Dracula's daughter. Still trying to process all this, Jim collects Lucy from work and takes her to the bar next to her workplace—which is where she met Nadja. In a rather obtuse manner, he tells her he can forgive her seeing someone, but Lucy replies even more obliquely that life is the "pain of fleeting joy" (Almereyder, 1994) and pulls him to her as if to kiss him, then throws him across the bar. Still not willing to let her go he takes her with him and his fellow vampire hunters to Transylvania where Lucy saves him from being killed by Nadja's assistant.

In a curious way this mirrors the knockout punch that began Jim's story in the film, making his journey something of a loop that gives him time to assimilate the past. In fact one can see the young man's narrative as a continual boxing match where each new revelation/distraction keeps him forever on the ropes, never able to fully assimilate new information or bring his identity into sharp focus. These distracting blows can be seen to be caused by the abject otherness of the vampire, not just Nadja's self-possessed femininity but the undying and resurrected past of her father's spirit within her, that manifest themselves in their influence on Lucy and Jim's own traumatic family history. And while these revelations never possess him in the way that Nadja's traumatic past does Lucy, they push and pull him further and further away from the identity he thought he had. Even when the narrative ends, one is not sure exactly where it leaves Jim and Lucy; while his wife is no longer possessed by the past, his own ancestry is only just beginning to catch up with him.

The next movie is one that changes the traditional narrative of *Dracula* even more drastically, but still centers on the troubles caused by a traumatic past erupting in the present.

Let the Right One In, Tomas Alfredson, 2008

At first glance, the Swedish film *Let the Right One In* appears to be about two pre-adolescent children in Stockholm in the 1980s, except one of them is a vampire who has been twelve "for a long time" (Alfredson, 2008). Its relation to *Dracula* seems minimal at best, and indeed the story feels to have more obvious connection to Le Fanu's *Carmilla* than Stoker's novel, with its dreamlike atmosphere and the illicit relationship beyond the world of patriarchal/parental control.[31] However, enough details resonate with *Dracula* to draw some interesting parallels and conclusions—the analysis of different characters which follows often repeats various scenes to examine them from a different perspective.

The film, adapted from a novel of the same name by John Ajvide Lindqvist, tells of Oskar (Kåre Hedebrant), a lonely 12-year-old boy who is bullied at school, distant from his divorced parents, and filled with anger at his own emasculation. Seemingly from nowhere a mysterious 12-year-old girl, Eli (Lina Leandersson), and her "father," Håkan (Per Ragner), move into the same apartment block as the boy, and they strike up an unlikely friendship which culminates in the wholesale slaughter of his tormentors and Oskar leaving home with Eli, his new vampire best friend. Many see the pair as "alter egos" and that Eli is the "manifestation of his rage and pain and thirst for revenge and affirmation" (Weinstein, 2012, 4)—he is extremely pale, and she is dark; he lives in the daytime, and she at night.[32] This reading suggests that the vampire, as an already existing entity, was invited, or drawn, into Oskar's life by his emotional excess. In this way Eli can be seen in the mold of Count Dracula, who too responds to emotional invitations.[33] Harker/Renfield "invite" the vampire into their home due to avarice and a need for self/professional affirmation. If we carry on that reading then the taxi arriving at the apartment block where Oskar lives is the Demeter landing at Whitby, and Eli's "father" is Renfield. The vampire/Eli then takes up residence next door to the young boy, just as the Count did to Seward's Asylum and the home of the Westenras. Oskar is then something of a Lucy or Mina character, and certainly Lucy's sexual excess—for the Victorian period—is a beacon for the vampire, just as the young boy's rage and need for revenge attract Eli. While no blood is exchanged between the two maybe something just as precious is, at least in regard to Eli.[34] Oskar gives the vampire his Rubik's cube, in part symbolic of the times the film is depicting but also as a time-consuming puzzle. We later discover that Eli, who is possibly 300 years old or more, collects such toys as a way to cope with eternity; the puzzles themselves become containers/symbols of temporality, so that Oskar has literally given her a gift of time, not to add to it but to lessen its weight. Eli reciprocates by lessening the weight of time on Oskar by killing his tormentors. This exchange reenacts the kind of exchange that took place between Mina and the Count and which subsequently binds the two together forever.

This paints a darker picture of Eli, who can then be seen as extremely purposeful in her seduction and eventual abduction of Oskar—something the Matt Reeves adaptation of Alfredson's film makes more explicit in *Let Me In* from 2010. This also begins to delineate the nature of the vampire's absolute otherness in the film as she then becomes a monstrous child who exploits and, literally, feeds on the adult society around her. Much of this otherness is constructed around her relationship to her "father" Håkan who, as more clearly stated in the novel, is a pedophile.[35]

Pedophilia is a popular category of monstrosity in the 21st century, demarcating those who are outside of normalized society as corrupters of innocence/innocents and its hopes for the future, yet equally manifesting the ambivalence of that same society to its own exploitation and sexualization of those very children. The vampire's relationship to pedophilia is a complicated one, mainly due to the great age of vampires, especially those that look like children, in comparison to their human prey. Edward and Bella from *The Twilight Saga* (Meyer, 2005–8) being a case in point, where he is over 100 years old and she 17 when they first meet; more obvious cases are Claudia from *Interview with the Vampire* (Jordan, 1994) and Shori from Octavia Butler's novel *Fledgling* (2005). As such they are often known to exploit their eternal youth to attack and kill those who would exploit children—sometimes facilitating something of a softening of their undead otherness. Alfredson's film suggests that Håkan and Eli have been together for a long time, even maybe since he was a teenager and that he is just a tragic figure rather than a truly monstrous one,[36] even though we see him killing people and draining their blood so that Eli might remain undiscovered.

As such the vampire's treatment of her "father" seems ambivalent at best, though this is in part due to his increasing carelessness when collecting blood—Wheeler W. Dixon goes so far as to suggest that these scenes of Håkan's blunders are "played for laughs" in the film (Dixon 2010, 178)—and it is difficult to read whether her final goodbye to him is a compassionate kiss goodbye or a coup de grace delivered by a stone-cold killer who breaks the neck of her victim.[37] Either way, Oskar has definitely been lined up as his replacement, which of course then makes Eli the pedophile character as she is a few hundred years older than the boy. Rather neatly, then, the vampire configures the object of transgressive sexual desire, the predator that preys on this symbol of societal innocence and goodness, *and* the vigilante that takes revenge for breaking such taboos; she is both the mirror image of society and its dark reflection.

Her monstrosity as a child/not child—this in itself makes her difficult to categorize and therefore abject (Kristeva, 1982)—is further reinforced by her foreignness, as her description as a dark other also speaks to her embodiment of the outsider/immigrant, not unlike Count Dracula before her. In Lindqvist's novel, Eli is described as having black hair and is more elfin in her features, to contrast with the very blond Oskar. In Alfredson's film however, he specifically chose Leanderssen to play Eli as she was of Iranian descent, casting her not just as the dark half of Oskar's psyche but of Sweden itself; the foreign other. While issues with immigration from the Middle East into Europe seem more a problem of the 21st century, issues were arising in regard specifically to Sweden in the time that the film is set. As I have noted elsewhere, there was:

> [a] sharp increase in Iranian immigrants into Sweden during the 1980s, making them suddenly not so desirable aliens entering the country.[38] Eli's dark hair and complexion ... [configure her] as something exotic and different, and a contagion that has come from outside of Sweden [Bacon 2016, 53].

The construction of Eli as a dangerous other from the East strongly parallels that of Count Dracula himself, where he represents an old-world monster coming to a new land to feed on it and corrupt its future. Eli moves to Blackeburg, a suburb of Stockholm, and the original influx of immigrants from Iran lived in such areas of the capital.[39] Something of this hangs around Eli, and while they might just seem like a couple of "troubled creepy children" (Gelder 2012, 34) she is actually busy about her work converting the youth to her own "religion."

Of course, there is always the possibility that Eli has great regard for Oskar, and the film does much to try and emphasize this aspect so that they rather configure the notion of hybridity and multi-culturalism, something that comes together in the movie's culmination. After killing the bullies that tormented Oskar, Eli leaves Blackeberg with him on a train. The final scene of Oskar sitting alone in a carriage with a large box in front of him is both dreamlike and disconcerting—Eli is apparently in the box but this could equally only in Oskar's mind; the former as the train seems empty, apart from the conductor and a soft breeze blowing through the sun-filled compartments; the latter because it mirrors the scene in Browning's *Dracula* where the deeply troubled Renfield scratches on and talks to the box containing the vampire in the hold of the Demeter. Eli, the dark other and immortal vampire, is leaving with her new assistant to find a new world to call home.[40]

The most obvious person to be troubled by the appearance of the vampire is Oskar, though it is questionable whether he is troubled or distracted into a new self, or if the appearance of Eli just allows him to become who he really is. Unlike Renfield in Browning's film no dramatic character change occurs between his former and later selves, though potentially there is one scene where he decides to embrace what he will be with the vampire rather than exist without it. This occurs in the latter half of the story after Oskar has already passed important milestones in their relationship, such as following Eli's advice to "hit back harder than you dare" and splitting the ear of the main bully, and sharing his bed with her all of which distract him further and further away from his former life and into the new one with the vampire. Consequently, when the crucial point comes, he is already in a place where the new life is closer than the old one. Still, it is still a choice he has to make, and it comes when Lacke discovers where Eli is sleeping.

Lacke (Peter Carlberg) is the friend of Jocke, who was Eli's victim the night Håkan first bungled his search for blood, leaving her unfed. Desperate for food she went out alone and attacked Jocke, a local man, by pretending to be a lost, distressed child. Lacke is the only person concerned over his friend going missing. Later, Eli also attacks Lacke's girlfriend Virginia and while he quickly kicks Eli off of her, it is not before Virginia has been bitten. Infected by the wound, Virginia begins to turn into a vampire, and when Lacke takes her to hospital to treat her mysterious illness, she bursts into flames when a nurse opens the curtains in her room, exposing her to sunlight. Filling a makeshift Van Helsing role, Lacke follows the trail that eventually leads him to Eli's apartment where Oskar is waiting for her to wake up as soon as the sun sets. Oskar remains hidden while Lacke searches the apartment. When he reaches the bathroom and starts tearing the newspaper away from the windows—Eli sleeps in the bath during the day covered by cardboard, with the bathroom windows blacked out with newspaper—Oskar leaps out of hiding, shouting for the girl to wake up. Eli jumps up and attacks the intruder, easily overpowering him, and Oskar leaves the room, closing the door to let her finish. As Anne Billson observes "it's an action, or absence of action, which draws the two children together, from now on, they'll be looking out for each other" (Billson 2011, 96). Yet it is more than that, as while Oskar might not have killed Lacke himself he is responsible and in many ways it is the final test for him to take over Håkan's role. They may be looking out for each other, but Eli is the one who controls the nature of their "together"-ness, as is shown when she rewards him for his good work with a kiss, leaving Oskar's mouth smeared with blood.

In many ways the final scenes of the film are superfluous to the outcome as Oskar has already been distracted enough to embrace his true nature, or at least his true nature with the vampire. Even the massacre of the bullies in the swimming pool only serves to prove to him that he has made the right choice and that, as he thought, he will never be bullied again. All that is left is for him to leave his mother and Blackeberg and find his new home.

Home is an important concept for vampires, though it is slightly different for Eli than it was for Count Dracula. The Count required soil from his homeland to sleep in every night[41]—actually earth from a chapel that was part of his dilapidated castle—but Eli seems to travel much lighter, just taking her collection of puzzles and "trophies" from victims with her.[42] More interestingly, vampires have an almost symbiotic bond with their environments. Dracula affects the weather and animals around his home, and even around the Demeter on his trip to England; indeed, one can argue it was Carfax Abbey itself that called to him to come and take residence there. Eli has a similar effect on and bond with Blackeberg, though it is both subtler and more unsettling than Stoker's Count.

Blackeberg, a ghost town for a ghost boy (Kåre Hedebrant). *Let the Right One In*, dir. Tomas Alfredson (Sandrew Metronome, 2008).

The film opens on Oskar, wearing only a pair of white underpants and standing in front of a large window, staring out into the darkness watching the snow fall. His reflection dominates the screen making him seem ethereal: as Billson notes, "he looks like a ghost child, already half lost to the real world" (Billson 2011, 30). The world outside his window is white, and cold, and still, and then the vampire arrives.

The film's version of Blackeberg echoes that of the real place which is a working-class suburb of Stockholm and is unprepared for its undead visitor. Built in 1952 it was, as Billson comments, "the height of modernity" but almost 30 years later "the angular construction has become shabby and slightly seedy in the way of much modernist architecture" (Billson 2011, 30). Blackeberg was originally built when Sweden felt like it was on the move to better times, and as Franziska Schneider observes, people moving there "wanted to lead good and respectable lives there. They all shared the same dream of equality and wealth. They were pioneers" (Schneider 2015, 107). But the economy faltered, and the dream became a nightmare as the suburb become something of an embodiment of a national trauma, and a community forcibly made unemployed without the possibility of the work and dignity it was promised. This sense of detachment is even more pronounced due to the fact that Blackeberg was specifically built for this purpose and has no past or roots in a shared heritage that might bind people together. Lindqvist writes: "where the three-storied apartment buildings now stood there had been only forest before. You were beyond the grasp of the mysteries of the past" (Lindvist 2008, 2). Consequently the memory-less environment has no defense against the memory-full vampire when it arrives,[43] as Schneider further notes: "Blackeberg stands for these values [modernity and progress]. It is most effective to destroy this idyll with a horror that represents the total opposite of modernity, health and progress ... causing its downfall from within" (Schneider 2015, 108).

As such, Eli arrives at a place that is summoning her almost as much as Oskar himself is, but rather than being given a new life, as the boy is, the city wants to be put out of the misery of its old, troubled one. This sense of brokenness is seen everywhere in the narrative; the group of friends that meet in the local bar to drink the day away; Oskar's parents who are divorced; the children who bully Oskar at school; and the drinking "friends" of Jocke who don't care that he has suddenly disappeared. Even the snow smothers the life of the community, leaving it cold and unwelcoming. It is not surprising that those who venture out soon become victims of the vampire and her assistant—the suburb is trying to kill any vestiges of vigor or hope. News of the sudden and mysterious deaths spread, and it is not long before the police arrive at Oskar's school warning the children not to wander out at night, and the despondency of the community is exacerbated by fear of an unknown and unseen attacker. It is not unexpected then that the denouement of the story sees a group of children horribly murdered at the local swimming baths. Though we are never shown what effects this has on the surrounding community it is an attack on the continued viability of the area, not just in the deaths of the children as an embodiment of the future, but also in making it a highly undesirable area to move to or stay in.[44] The suburb, almost literally, wants to trouble itself out of existence. In a somewhat contrary manner, the attack of the vampire, as traumatic memory bursting into a present unprepared for it, provides a traumatic memory for Blackeberg itself—a history that will stay with it forever. To confirm the existence of the oppressive cloud that hangs over and smothers the area, as Oskar leaves on the train with Eli, the carriage is flooded with air and light as noted above; Blackeberg might now be as undead as the vampire that is leaving it but the horizon is full of new homes to find.

The Strain (del Toro and Hogan, 2014–17) also sees the presence of the vampire cursing its surroundings largely through a traumatic memory that distracts the city from seeing what is occurring in its midst.

The Strain, del Toro and Hogan, 2014–2017

The Strain has appeared as a trilogy of novels, a series of graphic novels, and most recently a television series. The authors/creators Guillermo del Toro and Chuck Hogan had supposedly intended the story to be made as a television series, and indeed its novelization has moments which feel as if they were written to be watched rather than read. That said, the series that finally emerged on the small screen varies somewhat from the books and, as will be argued here, is consequently more about American politics since the election of President Trump than are the original books that came out between 2009 and 2011. Regardless, the main impetus in the narrative(s) is del Toro's vision to return to an older version of the vampire—at the time of the first novel's publication popular culture had been saturated with romanticized, vegetarian, and "sparkly" vampires for some time, reaching its apotheosis in *The Twilight Saga*—and as such, the King Vampire in del Toro and Hogan's story harkens back to both Stoker's and Murnau's vision of the undead while mixing in a flavor of Eastern European folklore and a large dash of del Toro's own vampiric mythology. Consequently, the Master is both immediately recognizable but also unknown, or as the tagline for the story across all mediums describes it, "This is something new.... Or—something very, very old" (del Toro and Hogan 2010, 164).

The story,[45] particularly in relation to the vampire, contains many flashbacks, emphasizing the constant presence of the past in the current moment, as well as the weight and importance of historical trauma that continually repeats when not sufficiently recognized or dealt with. Within the series, this is seen both in the repetition of fictional precursors, as well as in echoes and direct references to actual historical events, which position character types and tropes from *Dracula* and the Holocaust as intersecting with 21st century American politics. As mentioned, Stoker's work in particular casts a huge shadow here, with the Count from Europe being copied in the form of the ancient vampire, the Master, who conspires to procure an invitation into the heart of the world's dominant Empire. He too requires a coffin of his own soil to survive in and quickly starts to influence those around him.[46] The crew of light arrayed against him all find modern-day equivalents with Jonathan being replaced by Ephraim Goodweather, Mina by Kelly Goodweather, and Seward, Holmwood, and Morris by Vassily Fet, Augustin Elizalde, and Nora Martinez/Dutch Velders respectively.[47] Renfield is replaced by the far more influential character of Eldritch Palmer who is both enthrall to the vampire and trying to manipulate it for his own ends. The Van Helsing role is possibly the most important as it continues the original tensions between ideas of good and evil, and an educated man who believes in and utilizes the powers of esoteric knowledge. Here the updated Professor also strengthens the ideological links to the Holocaust and its ongoing trauma, as he is a survivor of Treblinka and although over 90 years old continues his fight against the forces of far-right racial supremacy (as 21st vampirism is constructed in *The Strain*). As such, del Toro and Hogan's tale re-envisions *Dracula* from the moment the ship lands in the Empire but allows the vampire to succeed in his plans to turn America's might and power into his own "bountiful wine-press for a while" (Stoker 1996, 311).

The narrative itself is set in present-day New York with a mysterious aircraft landing at JFK airport seemingly full of dead passengers. This prompts the authorities to call in the CDC (Center of Disease Control) to investigate. A team lead by Ephraim Goodweather arrives, and what seems already an impenetrable mystery gets increasingly complicated as passengers begin to revive and changing into vampires. The Master has arranged for his coffin to be "disappeared" from the airport and taken to a site under the city to create his lair and surround himself with the increasing number of undead—the Master, like the Count, is telepathically linked to all those he infects. The Master eventually manages to take control of the city, after moving between various host bodies, and sets up processing plants to "farm" humans; these plants are supervised by Thomas Eichhorst, former commandant at Treblinka and undead right-hand to the King Vampire. To facilitate his own superiority and free movement during the day, the Master arranges for a nuclear explosion near the city so that it is covered in a permanent dust cloud, occluding any sunlight. However, the Professor and the crew of light manage to lure the Master into a trap and use another nuclear weapon to destroy him. The Master in his role as Count Dracula is obviously the most troubling, and his absolute otherness is constructed specifically around the idea of historical trauma that gets increasingly violent and destructive as it repeats over time.

The King Vampire is described as being one of seven original ancients that are responsible for the vampire race. In the novels they are directly linked to fallen angels, but the television series never fully explains this, only suggesting that they have always existed alongside humans. The main introduction to the Master comes through the legend of Jusef Sardu as told to a young Abraham Setrakian by his grandmother in 1932. Sardu, a gentle giant of a nobleman—he was over 8 feet (2.4m) tall—went hunting for a wolf with his brothers, as it was believed the blood of such a beast would cure him of his gigantism. However, the wolf turned out to be the Master who killed the brothers and took Sardu's body for his own. On returning home, Sardu used his former, gentle reputation to abuse and infect the town's children, showing this as the monster's originating traumatic act and somewhat replicating the trauma of Eli in *Let the Right One In*.[48] Setrakian later encounters the beast himself when he is imprisoned in Treblinka during World War II and spies a mysterious creature taking ill prisoners during the night. Not long after this, Eichhorst, the camp's commandant, requisitions Setrakian to build and ornately carve a huge wooden box. It later transpires that Eichhorst has chosen to become part of a new master race as the Third Reich is falling into disarray, and that the box is for the Master himself.

The body of the vampire then embodies the corruption of innocence and racial purity as manifested in anti–Semitism and its recurrence though Western civilization. This becomes even more pronounced in 21st century

America once the vampire arrives in New York at the invitation of Eldritch Palmer, a terminally ill billionaire who thinks the Master can save him and make him immortal. Palmer himself is as white as the vampires, constructing him as equally exemplifying undead whiteness. The arrival of the vampire into the city via airplane, and then the Master's brief connection to Ground Zero, the site of the 9/11 Terror attack—this is more explicit in the novels— makes a direct connection and correlation between the War on Terror and the Holocaust, with the added corruption of innocence and pedophilia.[49] The absolute otherness of the Master is one born of racism and anti–Semitism which manifests as undead, white, nationalist supremacy.

The vampiric infection itself is possibly the biggest signifier of white purity as the victims get progressively hairless, sexless, and extremely white regardless of their original ethnicity.[50] This transformation is particularly interesting as it completely changes its human host. It does not just give the new vampires a thirst for blood and power to glamour people, or even turn into a bat or some other creature, but makes them a corporeal, flesh and blood monument to historical trauma. The body of the Master graphically shows this as his bestial, pure white, almost lizard-like torso seems both monstrous and inhuman; a once-human body desiccated by repetitive violence, leaving only a tortured looking creature behind. This is emphasized by the wattle of skin that hangs at its throat—the older the vampire the more this wattle looks like a large pair of testicles—which allows space for the huge tongue that explodes from the vampire's mouth when it eats. Indeed, the body is more of a carved-out husk for the anaconda-sized appendage to reside within. The final look of the Master, very much like Murnau's Orlok before him, is the creation of hundreds of years of living in the dark, violating and destroying humans, and spreading its deadly contagion at sites of human atrocity and violence. This is shown most clearly when the vampire changes hosts by shoving dirt containing worms into its victims mouth and then vomits white worms into the same orifice, at which point its wattle deflates making the act a form of oral rape and pseudo-sexual trauma; the past literally violating the present. So when the Master's victims begin to look like him, it is not just that they have been infected with vampirism but with the weight of the historical violence and trauma that he has committed.

Unsurprisingly then, the Master increasingly troubles the entire population of the city due in part to the metropolis's increasing distance from its own past and its concern with a consumerist present, but also to the vampire's manifestation as a monstrous intersection of ideas around history, Nazism, terrorism, pedophilia, and white corporate America. This last is seen specifically through the figure of Eldritch Palmer who is both distracted and troubled by the vampire, so before talking more of the Master it is worth considering his Renfield.

The Master (Doug Jones) repeating historical trauma in *The Strain*, created by Guillermo del Toro and Chuck Hogan (20th Television, 2014–2017).

Palmer is a very Trumpian character, even though he was first imagined before the rise of the current President of America. He is an amazingly wealthy, old, white man who thinks money can give him power over not only people but life itself. When this fails he decides to facilitate the safe entry of the Master into New York and assist in his rise to worldwide dominance so that he himself will become healthy and immortal at the vampire's side. Like Renfield, he chooses to betray his own kind in favor of more selfish rewards, and like his precursor he is constantly troubled between his old self and being what the vampire wants him to be. In the book, Palmer never becomes a vampire but in the series, circumstances dictate that the Master invades the billionaire's body. This immediately sees white corporate America correlated not just to *historical* traumas around the Holocaust but to their continuation in current day politics in relation to wider racial discrimination, vilification of immigrants, and the corruption of children.

Just as with Browning's Renfield, at various points in the story it appears that Palmer is trying to help Setrakian and his vampire hunters, and that he is not totally in control of his own mind. Once he begins to realize that the Master has little or no intention of turning him into a vampire he actively seeks the Professor out, though more to gain access to the illusive "white" than out of altruism of any kind; "white" is the vampire's blood, minus the infectious worms, that can regenerate those who consume it, but it needs to be filtered in some way or it kills humans.[51] Even then however, the troubling presence of the Master, specifically seen through the fascistic Eichhorst—a figure who embodies contained/repressed violence—keeps Palmer from returning to either his normal selfish ways or building on the occasional flash of human compassion. Eichhorst in fact forms something of a dark reflection of Palmer, and the series shows them both as unloved when younger. Whereas the former commandant found an outlet for his personal revenge through a sense of history and conviction to an ideal, the billionaire can see nothing beyond himself. As such, the past means little to Palmer as he is only concerned about what is happening to him in the present. This is why the history of Eichhorst, as representative of the Master, troubles him so much. The irony is that by series end Palmer has become the Master while the German remains the assistant. The billionaire himself is taken by surprise by the transformation, almost expecting to die unfulfilled, as his predecessor does in Stoker and Browning, but he is finally given the ultimate gift; not just vampirism but the essence of the Dark Lord himself.

Palmer is not the only character to join the side of the Master and to subsequently be troubled by that association and changed into a different version of him or herself. This happens to Dutch Velders who finishes up strictly on the side of the slayers.

The character of Dutch does not appear in the novels but in the television series she is brought in as computer hacker hired by Palmer to take down the city's communications systems, so the population will have no idea what is occurring. This is something of a reversal of *Dracula* where the slayers utilize the wonders of modern communication systems to outwit and track the vampire. Here, the Master takes control of technology and the means of communication to prevent his being discovered. This updating of the vampire is seen as well in its use of an airplane to travel the world rather than a boat—though in the Balderston/Deane play from 1927, from which Browning's film was largely taken, the vampire uses an airplane to fly to London so it can complete the journey in one night[52]—and in its use of a nuclear weapon to create a continual cloud cover for its horde of vampires to roam the city unimpeded. Dutch very much takes pride in her ability to break into secure systems and crash the internet and expects to be accordingly very well paid—aligning her to the amoral/immoral nature of corporate greed and control and the complicity of those who facilitate it. Even though she begins to be aware things are not quite right, it is not until she becomes trapped in an all-night garage with her girlfriend and needs to be saved from vampires by Ephraim and Vassily Fet that she reassesses her position. Eventually she joins the team of slayers and attempts to undo the work she had previously done. This culminates in her taking control of all television channels for a brief period so that Ephraim, as a member of the CDC, can try and warn the population of the fatal contagion spreading through the metropolis. This begins to analyze the way in which the Master troubles Dutch through his embodiment of the traumatic past, which controls the present and disrupts any moment into the future.[53] In part this is the Master's plan so that Dutch, as representative of modern technology, is either under his control or forced to revert to more simple/basic means of technology.

This reaches a climax when Eichhorst captures Dutch and chains her up in a feeding cell he has prepared for his personal victims. Here, he feeds on/violates Dutch, giving physical form to the violence of the past corrupting the mind and body of the present. However, Dutch manages to escape and to create a device, with Ephraim, that will disrupt the Master's own means of communication. As mentioned earlier the Master has the ability to contact all of his "creations" through telepathy, although as the series develops, this changes slightly to become a sound wave that is higher than humans can ordinarily hear. Ephraim and Dutch manage to isolate this communicative sound wave and make a device that can produce a sound to block it; it further transpires that when this blocking sound is played normal vampires become disorientated, no longer connected to the source, the historical trauma, which guides them. This moment is instructive in the series as it highlights the contrary effects of being troubled by the vampire. For those infected by him it means they can never escape the violence of the past and are forced to continually repeat it, it literally guides their every move[54]; however, this actually has the effect of making Dutch remember herself, troubling her into remembering her own humanity beyond the trauma of history.

In many ways this is the lasting effect of the Master on the city itself, making it remember the importance of the traumas it has itself suffered and reinforcing that they should never be overwritten by commercial or corporate needs. With this memorial imperative it is no surprise that to kill the Master, he has to be taken deep underground to tunnels that were built in the city's past, symbolizing the violence and trauma on which the metropolis was constructed, and a nuclear device exploded that allows the historical and violent excess of the king vampire to dissipate.

The ending of the series is particularly interesting as, unlike the novels, it was written just as the effects of populism and the alt-right were taking effect in the American elections, and although it is speculative to suggest it is direct social commentary it can certainly be read as such. Unlike the novel where victory is complete, the television series leaves a peculiar unsettling possibility hanging at its end. First, although the Master is dead the vampires are not, and while they are leaderless there is the potential that one day, they might continue the infection[55]; it is as though the original trauma has not been fully dealt with and might return unexpectedly. Secondly, and connected to the first, concerns the speed with which civilization returns to normal; seemingly within months the sky is pure blue above a rebuilt city and Dutch and Fet are both working at jobs and meeting for lunch. In the books, civilization has to slowly rebuild and remains in tatters at the story's end. Something in the series ending suggests that the problems caused/represented by the Master have been glossed over, that the real damage caused has been ignored, and that the old corporate consumerist ideologies that caused the problems are already back in place, if they ever left. One has the impression that the narrative might end on a sunny day, but the eternal night of the vampire's absolute otherness is ready to fall once again.

Two

The Land Beyond the Forest

In which the figure of Count Dracula embodies an ethnic absolute otherness which "troubles" Western society from early 20th century anti–Semitism to the War on Terror and Islamic/religious extremism.

Nosferatu, F.W. Murnau, 1922

If Stoker's vampire Count dreamed of being in the midst of humanity and not marked as "a stranger in a strange land" (Stoker 1996, 22), Murnau's Orlok (Max Schreck) has no such compulsion. Unlike his Victorian predecessor or his Hollywood descendant, Count Orlok could never be lost in a crowd or blend in with the daily life of Wisborg, where he travels to, as he is conspicuously marked as being an absolute other from a world beyond our own. This is curious given that this story's visitor, Thomas Hutter, does not need to travel anywhere near as far as Harker (Stoker) or Renfield (Browning) to reach the "land beyond the forest" (Stoker 1996, 259).

Murnau makes dramatic changes to this journey by making it begin in Wisborg, Germany, rather than London—appealing to a home audience while also trying to avoid copyright infringement—and altering the setting to 1838. The date is interesting as it definitely sets the story in the past—Browning's vampire seems extremely modern in comparison—and envisions the adventure that Hutter (Gustav von Wangenheim) makes less a trip back in time, as both Harker's and Renfield's journeys are, but more like being transported somewhere imaginary or otherworldly; Hutter almost transcends to the vampire's lair. Unlike Harker, Hutter is continually part of the landscape as he travels, mainly on horse or by foot. As his journey continues the landscapes seem to get more and more panoramic and romantic; as Kevin Jackson notes, "it is from here on that Murnau's deep affinity for the German Romantic landscape tradition in general, and for the paintings of Friedrich in particular, become manifest" (Jackson 2017, 50). The landscape is both sublime and "elemental" (Allen 2007, 180), making the young man's trip spiritual in nature and taking him beyond the realm of the living, though rather than meeting the angels he becomes entrapped by death itself.[1] Hutter is used in the film to embody German manhood and hope in the future, not unlike Harker did for the British Empire in *Dracula*, and his corruption by the vampire, aided by the young man's employer Knock (Alexander Granach), signals an attack both on the mind of Hutter and on the hopes and virility of Germany. This specifically constructs the vampire as a dangerous, shadowy creature that is less than human, not only a danger to Hutter and the residents of Wisborg but an enemy of the German state itself.

Orlok's absolute otherness is shown in many ways, firstly and mainly in how he looks, secondly in the way he inhabits/exists in the film, and lastly how these two elements racially identify him as Jewish. Browning's film painted a very romantic vampire in comparison to Stoker's novel which saw him as having a very prominent nose and wild unkempt hair and eyebrows— at least while in Transylvania.[2] Murnau goes to another extreme and makes his vampire hardly human in appearance, as Anton Kaes observes:

> The physiognomy of Count Orlok is replete with animal features: besides rodent-like fangs and ears like those of a bat, he has long claws ... a beak-like nose, and hollowed-out eyes. He wears a long black coat and tight pants that give the impression of skeletal limbs tightly wrapped in funeral clothes [Kaes 2011, 105].

This look is intimately tied up with ideas of anti–Semitism; the nose and ears being used by Stoker for similar purposes 25 years earlier in Victorian Britain alongside the idea that "the malevolent powers of hypnotism, suggestion, and seduction" (Kurtlander 2017, 77) were inherently Jewish qualities.[3] Both nations had felt the impact of pogroms against the Jews in Russia with many relocating to nations toward the west of Europe. Jews in Germany had achieved a level of social integration during and after World War I; indeed Jews formed the largest ethnic, religious, or political group fighting for Germany, and suffered 12,000 deaths.[4] However, among nationalists the defeat was seen as due to a lack of patriotism and was instantly blamed on the Jewish contingent of the army. Even though the Jewish community were an integral part of German life they soon came to be seen, by some groups, as a threat from within that preyed on the wealth and future of the nation. Eric Kurlander observes that for many of a certain mind:

> Murnau's *Nosferatu* simultaneously became the embodiment of racial (Jewish) difference "weirdly human and yet terrifyingly other ... abjectly *wrong*, unseemly, unnatural, anathema." Orlok's vampiric practices—bringing plague, drinking Aryan blood, or corrupting German women—were inherently demonic and unholy [Kurlander 2017, 77].

The corruption of women and the land—both emblematic of the National future and prosperity—quickly becomes the focus of the film. Once Hutter arrives at Orlok's castle the strange looking client—as with *Dracula* he is buying a property in the homeland of the agent sent to him—spies a picture of the young man's wife, Ellen (Greta Schröder), and suddenly the property he most desires is this woman's life. Not long after this the vampire leaves Hutter trapped in the castle and leaves for Wisborg, finishing the trip on a schooner. Once aboard the ship the crew begins dying of plague—Orlok is constantly accompanied by rats—and in an iconic scene the vampire's intentions are explicitly clear as, "when Orlok rises abruptly and mechanically from his coffin, he resembles a monstrous penis: his nocturnal passage through the arched gates of Wisborg conjures up the act of sexual penetration, and the film culminates in the invasion of a sleeping woman's bedroom" (Butler 2010, 160). Of course, this is not only about defiling German womanhood but the simultaneous emasculation of its manhood, for Hutter is totally unable to prevent the monster from doing exactly as it wishes. However, the power of the vampiric other is not just made manifest by its physical presence but goes before it like a ghost or phantom.

Murnau makes much use of editing and quick cuts between shots to give the impression that even while still on board the schooner the vampire has already made psychic contact with Ellen who is waiting for her husband onshore. This dark presence seems to gain a life of its own once the ship has landed and the vampire's shadow travels the distance between the monster and Ellen to invade her dreams and even clutch at her beating heart. The notion of shadows is used to hint at the vampire's (Jewish) racial otherness and dark forces at work within. After World War I, as noted by Kaes, shadows "assert an independent existence, exemplifying the degree to which the self had been shattered and the unconscious had seized power" (Kaes 2017, 36). *Nosferatu* perfectly captures this notion where the "unstable materiality and precarious referentiality" (Kaes 2017, 36) of the darkness speaks to the threat of the dangerous outsider who is simultaneously part of the self. Consequently, the vampire here troubles everyone it comes into contact with as it either resonates with their dark selves or attacks their innocence and purity. As such it is worth considering one case of each of these with the former most clearly seen in Hutter's employer Knock, and the latter in the symbol of innocence and goodness, Ellen.

Knock is a peculiar figure. In many ways he fulfills the Renfield role as the vampire's assistant but is more proactive than Stoker's madman and more scheming than Browning's salesman. Early in the film it is Knock who sends Hutter to Transylvania, tempting him with the prospect of wealth: "You could earn a tidy sum, even though the effort may involve a little trouble … a little sweat maybe … a little blood" (Murnau, 1922). And money certainly seems a driving force for the man who, as Butler comments, is "willing to do business with anyone if the price is right" (Butler 2013, 127). But this lust for money can be seen to be slightly different than pure avarice and more closely linked to derogatory opinions of Jewish greed in post–World War I Germany. This link to the Semitic otherness of Orlok correlates directly to Knock, as further described by Butler: "He even looks like a vampire in squat, Germanic form: he is bald and has wild eyebrows; he casts sly, sideways glances and grins maliciously through rotten teeth" (Butler 2013, 127). Arguably he is more gnome-like, but his deviousness is obvious and this alone casts him as opposite to the naive Hutter and aligned with the vampire, which is further corroborated by their correspondence.

Orlok (Max Schreck) rising from his coffin in *Nosferatu*, dir. F. W. Murnau (Film Arts Guild, 1922).

Once Hutter has agreed to go on the journey, Knock hands him a contract to sell Orlok an abandoned building in Wisborg—coincidentally situated opposite Hutter's own house. However, the document is written in occult-looking symbols which the clerk, and we as the audience, are unable to read (reading is actually important in *Nosferatu* as will be seen with Ellen). This identifies the Count and Knock as sharing a language, and a magical one at that. Such an esoteric form of communication would have been naturally linked to the Jewish community and spurious historical ties to rituals and magic. This would identify Knock as being a Jewish sympathizer, or even a Jew himself, who has been accepted into the community and yet plans its downfall to increase his own personal wealth. His actions infer the former as the growing influence of the vampire makes him lose his sanity and he becomes a raving madman. As such his Jewish sympathies quickly turn against him once they increase out of control due to the troubling presence of the vampire itself—his personality divides, shutting out the light and leaving only darkness and insanity.[5]

The degeneration of Knock into madness sees him institutionalized in an asylum where he continues the tradition of fly-eating established by Renfield. The exact and ultimate nature of his madness is shown by Murnau slightly earlier in a montage of images made up of Knock, a Venus flytrap and a polyp, all part of a lecture given by Professor Bulwar (Gustav Bots)—something of a backseat Van Helsing figure—to demonstrate the vampiric qualities of nature and equating "carnivorous plants and beastly humans such as Knock" (Janzen 2016, 158). Janet Janzen further describes how this is seen as a natural part of nature in the film, however, it can also be seen as suggesting that vampirism is a natural part of, or inherent to, people like Knock, suggesting that all Jewish sympathizers would become dangerous and destructive. Unsurprisingly the townspeople quickly believe that the madman is in some way responsible for the plague deaths that are afflicting the town[6]—which of course in a way he is for inviting the vampire there—but before they can take any action against him Knock kills his guard and escapes from the asylum, leading the agitated mob a merry dance around the countryside. This of course works as a distraction away from the true source of mayhem and death in the town, the vampire who lives secretly and silently in their midst. The troubled Knock, who has arguably been made more himself by the presence of the vampire, or allowed the other within him to take control, then acts as a distraction to the people around him. That is, everyone but Ellen who, as Thomas Koebner notes, is the only one besides Knock "that seems to know that the spreading of the fatal epidemic has to do with the vampire's presence" (Koebner 2006, 116).

Ellen is central to the film, and potentially the vampire knows of her existence before the narrative begins. As Jackson notes, Knock purposely suggests to Hutter that he sell the disused buildings across from his own house to the Count, thereby inferring that the vampire has "by supernatural means, learned about Hutter and Ellen and has dark designs upon them."[7] (Jackson 2017, 49). Curiously, Ellen has an almost psychic connection to the vampire that is not unlike that of Mina Harker in Stoker's novel, though of course there they shared each other's blood to achieve this. Here it carries a suggestion that on some level they are of the same order, beyond a simple predator/prey symbiosis. Some of this is seen in her mirroring the vampire and although not exactly its double she does represent the spiritual light of the land that the darkness of the vampire wishes to bleed dry. From the beginning of the film she is shown to have an affinity with life and nature, and even cries when Hutter cuts her some flowers as it means they will die. Their perfect life together is marked as over from the very moment Hutter decides to go on his journey; Ellen senses this and she is troubled from this point on. Not surprisingly she is increasingly troubled the closer the vampire gets, and Murnau again uses images intercut between Orlok and her to suggest that their meeting is inevitable. In fact, there is much in the film that infers that an element of the natural exists in the vampire's attraction to her and that they perform an almost spiritual battle where death consumes life, but the light of day destroys the dark of night, constructing a creation myth for the new Germany.[8]

This connection to the land and natural processes makes Ellen's awareness of the vampire's approach inevitable and once it nears the coast outside Wisborg, she faints as its power gets overwhelming. A strong sense of destiny pervades the film, as explicitly noted by Professor Bulwer who says to Hutter "Not so hasty, young friend! No one can escape his destiny" (Murnau, 1922). Once the vampire has moved in across from Ellen the strength of his presence builds to a climax seemingly out of the girl's control—death will inevitably consume her. However, illicit knowledge once again plays a central role in the narrative and Ellen discovers a way to undo the power of the vampire, if not save her own life.

Early in the film on his way to meet Orlok, Hutter is given a small book by the landlady of the hotel he stays at. This is a volume on vampires, and Hutter pays little attention to it, finding its contents laughable. His inability, or refusal, to read consistently has important consequences throughout the narrative. However, he takes the book with him and Ellen later finds it. Interestingly he has told her not to read it because of the nature of its contents, but she disobeys him and studies the whole book, and discovers that "only a woman can break his frightful spell—a woman pure in heart who will offer her blood freely and will keep the vampire by her side until after the cock has crowed" (Murnau, 1922). This knowledge, which seems to be entirely the remit of women in Murnau's film, is thereby passed on from the landlady to Ellen via Hutter (though as noted he does not read it) and it gives her power over the fate of the vampire, if not over herself. She puts it into action, sends Hutter away, and prepares herself for the vampire, an invitation that the "infatuated" Count cannot resist.[9] He arrives not unlike a nervous suitor and begins his grisly night's work. At one point he seems satiated and on the point of leaving, but Ellen makes sure that he stays to complete the ritual—and in many ways the fact that it is a ritual indeed is important. As Deborah Christie notes, this almost wanton offering of herself, as a married woman, to the vampire rather complicates her status as being "pure of heart" (Christie 2015, 280), however the giving of herself as part of a ritual does not corrupt her status. Indeed, once the process is under way it becomes almost alchemical, symbolizing male and female aspects, life and death, purification and rebirth. At its end the ritual requires an act of re-purification which is seen in the vampire vanishing in a cloud of smoke and ash, leaving only the light of the new day rising over Ellen's prone body. Christie describes this process in relation to Murnau's own text: "The final title of the film reads 'And at that moment, as if by a miracle, the sick no longer died, and the stifling shadow of the vampire vanished with the morning sun.' In part redemptive, the effect of the sun purges the town of contagion; sunlight which has a long standing" (Christie 2015, 281). Ellen's passing, her sacrifice for the nation and its land, takes the contagion with her, not just stopping its spread but removing it from those already contaminated. The new dawn contains neither the vampiric other with its associated corruption, or those who sacrificed themselves for the sake of the people of Wisborg (Germany) though they died with the knowledge of the worth of what they were doing. In a sense, *Nosferatu* is equally a parable for those who survived World War I and a warning for what is ahead, and a suggestion that ritual will be needed to cleanse the land and its "volk" once more.

As such, then, the vampire troubles Ellen into being even more herself, mirroring Knock, but in contrast her true self is for life and peace rather than death and chaos. As the film ends we see Hutter in tears holding his now dead wife, and Professor Bulwer looking lost, neither aware that they were witnesses to an event much larger than either of them knew. Such nationalist interpretations are not uncommon in vampire films, as Jack Halberstam observes, as monsters take the scars of their monstrous creation with them, and when they are born of racism (Halberstam 1993) it is a past they rarely totally cast off.

The next film sees the vampire traveling slightly further afield to find its "love" and in a much less serious story, but it still symbolizes a conflict with ideological (racial) implications.

Love at First Bite, Stan Dragoti, 1979[10]

Dragoti's film is a very different one from *Nosferatu*, not least in that it is intended as a comedy rather than a critique on post-war Weimar Germany. In line with its playful nature is the casting of the extremely suave George Hamilton who was, as noted by James Craig Holte "an actor best known for his perfect tan" (Holte 1997, 77). However, for all its light-heartedness the vampire's otherness is still extremely particular to the times the movie came out, and explicitly references a war that was as serious as it was deadly, the Cold War between the United States and the Soviet Union.

As the film begins, we see Count Dracula in his Castle in Transylvania, but things are not well as he is not only bored of where he is and pining for his lost love, but the local peasants are trying to break into his home. While spoofing original Universal Pictures monster movies such as *Frankenstein* (Whale, 1931) where the local villagers rise up against the evil scientist and his creation toward the end of the film, here in a knowing reference to the Communist regime in charge in Romania in the 1970s, the peasants are part of a workers' cooperative that need the space in Castle Dracula for living quarters.[11] When they force their way in the leader of the group, a female Commissar dressed in an androgynous uniform, informs the Count that "Either you spend the rest of your life in an efficiency apartment with seven dissidents and one toilet, or you gather your aristocratic shit together and split!" (Dragoti, 1979). This specifically builds on the notion of countries under Communism being extremely poor with the money being siphoned off by wealthy officials, something intimated in the brief exchange between the Count and his servant Renfield[12]:

> RENFIELD: I think they're from the government.
> DRACULA: How do you know?
> RENFIELD: They're wearing shoes [Dragoti, 1979].

The humor would feed into a well-known narrative in the United States at the time that viewed Soviet Russia and its satellites, such as Romania, in derogatory terms and framed their social hierarchy as aggressive and violent and the vast majority of workers as extremely poor, purposely kept unintelligent and hugely exploited, all points that are touched on in the brief exchanges between the Count and the townspeople.[13] This discriminatory view of Romania found its climax in the Dan Simmons novel *The Children of the Night* (1992) which painted a bleak picture of the nation post-communism but also as one infested with vampires that, just like Communism, drained the life blood from its people. Unsurprisingly this negative view of Communism found expression in other films. Ralph Donald notes how many represented their "evil" characters, either literally or metaphorically, as Soviet, as America's "Great Satan" (Donald 2014, n.p.) a devilish being that purposely thwarts/targets the United States and/or the "American" hero of the movie. The vampire quite readily fits such a reading and Simmons' book very much fits into such a framing. This interestingly proposes film production as an expression of American foreign policy, and in relation to Soviet Russia in particular Donald notes that this devil in Cold War–influenced films can take on a bear-like image to more clearly symbolize Russia to the American (Western) audience (Donald 2014, n.p.). Hamilton might be more of a cuddly bear but that does not mean that he has lost his claws.

Indeed, Hamilton's Dracula is rather too much of a playboy, an inveterate capitalist, to thrive in such an environment and leaves home for America— the new center of Empire in the late 20th century. He flies to New York with Renfield but his otherness becomes more and more obvious. People find his thick Eastern European accent difficult to understand—Hamilton spoofs Bela Lugosi—and the vampire himself feels more and more out of place.[14] Although this is superficially suggested this is due to his great age making him out of step with the modern world, it becomes increasingly obvious it is in fact because he comes from the backward and unsophisticated Romania. This initiates a string of events that, while highlighted for humor, are actually used to display the difference and outsidership of Communism itself; people mistake the Count for a headwaiter due to his evening dress; he drinks the blood of a homeless drunk and becomes intoxicated himself; and he gets mistaken for a flying black chicken in Harlem. This is all before he sees the socialite and fashion model Cindy Sondheim (Susan Saint James) who appears to be the reincarnation of his lost love Mina Harker, echoing the same plot line as in *Blacula*.

The Count then becomes extremely focused in his endeavors to make Cindy fall in love with him and leave her current boyfriend, Dr. Jeffrey Rosenberg (Richard Benjamin), who is the grandson of (Fritz) Van Helsing, renowned vampire hunter.[15] Cindy seems extremely unfocused and after much wooing, is finally won over by the vampire's persuasion—part of which is biting her during sex so that she will eventually become a vampire (three bites being enough). Just as with Mamuwalde before, turning the reincarnated love object into a vampire also returns her (immortal) memory. For all the joking and bumbling that occurs along the way, the Count is determined to get his intended victim by any means possible, and one can read the act of turning her into a vampire as much an ideological transformation as it is a biological one—brainwashing in fact.[16] The vampire turns her into a political other just like himself.[17]

Dr. Rosenberg has suspected Count Dracula of nefarious deeds from the beginning, and eventually persuades Lt. Ferguson that the foreign visitor is behind the recent and mysterious vampire attacks and blood bank robberies, and they attempt to catch him. Now that he has his intended victim, Dracula chooses to flee New York with his "bride" and they both turn into bats and fly away, following their misdirected luggage to Jamaica.[18]

The Count's positioning as a Communist pestilence is complicated, as he appears to be against Communism while still in Transylvania—indeed more aligned with aristocratic decadence than socialist equality.[19] But in terms of the film he is used to highlight the otherness of Communist practice itself, a system he quite happily existed alongside until it threatened to impinge on his own lifestyle. He might have been aware of the absurdities of the ideological world he lived in back in Romania, but once he leaves, he is the one shown as being absurd and out of step with the capitalist, consumerist world of the West. Once there he uses a feigned gaucheness as a cover for his real mission which is to convert/subvert the future of America. Cindy somewhat denies the trope of being a "mother" of the nation but her becoming a vampire definitely stops any chance of her giving birth to future Americans, and she seems to represent American youth in her particular kind of self-obsession and existence as a late 20th century socialite. Consequently, the most troubling aspect of this Dracula is that his obvious, almost comic, difference hides his true otherness; he is the source of ideological contagion. Unsurprisingly, the people he troubles most are Cindy and her boyfriend, although arguably Dr. Rosenberg is just as much distracted by his former career as he is troubled by his new (old) profession as a vampire hunter.

Cindy Sondheim is probably more like Stoker's Lucy Westenra than she is Mina Harker, as the former was far less concerned with social proscription than the latter. Dracula's reincarnated lover is constructed as a typical New Yorker, extremely glamorous and self-obsessed, in stark and purposeful contrast to the androgynous, indeed almost masculine figure of the Commissar seen in Transylvania. Cindy is more lost than found in the city as well, and rather narcissistic. In fact, she is not unlike Lucy from Almereyder's *Nadja*, who seems cut adrift and not really connected to anyone or anything. As such, she can be seen to be ready for a stronger personality to take control of her and give her the instruction/direction she lacks. This is something her current boyfriend/fiancé is unable to provide, again not unlike Lucy and Jim in *Nadja*, though this is partly because she purposely keeps people at arm's length. Actually, this is exacerbated by her boyfriend Dr. Rosenberg as he is a psychiatrist and makes decisions over-complicated; this just increases Cindy's inability to decide, which positions her situation as representative of city life but also of Western culture in general. In fact, it captures something of the crisis in New York City in the 1970s which threatened to tear itself apart due to rising crime, corruption, and financial mismanagement, all of which sparked something of a migration out of the center to the suburbs.[20]

The Count then offers her the solution of safety, simplicity and belief in a totalitarian system. This he first does by addressing her sense of worthlessness:

> DRACULA: Do you think of me as special?
> CINDY: Yes, of course.
> DRACULA: So how can you think of yourself as nothing, when I love you? [Dragoti, 1979].

With him, and what he represents, she will always have value. And then he argues that she is in the wrong place, one that will be detrimental to her health and mental wellbeing:

> DRACULA: You were born in the wrong time, Cindy Sondheim. In the other age things were simpler, less complicated. Do you know how many women had nervous breakdowns in the fourteenth century?
> CINDY: No.
> DRACULA: Three! [Dragoti, 1979]

The idea of going back in time represents both Dracula and the land that he comes from, where choices are far fewer and decisions are often made by others.

Of course, during this time, she has been having sex with the vampire—for Cindy, sex is all right but commitment is not—and being "indoctrinated" without realizing it. By the end of the film she has been unknowingly totally vampirized and is more than happy to head back to Europe with her "handler." However, their luggage and the all-important coffins—both now need them to sleep in—have been loaded on a plane to Jamaica, rather than London as intended, and they are forced to change into bats to pursue them. The ending oddly mirrors the final scenes of *Blacula*, with the vampire turning his true love into one of the undead so that she will remember who she is and be with him forever; the lovers are even pursued by someone who now believes in the vampires (Dr. Thomas in *Blacula* and Dr. Rosenberg here) and a police lieutenant who originally scoffed at such things (Lt. Peters and Lt. Ferguson respectively). Beyond this though the climax is vastly different. As mentioned before, Blacula's lover is killed, and he immolates himself as a last act of autonomy; here Cindy survives and is rather happy about her new (old) self:

> CINDY SONDHEIM: Oh, this isn't so hard. I think I'm going to love immortality.
> DRACULA: There is one small disadvantage. We can only live by night.
> CINDY SONDHEIM: Oh, that's all right with me. I mean, I could never really get my shit together till 7:00, anyway[21] [Dragoti, 1979].

More importantly the vampire survives, and not just as an atmosphere of unease that suggests an eventual return—as is often the case in vampire narratives—but as a fully embodied self.[22] This also has ramifications on his otherness as here the threat is not destroyed, only deferred or displaced to a Caribbean island—and of course Cuba, which they will fly over to reach its close neighbor Jamaica, has well-known Communist connections—the ideological threat will always remain close at hand. Cindy's choice of going with the Count in some ways highlights the failure of Western society in general and New York in particular (see mentioned earlier), even though she is heavily "persuaded" by the vampire to do so. We might say that it is the West itself that is troubled by Dracula's presence, something made even more explicit in the character of Dr. Rosenberg.

Cindy's boyfriend/fiancé is a troubled man, both in terms of his relation to his own past but also in his role as being representative of Western culture—following on from Harker, Renfield, and Hutter. The troubled figure of Dr. Rosenberg presages Almereyder's character of Jim who similarly seems unable to process his own heritage which constantly "knocks him down" with each new revelation. Dr. Rosenberg is slightly different in that he knows who his ancestor was, but attempts to deny it—for example, changing his name from Van Helsing. Even his choice of profession is one that would denounce the idea of real vampires and explain them in terms of dreams or mental psychosis.[23] As such it reinforces the idea that his past is in direct conflict with his present, which seems to add to his high levels of indecision and sense of being ineffectual; Cindy is unable to make decisions as she sees no choices, Dr. Rosenberg cannot do so as he sees too many possibilities. Yet, curiously, even once he accepts his destiny, largely predicated on Count Dracula's name which he already knew from his grandfather, and jealousy over Cindy, he still manages to be misinformed. In one scene he confronts the Count with a religious symbol:

> DR. ROSENBERG: [triumphantly] Well, Count, what do you say to that?
> [Pulls out a Star of David]
> [Dracula hides his face, then realizes what it is and removes his hands]
> DRACULA: I would say, leave Cindy alone and find yourself a nice Jewish girl, Doctor!
> DR. ROSENBERG: Huh? [looks at star] Ah shit! It's the other one, isn't it? [Dragoti, 1979]

Rosenberg tries to kill the Count again, this time in a restaurant where the Count and Cindy are eating, declaring "The second way to kill a vampire, Count; three silver bullets through the heart!" The doctor shoots him three times before the Count tells him "No, Rosenberg, that is a werewolf," after which Rosenberg is escorted away by guards. The doctor's incompetence begins to take on more meaning than just his detachment from his own past when it is seen in light of the West's inability to kill off the pestilence of Communist ideology, highlighting that the main reason for this is that people like Dr. Rosenberg do not understand it, or have not learned their history. This strengthens the idea that Rosenberg actually stands a representative of the culture within which he lives.

Rosenberg plays a hybrid character in relation to Stoker's novel, embodying something of a mix between Van Helsing himself and Jonathan Harker, eventual husband of Mina—again not unlike Jim in *Nadja*. But it is more the Harker aspect that is of interest here, as he was specifically constructed to represent the British Empire and its future at the end of the 19th century; he is a professional, he's well-educated and, although not wealthy, an aspiring family man and upright member of society. Dr. Rosenberg performs a similar function for late 20th century New York and Western culture in general. He is a professional, places a high value on monetary wealth—the Count pays off Cindy's psychiatry bill to Rosenberg as they escape to Jamaica, knowing it will stop him pursuing them—has a complicated relationship to ideas of family and procreation, and believes in democracy and free-speech and expression but ultimately finds them confusing. In many ways he is in a similar predicament to Harker in that he is in an era on the cusp of change; if *Dracula* was written in a time when the New Woman and the struggle for women's rights were seen as potential threats to manhood and the nation's potency, by the time that *Love at First Bite* came out America was experiencing

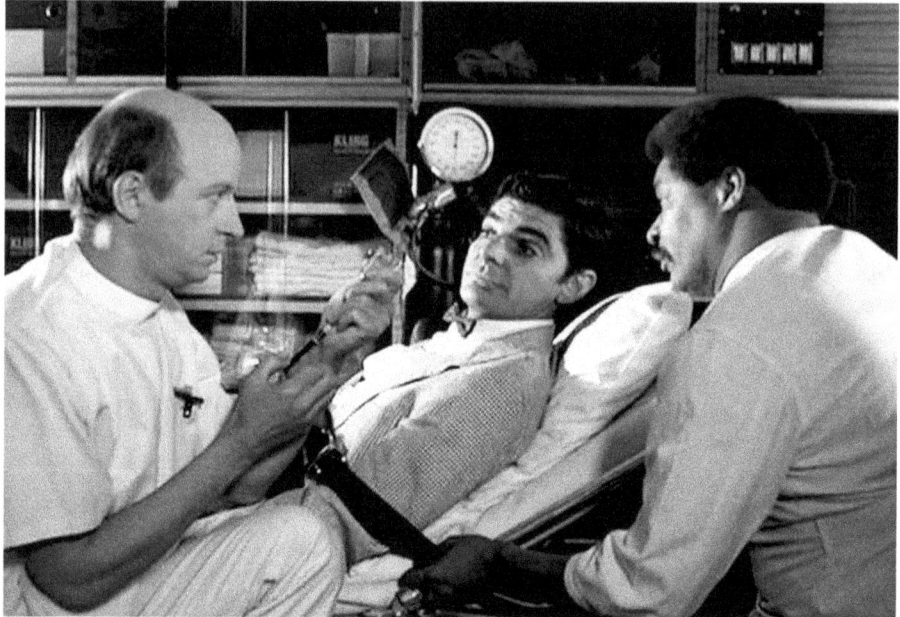

The troubled Dr. Rosenberg (Richard Benjamin) on a gurney (the other two actors are unidentified) in *Love at First Bite*, dir. Stan Dragoti (American International, 1979).

second wave feminism,[24] and while the nation felt secure, masculinity still remained troubled and in crisis with its own perceived emasculation.[25] Dr. Rosenberg very much feels this in terms of his identity as a man, and even more so when the Count arrives upon the scene to become a rival for Cindy's affections. Theirs immediately becomes a fight between masculine egos and ideologies, as explicitly shown when the Count forces his way into Cindy's apartment while Rosenberg is there:

> CINDY: I told you, I have a man in here...
> DRACULA: [forces his way in] **Now** you do [Dragoti, 1979, emphasis in original].

This continues throughout the film with the Count continually getting the upper hand over the Doctor, and it is only once Rosenberg accepts the nature of the vampire (its motivating ideology) that he begins to vaguely threaten it, as shown when he sets fire to Dracula's coffin and says "This is a perfect example of a man taking charge of his own life. And I feel ... pretty good!" (Dragoti, 1979). Though of course the coffin is empty. As such, in contrast to Abbott's view of Hamilton's parodic Dracula being "anachronistic and ineffectual" (Abbot 2006, 125) the vampire here, as an example of masculinity and ideological conviction, turns the tables and serves to make the vampire hunter appear as such. This is graphically shown in the final scene, touched on earlier, where Dracula in his bat form drops a check with Dr. Rosenberg to cover Cindy's bill and the doctor says "Look, a check. She paid me everything she owes me. She left me, but she learned something. She's a responsible person, or whatever" (Dragoti, 1979), a statement which simultaneously reveals his anxiety over both his status as a man and the validity of his profession (ideology). As a consequence, a film that sets out to parody the vampire genre and poke ideological fun at the Soviet Union is itself troubled by the otherness of Count Dracula which subverts this intention, with the result of revealing America's anxiety over its own identity. This sense of a troubled American identity informs the next film, though in a far more overtly nationalistic manner. It also features Dracula but only in a minor role, leaving most of the story to a vampiric crew of light.

Modern Vampires, Richard Elfman, 1998

If Browning's *Dracula* expressed an anxiety over American identity and involvement with émigrés from Europe, *Modern Vampires* stridently declares the supremacy of the U.S. over any "foreign bag of shit" (Elfman, 1998) sentiments that seem all too familiar from the growing prevalence of populism and far-right extremism in contemporary America. The film itself, in its rather unique way, takes character traits of the various characters to extremes—Van Helsing's need for control in Stoker is heightened to outright fascism here—and more interestingly, all of the main characters are vampires. This does rather complicate the ways in which the stock figures and tropes from *Dracula* can be applied to the narrative. However, as seen in earlier examples, while some figures in the newer story have characteristics of more than one original character there is usually an overriding one in relation to the meaning of the overall narrative. Consequently, the figure that is named Count Dracula in the film does not necessarily represent the same troubling entity as in other narratives. Here, the King Vampire is not the aristocrat from Stoker's text but rather is representative of the dominant hierarchy in Los Angeles,[26] who keeps strict control over what the vampire community does. In this role he is represented as a mob or mafia boss, an undead Godfather who is more Italian than Transylvanian (alluding to the Italian community in America) but is represented as a foreign influence controlling the internal affairs of the U.S.[27]

The person that more clearly represents "Dracula" in this film is Dallas (Casper Van Dien), a young American soldier who was turned during World War II and is forced into exile by the Count because he sired a new vampire—Van Helsing's crippled son—without Count Dracula's permission. Years later (1989) he covertly returns to Los Angeles only to discover that a young girl he secretly turned 20 years earlier has gone feral and is causing a stir around Hollywood, threatening the secrecy of the vampire community. Count Dracula (Robert Pastorelli) wants Dallas to bring her to him so he can kill her but, inevitably, the exile has fallen in love with her. To make things even more involved Frederick Van Helsing (Rod Steiger) has come to town to kill vampires, attracted by newspaper headlines of savage murders and blood-drained bodies. Dallas tops the slayer's revenge list, as he was the one who turned his son into an undead abomination that he had to kill. Dallas then, at least in terms of the film's motivation, becomes the absolute other; the outsider who breaks all the rules and threatens to bring down the dominant order, and because of this will be looked at further in his role as a "modern" Dracula.

Dallas is shown to be a "true" American in that he served, and indeed died for, his country. He also has a mind for the open road and adventure—much of his character speaks of the Wild West and a frontier spirit, and of one who travels and rarely settles anywhere for long.[28] The importance of the idea of "frontier spirit" to American identity is noted by Cynthia J. Miller and A. Bowden Van Ripper: "The frontier ... is seen as one of the defining elements in American national identity—the catalyst and proving ground for the course, individuality, and dynamism of the American character"[29] (Miller and Van Ripper 2013, xii). This idea is further played out when Dallas reclaims the "frontier" in the name of America. In this sense at least he fulfills the Harker role of being representative of his country—a bit of a grifter and an adventurer but straight-talking, good to his friends, and always willing to give someone a break. Interestingly it is also suggested that he originally invited Count Dracula into America and so introduced vampires to the New World,[30] however the Old World vampire has now overstayed his welcome.[31] Once back in Los Angeles, his home before his exile, Dallas calls in to see his old friends Ulrike (Kim Cantrell), Vincent (Udo Kier), Richard (Craig Ferguson), and Panthia (Natalya Andreychenko)—she is Richard's wife and has always been pregnant as she was made a vampire while carrying a child—and they go out to a night club. Count Dracula spots them and tells Dallas he has three days to leave town. Curiously the friends are all European—Ulrike and Vincent are German Jewish, Richard is English and Panthia is Eastern European—yet are categorized as being American, something of a reference to the European émigrés who fled the Nazis and came to America, and Hollywood in particular, before and during World War II. Van Helsing is one of these. Count Dracula appears to have come to the U.S. specifically to suck the life out of the New World and so is not considered part of the home nation.

During this time, Dallas also runs into Nico (Natasha Gregson Wagner) who, it transpires, is the rogue vampire creating headlines in the newspapers and was in fact sired by him—in theory this makes him her father but that does not stand in the way of their growing relationship. Her role then is something of a Lucy-type character with a more open idea of relationships and sexual partners, but one who escaped being staked, as in Stoker, and becomes an adult-orientated Bloofer Lady who lures the unwary to become her victims—whereas in *Dracula* Lucy preys on young children. Dallas takes the young vampire under his wing and introduces her to his friends, so they can help socialize her to be accepted into the wider vampire community—enacting something of a vampire version of *My Fair Lady* (Cukor, 1964). Dallas meets with Count Dracula to try and convince him that he can train Nico to join vampire society, but the patriarch will have none of it and demands that the girl be brought to him or all those whom Dallas loves will die screaming.

In the final scenes of the film Van Helsing and his African American mercenaries attack and kill Dallas's friends. But the Count's henchmen intercept them afterwards and take the Professor and Nico to Dracula's club. Once there Nico and the Professor are restrained, ready to be killed, but just in the nick of time Dallas crashes into the club where all this is happening and with the help of Van Helsing's hired killers he kills the Count and his mob. Now that Dallas has destroyed the foreign threat, he, Nico, and her new friend Rachel leave Los Angeles to try out New York, hitting the road like the true Americans they are.

Dallas himself seems to have little ideological agenda beyond individual freedom, which informs his own sense of what being American is, and so in this light by trying to control and enforce a personal ideology on the vampire community, Count Dracula marked himself as being unAmerican, and even worse "foreign." This is a designation reserved for those who are decidedly not American. As Nico succinctly declares (and as was mentioned previously): "I'm an American citizen, no foreign bag of shit is gonna run me out of my own goddamn country" (Elfman, 1998). In light of the film's ending, being foreign makes one not only not American but even *anti*-American, and no longer fit to be alive, or undead. Dallas himself would not necessarily feel the need to be so extreme in the expression of his own ideological standpoint but Nico has a much more emotional response to perceived danger, so much so that it would be fair to say that it is she who actually troubles her maker.

As mentioned, Nico is very much the Lucy character in the story but taken to extremes that Stoker would not have imagined. Unlike Lucy, Nico comes from a very poor family—she is very much portrayed as white trailer park trash. In *Dracula*, although the Count is shown to feed on the lower classes—he killed the crew of the Demeter and then a flower girl in London—he only spends time on those that are middle class or professional.[32]

The only profession Nico knows is the oldest one in the world and that is where she often picks and kills her victims. Indeed, much of what Nico does, particularly in terms of her sexual freedom, embodies what Stoker's Lucy fantasizes about and which frames her statement to her close friend Mina: "Why can't they let a girl marry three men, or as many as want her, and save all this trouble? But this is heresy, and I must not say it"[33] (Stoker 1996, 65).

As a way to explain the young vampire's behavior, the film shows that her mother was more obsessed with being with a man than caring for her daughter, and that her stepfather sexually abused her, and if Dallas had not made her undead, she most probably would not be "alive" today. Curiously, in this perspective she embodies the traumatic memory of a generation of forgotten children and families: those who were overlooked by the American Dream and the American government and forced to live brutal lives below the breadline—her undead self returning the abuse she suffered while alive. In some respects, she also manifests a slightly older version of Eli from *Let the Right One In*, as she looks quite young, late adolescence, is very dirty and sparsely dressed, and feigns a vulnerability that draws predatory men to her; her killing of these men enacts an ongoing revenge on her stepfather.[34]

Dallas, though, largely manages to temper the worst of her behavior to a level where it no longer endangers the local vampire community—although she does savage and kill a condescending shop assistant when Ulrike takes her out to buy new clothes. Her attacks are always accompanied by the sound of a leopard or large cat growling, suggesting she is still wild and largely uncontrollable. Consequently, Dallas feels that Nico just needs a little bit of "civilizing" to make her safe and he tries to persuade the Count to give the girl a reprieve, but the Count blankly refuses and demands she be brought to him. Dallas thinks the best course of action is for himself and Nico to leave town, but she puts her foot down and decides that the real issue here is Dracula's foreignness and the fact that he is telling an American citizen what they can and cannot do.

Nico's knee-jerk responses to situations can be seen to both reveal what she really thinks and to complicate any ultimate meaning of her outbursts. Her vilification of the Count and his foreignness bears little relation to her feelings for Ulrike, Vince, and Richard. In fact, as indicated earlier her issue is with those who have power over her, something shown in an earlier scene in the film when she first meets Dallas and pulls a gun on him saying, "Hey, I'm the one holding the gun, okay? So, that makes me smart and you stupid" (Elfman, 1998). Consequently, she embodies a very primitive form of nationalism where she can do what she wants and can get revenge on everyone who she feels has wronged her—rather echoing similar sentiments to those expressed by President Trump in some of his more spontaneous tweets, campaign promises, and executive orders. However, this rather personalized framing of nationalism, and the vampire's absolute otherness, becomes even more complicated in relation to African Americans in the film, and how they are used to constitute Van Helsing's crew of light.

Dr. Frederick Van Helsing is a very troubled character and, in many ways, represents the troubled nature of the film itself. It is suggested that he worked for the Nazis during World War II conducting medical experiments on vampires. Not long after this his crippled son was befriended by Dallas who, to make him well again, turned him into one of the undead. This was of course anathema to the Doctor who subsequently kills his own son rather than let him exist as a vampire. This caused Van Helsing's wife to kill herself and gave the Doctor an obsessive hatred for Dallas. After this he created the Van Helsing Institute of Vienna specifically for the hunting and destruction of vampires, and after hearing of the activities of the "Hollywood Slasher" comes to LA to investigate whether the undead are involved.

At this point the construction of Van Helsing as a fascist correlates Jewishness with vampirism—something compounded later when Ulrike is killed after being identified as a German-Jewish vampire. This gets more involved as the narrative continues. On reaching Hollywood, Van Helsing realizes there must be a vampire "infestation" and so puts an advert in the newspaper for a "strong and brave young man who's not afraid to get his hands dirty in a cause that is holy" (Elfman, 1998). The only person to answer the advert is an African American called Time Bomb (Gabriel Casseus) who is a member of the renowned Los Angeles gang, The Crips. Van Helsing does not know about gang culture but decides to take on the young man who is willing to do anything for money. On their first sortie they manage to kill Vincent but the doctor realizes he will need more manpower now he knows the scale of the problem. He asks Time Bomb if he has some friends that might be able to help, and so three more gang members join the crew of light. In Stoker's novel the gang of vampire hunters were signified as the soldiers of the (holy) Empire rallied against the forces of evil; here that gets rather complicated. On their next raid they manage to kill Richard and Panthia, and restrain Ulrike on a bed. What occurs next is possibly one of the worst-taste scenes in vampire film history as Ulrike taunts the black gang members into having sex with her as a white, German-Jewish other. The gang members oblige until Van Helsing comes in and stakes her. The punchline, which is supposed to excuse this, is that having sex with a vampire turns the human involved into a vampire as well. The difficult possible meanings behind this scene are worth touching upon for the film's view on nationalism and racism in general.

The setting of L.A. instantly links the film to *Blacula* and the position of the African American community within society there. If the earlier film suggested to the black community that the white police could come and go through their property as they please—as seen in the hunting down of Mamuwalde—then *Modern Vampires* purposely heightens the anxiety of the white community around black gang members invading their homes, and raping and killing them. Denigration of black characters begins with Time Bomb, the only person willing to work for such low wages and do work that is physical and violent; he is little more than a paid killer. This carries on with the introduction of his friends Soda Pop, Li'l Monster, and Trigger who are loaded into Van Helsing's van where they play very load rap music and smoke drugs. All this makes their transition into vampires inevitable as they are already shown to be feeding off the (white) society around them. Van Helsing then become complicit in this, using them specifically for degrading work that no white person in America would do—at least this is implied. This potentially creates a peculiar hierarchy of otherness in the film where white fascists are higher than black gang members, who are themselves higher than Jews and vampires (who are equal). Vampires themselves then divide, with Count Dracula's European vampires being the lowest, African American vampires being slightly higher, with the pinnacle being the white, American undead. Van Helsing, inevitably, becomes a vampire himself and we see him as the film ends pleading for his son's forgiveness as he becomes the new lowest of the low, a white, fascist vampire.

Van Helsing is deeply troubled by Dallas from the time he turned his son into a vampire, turning his already established racism into a driving obsession. His identity as a European who kills Nico's new friends, and indeed abducts the young vampire herself, sees him categorized as unwanted outsider just like the Count. Indeed, in many ways he embodies the same kind of fears that Lugosi did in Browning's film, an Old-World European that seeks to re-establish Imperial rule in the New World. This reinforces Dallas's credentials as representing (modern) America, one which needs to fight to regain its own identity, as seen when Nico and Dallas reclaim their freedom in the club by killing Count Dracula, a symbol of historical white European Imperialism. Dallas and Nico then trouble America into reclaiming its own identity once again, or as President Trump states it, "making America great again." This sees Dallas's otherness more aligned with populism and what might have once been termed "the forgotten right," a form of otherness that is not oppositional but rather excessively affective, as seen in Nico who rarely thinks but only acts. Ultimately then, the absolute otherness of the vampire here is to trouble those around it into excessively emotional responses, particularly in terms of individual freedom and nationalism. Curiously, the next example is completely opposite of such emotions, though rather confirms *Modern Vampires* fears over European émigrés wanting to, quite literally, eat the hand of the nation that feeds them.

Hannibal, Bryan Fuller, 2013–2015

Hannibal is not an obvious adaptation of *Dracula*, but there is much about Dr. Hannibal Lecter that corresponds to Stoker's vampire Count, and particularly in Browning's adaptation.[35] It is worth noting that this comparison is focused mainly on the television series and not the hugely popular films featuring Anthony Hopkins, though as part of the "world building" around *Hannibal* they will be mentioned.[36] In this respect there have already been comparisons drawn between the cinematic Hannibal and the Transylvanian Count, as Paul Meehan notes, "like Dracula, Lecter is a predatory killer who murders casually and without a hint of conscience. Both physically consume parts of their victim's bodies and both have superhuman powers of mind that allow them to dominate their prey."[37] These comparisons, though, are more about general similarities than exemplifying a direct correspondence between texts, which is argued here.

The first important point involves the actor taking the role of Hannibal, for just as Lugosi and his voice embodied the vampire king in the 1930s so too did the actor playing Hannibal Lecter in the 2010s come to represent the fictional psychopath. Jonathan Demme's amazingly successful *Silence of the Lambs* (1991) cemented the place of the highly intelligent, totally amoral, and sophisticated cannibal in the public imagination in a way that its source novel of the same name by Thomas Harris (1988), or Michael Mann's earlier film *Manhunter* (1986), failed to do. Anthony Hopkins' interpretation of the role made the character deadly and unpredictable, creating an anti-hero who filled audiences with awe but also the wish to be the one whom the cannibalistic killer would befriend, or at least tolerate. More importantly, the film portrayed him as American, and even though subsequent installments (one being an origins story) showed him to be European, he was categorized as U.S.–born and bred; a killer so dangerous, ingenious and intelligent that a nation could almost be proud of him.[38] Bryan Fuller's series totally changes this construction by using Mads Mikkelsen as Hannibal Lecter, a Danish actor who speaks the role using an often difficult to follow, European/Danish accent.[39] Of course, as show creator Fuller points out, Lecter in Harris's novels comes from Lithuania in Eastern Europe, so the accent is nearer to the source material than Hopkins' American one. More interestingly, at least in terms of this study, Mikkelsen's accent marks him as a dangerous outsider coming from the East, penetrating into the heart of Empire to fulfill his nefarious plan. In contrast to Stoker's vampire and even Hopkins' Lecter, neither Lugosi or Mikkelsen's characters want to blend in; as Abigail Burnham Bloom comments, "he makes himself charming and accepted into society through the use of … his accented English, his formal manners, his elegant clothes, and his manipulation of the politeness of others" (Bloom 2010, 174)—words that perfectly describe Fuller's psychopathic Doctor whose obvious foreignness becomes a cover for his true otherness.

The similarities between Lugosi's Count and Mikkelsen's Lecter do not end at the possession of a distinctive accent; each also has a very distinctive wardrobe which adds to their construction of difference. Where Browning's Dracula wore evening dress throughout the narrative—except when the vampire was masquerading as a coach driver—Fuller's Lecter always wears extremely distinctive and expensive clothes straight from a men's fashion magazine. Indeed Hannibal's attire has been featured in magazines such as *Esquire*[40] and *Gentlemen's Gazette*.[41] As one journalist, London McGuire, observes "he's a well-groomed, flawlessly-dressed, calculating genius" whose style is "a hybridization of the modern fit with bygone patterns and hues, peaked lapels that harken back to more sophisticated, refined days—when power was earned less by yelling and more by speaking eloquently."[42] Though he further adds "For how complete and formulated his entire style is, there's also something just slightly off."[43] So just as Dracula's theatrical evening wear seemed slightly out of place so too does the serial killer's fashion sense. While his voice and dress mark Lecter out as fulfilling a visual/aural difference very much in the mold of Dracula, the true nature of his absolute otherness makes this connection between the two even more pronounced.

The most obviousness point of otherness for Hannibal in all the versions of the story, novel, and films, is his cannibalism, and like Count Dracula, he often not only personally (intimately) knows his victims but makes them part of himself through consummation. In Dracula this means they become, like their master, one of the undead; for Lecter this can be, when considered literally, more problematic, but if read metaphorically the Doctor's prey are now transformed into being part of his body (an absolute other) and as such are now viewed as dead by their own society. More importantly Lecter's nefarious acts are undertaken under the very noses of those trying to catch him, in stark contrast to the often-flamboyant ways in which he often kills his victims. In this sense Lecter is more than just another serial killer as his murders are more critiques on society than a psychological necessity—even Dracula can be seen to have chosen victims for effect rather than necessity as when he exchanged blood with Mina in her marital bed while Jonathan slept next to her.

Mark Seltzer, writing at the end of the 20th century, calls America a "wound culture," one that is bewitched by the spectacle of "atrocity" and that one of its "superstars" is "the lust-murderer or the stranger-killer, or the serial killer" (Seltzer 1998, 2). And although the original novels and films do largely fit into that framework, Fuller's *Hannibal* does not. Lecter might provide spectacle but it is never, so he can get caught; he kills, but rarely to satiate the demands of an inner voice or desire. If anything, Lecter would consider himself an artist—a Banksy if you will—who makes bold and daring statements about the corrupt nature of the society within which he exists, but ensures his own anonymity. This conforms very much to the place he has made for himself within the higher echelons of his local society, not only as a renowned psychoanalyst but as a patron of the arts and a host with impeccable taste and culinary expertise. It is something of an honor to be invited to the good Doctor's soirées and partake of the exquisite meals that have taken hours, if not days, to prepare. Unknowingly, his guests are often consuming human flesh or organs as integral parts of the dishes being served.

Something of this plays into the Marxist trope, as noted by Franco Moretti (2005, 91), of Dracula representing the aristocracy (the wealthy) that literally feeds off the poor, or the nation, to sustain itself. Hannibal, as an arbiter of taste and fashion, and a leading member of "society"—the rich and well-to-do—consumes those who are of the wrong sort, who are less in some way. Equally, he is shown to despise the vainglorious, the empty bells that proclaim their wealth and status but lack class and good taste. In this reading, Hannibal becomes something of a hidden activist, a guerrilla fighter who reveals the corruption of Western capitalism while directly attacking it. In this way Lecter begins to be similar to Dragoti's Communist vampire, an ideological terrorist who hides in plain sight. Hannibal then makes his guests unwitting cannibals, and complicit in the savage acts he performs, subsequently destabilizing and troubling the morality of the society around him. This is most clearly seen in the figure of FBI's profiler Will Graham (Hugh Dancy) who is troubled into thinking he is just like Hannibal. Curiously Will is stalked by Lecter just as Count Dracula preys upon Mina Harker, and indeed much about the recovering profiler suggests he is a potential bride of the vampire.

When we first see Will he is teaching forensics for the FBI. He has retired from field work because his "gift"—he is extremely empathic and able to assume the state of mind of a killer when entering a crime scene—troubles the integrity of his personality. His boss, and Head of the FBI Behavioral Science Unit, Jack Crawford (Lawrence Fishburne), asks him to help solve a case involving eight murders. Will is reticent but persuaded to assist. However, it is not long before he starts to suffer under the stress of the case. His colleague, Alana Bloom (Caroline Dhavernas), recommends that her mentor, the renowned psychologist Hannibal Lecter, be brought in to help. Not unlike Count Dracula in Browning's film, the foreign guest goes completely unrecognized for the monster he is, not least by the Van Helsing character, Jack Crawford. Hannibal though, immediately recognizes Will, not just as a new victim but as a potential "bride" of his own ideological cause. As such Lecter immediately begins to trouble Will under the guise of helping him.

Predictably, Will becomes too involved in the murder case and begins to "lose" time, specifically he begins to hallucinate that he is the one actually killing people. Hannibal realizes this is in fact due to a medical condition called encephalitis, but he purposely neglects to tell the profiler this. Instead he tries an experiment to see how much he can influence and trouble Will, and to convince him that the reason he is able to share his mind with killers is because he is exactly like them. Much of Hannibal's "turning" of Will is similar in tone to the way in which Count Dracula takes control of Mina. Just as Harker slept unaware next to his wife, so do all Will's colleagues who literally doze or look elsewhere while the monster shares its lifeblood with the powerless victim. At one stage Hannibal has so much influence over Will that they almost become interlinked; the killer controls the pliant profiler's mind, planting images and ideas directly into his subconscious and making him believe that his troubled self is his true one. This is intimated by the following exchange between the two in episode 13 (Savoureux) of Season One:

> LECTER: Perhaps you didn't come here looking for a killer. Perhaps you came here to find yourself. You killed a man in this very room.
> GRAHAM: I stared at Hobbs and the space opposite me assumed the shape of a man filled with dark and swarming flies. And then I scattered them.
> LECTER: At a time when other men fear their isolation, yours has become understandable to you. You are alone because you are unique.
> GRAHAM: I'm as alone as you are.
> LECTER: If you followed the urges you kept down for so long, cultivated them as the inspirations they are, you would have become someone other than yourself.
> GRAHAM: I know who I am. I'm not so sure I know who you are anymore.

This mirrors the kind of connection between Count Dracula and (his) Mina, where she is becoming a new troubled self which is joined/equivalent to that of the vampire. This is described by Van Helsing—in the rather awkward English Stoker creates to show the foreigners of the vampire hunter—as follows: "it is to be seen if we have eyes to notice…. Her teeth are some sharper, and at times her eyes are more hard … there is to her the silence now often," which all intimate that "he who have hypnotize her first, and who have drink of her very blood and make her drink of his, should, if he will, compel her mind to disclose to him that which she know?" (Stoker 1996, 351). In fact much of the interaction between Hannibal and Will in season one enacts something of a courtship between the two, with the psychopathic Doctor seducing the profiler; a process which indicates a feminization of the latter.[44]

This is most obviously seen in the increasing levels of hysterical behavior Will presents as he loses time and is often unable to tell the difference between his hallucinations and reality. Hysteria is important for defining the role Will plays in the first season and indeed, in some measure, going forward throughout the series. Defined as "An old-fashioned term for a psychological disorder

Hannibal (Mads Mikkelsen, right) is the troubling voice in Will's (Hugh Dancy's) head in *Hannibal*, creator, Bryan Fuller (Sony Pictures Television, 2013–15).

characterized by conversion of psychological stress into physical symptoms (somatization) or a change in self-awareness (such as a fugue state or selective amnesia)"[45] it was also a condition with inherent feminizing connotations. During the 19th century it was seen as occurring only in woman—Ancient Greece originally framed it as being caused by a pathologically traveling womb.[46] Elaine Showalter further links it to shell shock victims in World War I: "In sum, then, the hysterical soldier was seen as simple, emotional, unthinking, passive, suggestible, dependent and weak—very much the same constellation of traits associated with the hysterical woman" (Showalter 2009, 175). All qualities that the troubled self of Will Graham displays under the controlling hand of Lecter. However, Lecter realizes that his murder spree, his ideological mission, will be best served by framing Will for the Chesapeake Ripper murders he himself has committed, and the still hallucinating profiler can do little to save himself.

Once cured though, Will manages to turn the tables on Hannibal, partly due to the acceptance of the troubled side of his own personality—not unlike Mina realizing she was under the influence of Dracula and using that knowledge against him. This both differs and confirms aspects of Stoker's story; it differs in that Hannibal is not destroyed as Dracula is—though the death of the Count is debatable for many reasons[47]—breaking the bond between the two characters, and it confirms in the very particular qualities of Mina herself which sees her as the only figure other than the vampire to combine gender characteristics. As Van Helsing notes, "'Ah, that wonderful Madam Mina!

She has man's brain—a brain that a man should have were he much gifted—and woman's heart" (Stoker 1996, 253). In *Hannibal*, Will successfully combines his old self (masculine) with his new troubled identity (feminine), which marks him out as equivalent to Lecter. This last posits what might have occurred in Stoker's narrative had the vampire survived and had some of the more romantic interpretations of the tale, as seen in John Badham's *Dracula*,[48] come to fruition. As such, the troubling nature of Hannibal/Dracula eventually has beneficial effects in this instance, though this might also be due to the distracted/distracting presence of Jack Crawford.

Jack, as noted above, is the Van Helsing character in this reading, and like his predecessor seems distracted by the presence of the absolute other to the point of not realizing who he is. In Browning's film it does not take the Professor long to discover the true identity of the foreign guest at Seward's home—though it was mainly by chance. Jack takes the entire first season before he begins to suspect that Lecter is not who he pretends to be, and in the meantime, Jack has Will jailed for the murders that Lecter framed him for. This also begins to construct the distracting qualities of Crawford himself as the overall plot suggests that, in some measure, the Head of the FBI Behavioral Science Unit, allows things to happen knowing what the outcome will be. In many ways this reading of him ties in more strongly to the correlation with *Dracula*, where Van Helsing and the vampire constantly battle to be the "Master" of the narrative; both are named as Master in the story. Once Stoker's Professor has recognized his adversary, he does much to remain central to the plot, though there are many times when it seems to proceed without him and he only intercedes to steer it back on course to its inevitable conclusion, the destruction of the vampire. Crawford can be seen to do much the same, especially in the film adaptations of Thomas Harris's books such as *Manhunter* (Mann, 1986), *Red Dragon* (Ratner, 2002), and particularly *Silence of the Lambs* (Demme, 1991) where he chooses Clarice Starling knowing she will fascinate the psychopathic killer. Something of the same can be seen to occur in *Hannibal* as Jack chooses Will to investigate the murders, knowing that he will flush out and/or attract the killer. Arguing that Crawford knew it was Hannibal from the beginning is problematic, but it is possible that once he became part of the investigation, the FBI Agent was distracted enough by the foreign doctor to keep him close.

Of course, Jack is also distracted by his wife's ill health, but it is the non-specified attraction between himself and Lecter that is pivotal—one might say that if Lecter is drawn to Will as his double, then Crawford is attracted by the killer as his opposite. Much of this attraction is seen as a kind of fascination Crawford has with Lecter, shown by his concern over Will's welfare but also so mesmerized by the foreign Doctor's lifestyle, and particularly his food. Crawford enjoys many meals at Hannibal's home, not all of them containing human flesh, and it does call into question just how knowing the agent is. It would require a monumental amount of dissembling on Jack's part to not show that he knows more than he appears to, even if he is head of the Behavioral Science Department. This would also show his fascination with Hannibal's culinary expertise not just as a means of questioning the suspect but of investigating his modus operandi; how better to interrogate a cannibal than through what he eats and how he prepares it? This equally means that Crawford allows Will's identity to disintegrate knowing that he will have the strength to remain intact in some way when he comes out the other end; something similar can be said of Mina, as no one quite knows how deeply ingrained the vampire is inside of her when Dracula is killed, and Van Helsing is fully prepared to kill her should things go badly.

As such, both Crawford and Hannibal are distracting characters with the former being the defender of the nation, a one-man crew of light who attempts to maintain the ideological integrity of the homeland; the latter, then, is the ideological terrorist who consumes the nation from within in an attempt to destabilize it and trouble it out of its former identity. Will is then part sacrificial lamb, part conduit, part unknowing double agent who can infiltrate behind the enemy's defenses without being detected, but he also intimates post-troubled identity positions; the self beyond terrorism. The absolute otherness of the ideological terrorist looms large in the next example but it configures terrorism more explicitly in terms of religious extremism and ideological death.

The Witch, Robert Eggers, 2015

Eggers film, like *Hannibal,* is not obviously a tale about Count Dracula and in fact the character that fills that role spends the majority of the narrative in the shape of a large black buck goat. The story is very different from those discussed previously in that it is an historical piece, set in the 17th century, and we never see the arrival of the Dark Lord; he has already travelled from the land beyond civilization and is fully installed in the family/society that he plans to destroy. Set in Salem, New England, in the 1630s, it predates the infamous witch trials that would take place there 60 years later, yet suggests that there might be some historical precedent for them. From its beginning it speaks of religious fundamentalism and shows a family being cast out of a Puritan settlement because they believe the family's patriarch, William, talks improperly about the word of God, and he calls the others false Christians. William, along with his wife and five children, is forced to set up his own small farm in the wilderness—the metaphorical land beyond the forest as described in Stoker's novel, where the supernatural holds sway. However, unbeknownst to the family a witch lives in the woods not far from their new farm and it is not long before she, under the influence of her Dark Lord, wreaks havoc on the farmstead leaving only the eldest daughter, Thomasin, alive.

In the film the family's black goat, Black Phillip, represents Satan but can equally be seen as a version of Count Dracula—in Stoker's notes for the novel he believes Dracula to mean "Devil" and connected the vampire to the Scholomance (where Satan teaches nature to select students) and even has the character use the pseudonym of "Count D'Ville" when purchasing other properties in London (see Eighteen-Bisang and Miller 2008, 31, 123, 245). Indeed, the otherness of both figures is configured in very similar ways. In Romanian folklore "the devil can change himself into an animal or a black bird" (McNally and Florescu 1972, 125), an attribute similar to those Stoker gave Count Dracula, seeing him able to become a wolf, a bat, and even "elemental mist" (Stoker 1996, 258).[49] Later adaptations have increased this range to include any animal/insect associated with vermin, disease, and the nocturnal hours. Equally they are united in their creation as absolute others to Christian, patriarchal society, their ability to beguile, mesmerize, and control others, and a desire to rule the world by filling it with their acolytes. As Mary Hallub observes:

> Those critics and writers like Stoker and Montague Summers who portray the Vampire as an enemy of God and the Good actually assign him a significant position in the universal order.... McGrath [Patrick] places the Vampire in the position of Satan, the great Opposite and Opponent of God [Hallub 2009, 95].

Francis Ford Coppola in *Bram Stoker's Dracula* takes this idea literally and mashes up Stoker's tale with the historical Vlad the Impaler's life—he was known as Vlad Dracula which can be translated as son of the dragon/devil due to a title given to his father—with the result that, as noted by Christopher Sharrett, "Dracula is angel turned devil; exactly how God turns Vlad into a vampire is unclear and unimportant, since the film opts for a simplistic equation of Dracula with Satan, with embodied evil"[50] (Sharrett 2015, 294). While Eggers' Dark Lord is nowhere near as excessive as Coppola's, he certainly hides in plain sight, concealed by his obvious otherness rather than being exposed by it, as Lugosi's Count also did. Still, in a Puritan society that truly believes in Satan, witches and their animal familiars are a real and physical presence in everyday life, so it seems strange that the large black goat with huge horns never falls under suspicion.[51] Goats were not uncommon with settlers in the Americas, as the film's director David Eggers observes: "… when the settlers came over here, they brought goats with them, and there was a lot of people with goats, because goats could clear the land very efficiently and they were small, to travel with" (Wickman 2016, n.p.). Yet, Eggers'

Two. The Land Beyond the Forest 75

The Dark Lord. Lucas Dawson as Jonas and Ellie Grainger as Mercy in *The Witch*, dir. Robert Eggers (A24, 2014).

Black Phillip is very large for a goat and particularly distinctive, even more so as the family's young twins, Mercy and Jonas, spend much time playing with him and singing songs about him "eating lions" and ruling the world. The fact that the medieval tradition of representing the devil as a goat or with goat-like features is not a particularly English one and was more common in Continental Europe (Jensen 2007, 155–156) perhaps allowed Black Phillip to evade suspicion, yet this very lack of suspicion is on a par with how long it took Van Helsing to recognize his nemesis in Browning's film. Unfortunately for William and his family there is no Van Helsing of note in this narrative and so there is little chance they will escape the clutches of the undead Master.

There are two other features of particular importance that link *The Witch* to Stoker's *Dracula*; the first is the brides of Dracula, called witches in Eggers' film. Although we never see Black Phillip drink from his wives to "turn" them he does require their signature in blood on a contract, performing a sanguinary transaction not unlike that of the King Vampire. The witches also feed on/kill babies and young children as a way to remain young and powerful, again not unlike the brides who are rewarded with such tidbits by the Count. Once rejuvenated, the witch who lives nearby, becomes like Stoker's Bloofer Lady mesmerizing the young, as she does with Thomasin's eldest brother Caleb.

The second similar feature is Phillip's obsession with Thomasin. He may not become besotted with her in the way Orlok does with Ellen or view her as a reincarnation of a lost love as Blacula does, but his sole goal of infiltrating the family is to make the girl on the edge of womanhood his wife. Similarly, the Count distracts his potential foes away from his true intentions by preying on Lucy—especially in adaptations where he sees Mina or her picture prior to arriving in England. In Coppola's film this is highlighted when Mina catches the vampire in his wolf form copulating with Lucy in the garden, and he reacts as though ashamed; his animal self suddenly has human eyes that will his true love to forget what she has witnessed. Once she is a vampire, Lucy continues to act as a distraction through her nightly excursions to Hampstead Heath to prey on children. Black Phillip does much the same here in Eggers' film, casting suspicion on Thomasin by getting the witch to steal Sam the baby while he is in the girls' care, as will be discussed further below. This is exacerbated when Caleb also goes missing while out with his sister and the young twins start to call Thomasin a witch. All of these events distract the remaining members of the family away from the true source of evil in their midst, not unlike Hannibal's framing of Will Graham. By the end of the tale Thomasin has little option but to embrace the life proposed to her by the Dark Lord, and he willingly accepts her blood offering to enter her into the coven of like-minded souls.

This gradual process of separating Thomasin from her family is an important aspect of Phillip's absolute otherness in the narrative as it identifies him as a male adult grooming a young child—one of the more emotive issues around children/young adults and social media in the 21st century.[52] However, Eggers specifically sets his film in an environment of religious extremism to further emphasize the effects of ideological grooming, especially of the young and innocent. As such it is possible to read the narrative in light of contemporary anxieties over Islamic extremism and online grooming of jihadi wives from Europe and the U.S.[53] While *The Witch* is set in 17th century America, the ideological environment and family dynamics it creates is not specific to that period. It sees an adolescent girl out of step with society and her parents' beliefs, too young to be an adult but not young enough to remain in the company of her siblings, and she yearns for acceptance and empowerment. Once her family are literally and/or metaphorically dead to her she takes the only choice left that allows for some measure of agency and control over her own life and offers herself to Phillip. He responds to her with a human voice, and briefly in human form. It is an important moment in the film as to this moment, Satan/Dracula has only been seen in his goat shape, and this opens up the possibility that either the beast is a form taken on by the evil one, or that it only assumes human form to lure the unsuspecting into joining its ranks. Curiously, the human figure it takes is of a man with long black hair and a beard and dressed in black period costume that is oddly reminiscent of a Royalist Cavalier, although the film's context predates that slightly. The figure has opulent clothing, but no shoes only cloven hooves, representing a luxury and decadence that has been withheld from Thomasin but which she yearns to embrace—she mentions earlier in the story her desire for a return to England and the less barren lives they lived there.

Consequently, Black Phillip's otherness is that of a religious and ideological deceiver, an inhuman beast that corrupts the young to join him in the war against civilized society. His witches/brides here are similar to Dracula's biologically non-reproductive women who "murder" the next generation of a nation both through their own infertility and in their need to kill babies to remain young. Similarly, Phillip as an ISIS terrorist steals girls on the cusp of womanhood, denying the reproductive capabilities of the Christian world as well as then turning them into "wives" of Islamic religious extremism—ensuring the "future" of the ideological terrorists. Thomasin is the perfect example of how this grooming works; Phillip has played on her fears and anxieties and she loses track of who she is or what she wants.

Thomasin is permanently troubled and never seems to be where she wants to be; she did not want to leave England to travel to the America's, but her parents made her; she did not want to leave the Puritan compound, but her father made her; she does not like their new home as she has to do most of the chores and her older brother and father are acting peculiar around her and her mother blames her for it. And that's even before Black Phillip starts to really trouble her. Once he turns his full attention to her things start going badly very quickly and she loses all control over the situation and indeed her own life.

Not long after the family have set up their new home Thomasin is near the edge of the forest looking after the baby of the family, Sam. She plays peek-a-boo with him but, in a blink of an eye while her face is covered, the baby vanishes leaving the young girl distraught. We know it is the witch who lives nearby that has snatched him but Thomasin's parents are not totally convinced by her story and suspicion hangs around the girl—the witch, who is an old crone, requires the blood of a baby to make her young and beautiful again. Not long afterward, the twins, who are much younger than Thomasin, accuse her of being a witch—the twins spend much time with the goats, Phillip in particular, so it is highly likely he planted this idea in their heads. Increasingly annoyed by their taunts, Thomasin declares that yes, she is a witch and will eat them, and the twins run off screaming. This adds to the tensions in the household and William decides to sell her to another family back in the settlement. The girl overhears this decision, making her feel even more estranged. A short time after this Thomasin and her eldest brother Caleb—he's slightly younger than her—slip out from the house to see if any rabbits have been caught in the traps the boy and his father set in order to supplement their food supply. Their crops have failed and what corn they have is covered in mold.⁵⁴ They get separated and Caleb is bewitched by the witch—she is now young and beautiful again after rubbing herself in the blood and flesh from baby Sam. Thomasin has to return home without Caleb, raising suspicions against her even higher. These get even worse when the boy miraculously reappears near the homestead but totally naked. He is delirious and goes into a rapturous state as though seeing a beatific apparition floating above him, then suddenly collapses and dies. Meanwhile the twins have started to convulse, and accusations fly between them and Thomasin. Their parents lock all of them in the barn with the goats, and during the night the witch visits, slaughters the animals, and disappears with the twins. In the morning the barn is destroyed, leaving only the girl and Black Phillip, and he attacks and kills Thomasin's father. Her mother emerges from the house and at the sight of her dead husband loses what little reason she had left and attacks the girl. Thomasin keeps repeating that she loves her mother, but as with her prayers no one seems to listen. She is left with no option but to kill her own mother.

In many ways the death of the girl's family is as metaphorical as it is literal, and the gradual demise of its members represents the process of the girl cutting them out of her life so they become dead to her—the death of her mother, who she repeatedly slices and stabs with a knife, seems particularly apt in this reading. David Crow though feels that she suffers from a level of self-loathing due to wanting things that are different from the desires of her family. "This ability to quietly covet worldly things is also why she hates her own weakness and, on a certain level, desires her family to loathe her too, hence 'spinning fantasies' to young sister Mercy about selling her soul to Satan and eating flesh" (Crow 2016, n.p.). Yet this too can be seen to prepare her for being converted by Phillip; as a girl brought up in an extremist environment the natural place to turn is another, if oppositional, form of extremism. As such, by the story's end Phillip has convinced Thomasin that her place in Christian society is no longer tenable and that she must join him in order to gain any kind of control over her life—the local community would never believe her version of events and would inevitably burn her as a witch.

Much of this is borne out in the final scenes of the film where Thomasin offers herself to Phillip and unlike her God or even her own father—who refuses to stand up for his daughter in the narrative—the Dark Lord both speaks to her and offers her worldly rewards. More, he gives her immediate and positive proof of his intent as, after she has signed his contract, he leads her into the forest where a coven of young-looking witches dances naked around a large fire. As Thomasin joins them they are all lifted into the air. It is an ecstatic experience, giving substance to Phillip's promise of a life lived "deliciously" while simultaneously hiding the grimmer realities of Thomasin's future which will inevitably require the murder and preparation of babies like Sam to retain her youth.

Consequently, she is troubled into this new identity not so much in that it replaces her old one but more accurately redirects it; she was already prepared for religious extremism and the only thing that changes is to whom or what this is directed. There is something here of Lucy Westenra whose vampiric identity is a continuation of her previous self in that her rather transgressive approach to Victorian sexuality is allowed full reign once she no longer is part of that society. Thomasin has always wanted to give herself to a cause, to have more control over her life, and be rewarded for it, all of which her new life as a witch will "deliciously" do.

Black Phillip, and indeed Hannibal, exemplify a different kind of Dracula as absolute other, one that is not destroyed at the end of the narrative but continues in his troubling existence. As mentioned previously, Stoker's novel ends with the lingering doubt that the vampire is not truly destroyed, and here that becomes explicit. Hannibal's powers might be curtailed but as Harris's series of novels suggest, this is only for a limited time. Phillip's power to trouble the world would appear to be endless, and *The Witch* suggests that, just like the Count, he might reappear in any form he chooses. Also, unlike Hannibal, but much more in line with the vampire, Phillip converts those he chooses to be like himself, and although we do not see the witches bringing any new followers into the fold it is highly plausible that they might, at the very least, be an example to others in a similar situation as Thomasin. Consequently, the Dark Lord here is able to make his presence felt over a much larger area, making the foreignness he embodies both excessive and pervasive. The anxiety caused by this is more than human; it is almost supernatural in nature which makes detecting him and his cohorts virtually impossible, resulting in a continuous, and troubling, sense of constant suspicion and impending violence.

Three

The Trouble with Money

In which Count Dracula's association with money and/or consumerism troubles the world around him and reveals the more troubling truths that beat at its heart.

The Son of Dracula, Robert Siodmak, 1943

Siodmak's film is a curious one. Himself a European émigré—he was on the last ship leaving France for America as the Germans began their occupation—he envisions the King Vampire abandoning the Old World for the New in search of better prospects. The movie itself was made and released during World War II but, unlike its two prequels, shows the Count (Lon Chaney, Jr.) taking residence in America itself rather than a metaphorical version of it. Consequently, the narrative becomes more about collaborators and the wrong type of Americans during wartime than a call to isolate the United States from a monstrous Europe. This idea becomes explicit when the movie's true monster is shown not to be the undead Count from Europe but the conniving, vampiric woman Kay Caldwell (Louise Allbritton), who invites the Count into America for her own nefarious purposes. In fact, the real Dracula in the film is not the Transylvanian vampire but the woman from the American Deep South, and so it is to her we turn first.

In many ways Katherine "Kay" Caldwell is a trans-Atlantic version of Lucy Westenra; she is a woman who knows her own mind and does not see why the rules made up by patriarchal society should stop her. Here though Kay does not want multiple husbands, just the same one for eternity. From the viewpoint of the early 21st century this might not seem such a transgressive idea—Bella Swan from *The Twilight Saga* achieves this and is allowed to have a baby as well—however, in America during World War II this was not something to encourage for many reasons. Probably the most important ones are that she is a woman, and an heiress to an estate. The first is the most obvious but her gender has increased importance during wartime, and particularly in America in the 1940s, as women were given far more power in the workplace while the men were away in Europe and Asia fighting[1] (Colman 1998). Consequently, women were no longer forced to stay at home and be supported by family and/or husbands but could do jobs that were normally done by/reserved for men, and they had the potential to be individually independent. With this in mind the government were very keen that women were not seen to abuse these new freedoms and that they remained loyal both to their husbands and to the nation (Dick 1985, 166). Films such as *Mrs. Miniver* (Wyler, 1942) were typical in showing a loyal wife who kept the home fires burning and the family together, even when forced to cope with the greatest sacrifice of losing a husband due to the conflict. Kay demonstrates the complete opposite to this and acts wholly for herself throughout the narrative. Secondly, Kay's father owns a large plantation called Dark Oaks in the Deep South which, although no longer staffed by slaves, seems to have many African American workers. Kay and her sister Claire (Evelyn Ankers) are the only beneficiaries in their father's will when he unexpectedly dies after being attacked by a large bat (Count Alucard).[2] The estate not only represents family (American) heritage but both land and wealth; much national wealth was provided by slavery and its aftermath. The plantation then symbolizes the idea of old money, violent national memory, and even America itself, not unlike Count Dracula's castle that hides piles of "dead" money (Moretti 1988, 92), has rooms that are decrepit, and contains old chapels from the distant past and soil that is integral to the vampire's identity that he cannot exist without. In this vein the plantation, which equally consists of many parts from the modern main building down to the decrepit shacks on its grounds, can be seen as a symbol of national vampirism which fed off the "undead" labor" of slaves—to repurpose Franco Moretti's idea of Dracula representing capitalism that feeds off the wealth produced by an "undead," zombie-like workforce; consequently a plantation is the perfect place for Alucard/Dracula to be drawn to.

As such it is not a total surprise that Kay is not interested in the financial part of her father's will but only wants the property. She realizes the importance of land, not only to individual identity but to national prosperity and heritage. Indeed, she plans on possessing it forever, quite literally making it "undead" property. This further describes the kind of alterity that Kay embodies as she not only wants to take total control of herself now but for evermore, removing herself (and her property/wealth) totally from the American, patriarchal system.

Her antagonism to male control is shown from the beginning of the story when we find out that she has been traveling around Europe specifically to find the vampire so that she can invite him back to her plantation. Once back home she plans to marry the Count, become a vampire herself, then dispose of Alucard/Dracula so that she can marry her true love, Frank (Robert Paige) and live with him forever. This is hugely transgressive in many aspects; first she shows herself to be a "vamp," a woman who preys on men, specifically wealthy men, for their money and what she can get out of them (see Berger 2002, 5)[3]; secondly she invites evil into the heart of America; thirdly she is a woman taking advantage of a nation at war, not only by abusing the increased power bestowed on her by the government but by being unwilling to sacrifice her man to the war effort[4]; and lastly, she is totally selfish, putting her own desires above the needs of family and nation.

This starts to configure the scale of anxiety around the figure of Kay, a female, Southern other who threatens to dissolve the Union, weaken the nation, and drain it dry of wealth. There is something of a subtext here with Kay symbolizing a return to the Southern past while her sister, Claire, though conforming to the structures of patriarchal control, is shown as more contemporary, hinting at a need to suppress old divisions for the sake of a united Nation. Consequently, one can argue that Kay troubles America, and the viewing audience, as much as she does the other characters in the film and, maybe unsurprisingly, to diffuse that effect she is constructed using similar tropes as those used to configure Stoker's King Vampire. Specifically, she is framed as a monster from the past who is obsessed with death.

In Browning's film the Count often speaks of death—"to die, to be *really* dead, that must be glorious,"—and he is drawn to old, ruined buildings such as Castle Dracula and Carfax Abbey. Similarly, Kay is described as having an unhealthy, "morbid" interest in the occult—she brings a fortune teller, Madame Zimba from Hungary back with her from Europe—and she wants the plantation house as a symbol of what it was, without any improvements. She represents an American past as much as Dracula does a European one. Even though her attempts at female agency suggest a look to the future and female equality, her misuse of it points to an unpatriotic and unwanted past rather than a dreamed-of, desired future. In fact, her assistance in the murder of Zimba and her attempt to kill Alucard constructs her as being even worse than the monsters from Europe. This leaves the Count as rather peripheral to the story and can be read as the reason he seems so troubled for most of the film. Subsequently the next character to be looked at is Alucard, the troubled vampire who is out-vamped.

Alucard, as played by Lon Chaney, is a very different character from Lugosi's Dracula. If the earlier Count was more sophisticated and unmistakably European, Chaney's vampire is "bulkier and obviously more American" (Hutchings 2003, 22). While more recent critics have argued for the quality of the actor's performance (see Hutchings, 2003 and Smith, 2004) there is a certain indecisiveness to some of his scenes that adds to the character's air

Whose vamping who? Lon Chaney, Jr., as Count Dracula and Louise Allbritton as Katherine Caldwell in *The Son of Dracula*, dir. Robert Siodmak (Universal Pictures, 1943).

of being in the wrong place.[5] This is certainly compounded by the fact of Kay's stronger character and vampire credentials, which at times makes the story strangely reminiscent of the earlier *Dracula's Daughter* (Hillyer, 1936) and the relationship between the vampire Countess Zeleska and her man servant Sandor.

The latter obviously desires his mistress but must maintain the distance between them due to social proprietary and the fact she has no feelings for him whatsoever. Kay similarly keeps Alucard at bay no matter how much he wants to consummate their impending nuptials—it is never suggested what this might entail exactly other than the exchange of property—which leaves him as a menacing bystander who bullies all those who threaten his fiancée. Indeed, it is never explained why he would want to marry Kay; perhaps it is to make himself the owner of the plantation so that its soil might have the restorative qualities he requires to remain safe during the day. In contrast to this, his reason for coming to America is stated by the vampire himself: "I am here because this is a young and virile race, not dry and decadent like ours. They have what I want, what I need, what I must have" (Siodmak, 1943). As such he could be in America to take its prosperity (virility) as much as to suck the blood of the population. Oddly though, he drinks very little blood during the film. The majority of his victims are attacked when he is in the form of a bat that causes heart attacks or strokes, rather than the classic symptoms of extreme anemia as seen in Stoker's novel.[6] This exemplifies the curious split in the vampire's personality. While being menacing and rather thuggish in human form, he causes far more anxiety when in bat or mist form, or even when sleeping in his coffin. For example, one of the most spooky scenes in the film is when Alucard's coffin floats to the surface of a swamp on the plantation grounds, referencing fear of the *idea* of vampirism (of having one's vitality drained) rather than the physical actuality of it. As such, the vampire is more himself when in non-human form and is less troubled by Kay's influence than when he is Alucard, where he seems always in her thrall. This is the opposite of Dracula whose "brides" are forced to comply to his will, and also suggests a deeper meaning to the reversal of the names in the film (Dracula/Alucard).

The idea of reversal seems prevalent in the narrative. Alucard is befuddled by Kay, as Dracula had earlier confused Van Helsing and the others at the opening of Browning's story. The Count seems to have no idea of Kay's nefarious plan to marry him just so she can become immortal and then kill him so she can be with another man; it seems that just as the men of the New World were unprepared for a vampire—and require a Professor from Europe to identify the undead killer in their midst—so the vampire did not expect the New Woman from America.[7] This suggests that it is the (female) monster within that is more dangerous than the one from Europe, or beyond one's borders. In part this can be seen to be a vilification of Nazi-sympathizers,[8] conspirators, and even pacifists—Kay and Alucard want nothing to do with events occurring beyond the plantation—though this theme often seems peripheral to the abjectness created by Kay's totally self-centered and selfish motivations. It is hardly surprising that Alucard does not survive the film and is dispatched by Frank, Kay's real love and the symbol of American manhood. Frank achieves this by burning Alucard's coffin, leaving the vampire to disintegrate in the light of the morning sun.[9] Curiously this figures something of a new start for the Count, a chance to become himself again after finding release from the troubling influence of his first American bride as his remains are scattered on American soil. America is now his place of rest ... and resurrection.

All the above frames the crew of light rallied against the vampire as fairly ineffectual. Indeed, apart from Frank they are all elderly gentleman or foreign, representing the past rather than the future. There is something here that configures the battle against the vampire as a synecdoche of the larger war occurring overseas, where old money is sending the youth of the nation to fight the evil from Europe. Frank is the representative of this youth, and the problems he struggles with during the film show what happens when the behavior of the nation's women serves as a distraction rather than as encouragement and support for their men. As such, Frank is the last character to be examined, focusing on how he remains distracted for large parts of the narrative due to his vampish ex-fiancée Kay.

Frank Stanley is the Jonathan Harker of Siodmak's story, and like the young solicitor he was engaged to be married. However, upon returning from her trip to Europe, Kay breaks this off for reasons unknown to him.[10] This immediately positions him as slightly distracted as, in this wartime narrative, he is constructed as being representative of American youth and the nation's future, indeed even its potential prosperity/virility. As such, his woman is supposed to stand by him. When questioned about why Kay is no longer with him, he has no answer other than she has been beguiled by the Count from abroad, even though we know the opposite is true. Kay organizes a party for the arrival of her new beau and speaks to Frank, trying to intimate to him that there is a plan afoot, but he is so distracted that he fails to understand. He departs and just afterward Alucard, who has failed to show at his own welcoming party, appears to Kay's father in his bat form. The old man dies of the resultant heart attack and, after inheriting the property Kay announces that she is going to marry the Count, which distracts Frank so much that he behaves erratically and confronts the couple with a gun. He shoots at Alucard but the bullets pass through him, killing Kay and leaving Frank so distraught that he runs off and turns himself in to the police. Not unlike Jim from *Nadja*, in the previous chapter, Frank is literally knocked off his feet by how much Kay, his fiancée no less, has disrupted the expected patriarchal narrative of a wartime woman. But things are set to become even worse.

Kay appears in his cell in the form of a bat and transforms into her human self—she was already part vampire when Frank shot her—and tells him of her plan to turn him into a vampire too after he has killed Alucard, and that they then can live together forever. Frank is clearly discombobulated by this and is so distracted from his old self that he partially agrees and allows Kay to begin his vampirisation. Soon he escapes from his cell and goes to try to kill the Count. After a scuffle Frank manages to burn the vampire's coffin, leaving him nowhere to hide from the rising sun, and Alucard is destroyed. Frank then goes to meet Kay as agreed earlier, in the play room at Dark Oaks. Once there he sees her asleep in her coffin and his distraction finally lessens. He remembers who and what he is and sets fire to Kay's coffin, killing her.

Although this sees Frank break down in tears, it marks a return to his "true" self—restoring his masculinity—as representative of American manhood and the national/patriarchal order; not only is the selfish and uppity woman dead but she serves as an example to those watching who might think of ignoring their responsibilities to the nation (and their men). More importantly, in this reading Kay's inheritance will now pass to her sister Claire who is a true patriot and who will reintegrate the land, its history, and its potential wealth back into the homeland.

The end to the narrative also works as a model for America after the nation's battle is complete, seeing the country come together to defeat the foe from over the sea in the form of Europe, but also references any nation wishing to "feed" off America's virility and future prosperity. The internal threat has been dispelled and an example made to ensure that women remain faithful and responsible to the patriarchal/financial order. World War II saw unprecedented numbers of women taken into the workforce with little union resistance, which subsequently helped to more than double national profit between 1939 and 1945.[11] This equally sees the future of the nation being secured since submissive, responsible women no longer threaten to emasculate the men and rob them of their potential to repopulate the nation or drive the economy forward. Yet, just as with Stoker's narrative, there is an air of unease that hangs over the ending. Kay was American born and bred, and steeped in the history of the nation, maybe too much so. Moreover, she believed in dead money and just as the Transylvanian aristocrat kept piles of gold in his ruined castle, Kay is prepared to keep unrealized wealth in her plantation house, removing her from the living flow of capital. The spirit of the vampire lives on in Kay's daughters who do not so much suck the life out of a country but remove its source of sustenance. Kay's legacy is not to create a nation of vampires but turn it into an undead nation.

The Satanic Rites of Dracula, Alan Gibson, 1973

The idea of inviting the vampire in for one's personal gain, as Kay Caldwell did, is at the heart of many vampire narratives,[12] especially those of Hammer Studios where the undead Count was continually raised from the dead by people or groups looking to improve their lot in the world.[13] *The Satanic Rites* features just such a plot with a secret devil-worshiping society bringing the Dark Lord back to life in London of the 1970s. It is actually the last Hammer film featuring Christopher Lee in the lead role of the vampire, partly because the actor felt the films were getting less and less about Dracula himself—and indeed the vampire king does seem rather peripheral to the story and oddly out of date as an Old-World vampire in swinging 1970s London (see Johnson and Miller 2009, 150). Understandably, the Count likes to keep out of the public eye and is constructed as a reclusive millionaire, D.D. Denham, who runs a business/property empire. Unlike Stoker's Count, who kept his own (dead) money out of the economic flow of "living" capitalism, Gibson's aristocrat invests, builds, and accrues wealth and power. However, after his untimely demise in the previous film in the series, *Dracula A.D. 1972* (Gibson, 1972) which was also set in '70s London, Dracula wants revenge on the human race and is recreating a virulent strain of bubonic plague to unleash on the world, which his associates/acolytes believe he is doing in order to extort large sums of money.[14] As such, the Count is constructed as a very different figure to Stoker's, while still representing a supernatural past in a modern world.

The film begins with cuts between a Satanic ritual and an undercover agent escaping from the Pelham House of Psychic Examination and returning to his headquarters to tell of Satanic rituals that feature five of the biggest businessmen in the UK who are all part of the British government in some way. Before dying he manages to identify four of the men in the photos from his hidden camera but the fifth remains invisible, even in the picture—this will later replicate the missing reflection in Van Helsing's cigarette box from Browning's film. Using the idea of secret societies in the '60s and '70s immediately calls to mind the Cold War and cells of "sleeper" agents hidden from view waiting to bring down the government. Kim Philby and Guy Burgess of the Cambridge Five still loomed large in the public imagination, and Anthony Blunt confessed to be a Soviet agent as late as 1964 (see Bird 2018). Such associations are mentioned in the film when Inspector Murray (the Harker character in the film) enquires if the society is run by Moscow or Peking, the last being intimated by Pelham House being run by a Chinese woman called Chin Yang.[15]

Alongside this is the idea of biological warfare and, though not an explicit part of the ongoing antagonism between the USA and the Soviet Union—they both signed a treaty outlawing such weapons in 1972[16]—it correlates to the unknown effects of nuclear testing and radiation. This connection to the Cold War is further strengthened by Professor Julien Keeley being one of the members of the cult and also a Nobel prize winning scientist who we later discover is making a biological weapon for the Count. Professor Lorimmer Van Helsing—and police expert working—remembers his former friend from Oxford University, making relatively evident the link to its equally famous competitor, Cambridge University, and its Soviet infection. Indeed, the idea of a global epidemic would not have been unfamiliar to audiences of the time, as the Hong Kong flu had killed a million people worldwide in 1968–1969. It is the intersection of all these ideas, spy rings and global epidemics, that can also be seen to feed into the notion of a mysterious corporation, a body that controls governments and the wheels of power in order to make money and is not accountable to any state or nation but only to its leader. As Abbott observes about the film "Dracula returns as a corporate executive, a move that positions the vampire as a metaphor for global commodity culture" (Abbott 2007, 82)[17] and, at least in this film, for its inhuman nature as an all-consuming greed. D.D. Denham is suggested to own much of London, if not the actual properties themselves then the people who own them. There are quite strong parallels here between much of *The Satanic Rites* and the series *The Strain* looked at earlier, seeing corporate vampirism as an undead plague that infects the land/environment itself.

Not coincidentally, London was experiencing a boom in the building of office properties at the start of the 1970s due to a change in government policy[18]—the exact kind of thing intimated in the film—and the scenes in Denham's office were filmed in the empty Centre Point in the heart of the capital, positioning Dracula as an undead eye surveying the city and its inhabitants. The tower block contains many CCTV cameras, unusual for the times, mirroring the use of surveillance cameras throughout the movie and foreshadowing 21st century consumerism and the ownership of public spaces, where all are seen except for the vampire himself; this embodies the hidden consumerist ideology behind the system. Presciently it also foreshadows the ideas that banks and money never sleep, and that one can be constantly tracked and monitored through one's financial transactions.

The idea of Dracula as a reclusive millionaire would also see him correlated to the then famous Howard Hughes, though maybe equally well known to a British audience at the start of the 1970s would have been John Poulson, a wealthy architect and businessman who cultivated connections to government ministers. At his height he was earning over a million pounds a year, worked on constructions at London railway stations, and was himself a Commissioner of Inland Revenue. In 1972 the Metropolitan Police instigated an investigation for fraud which placed Poulson at the center of a huge corruption scandal, which caused the resignation of the then Home Secretary who was also nominally in charge of the police; one of the "Satanic" businessmen in Gibson's film is identified as being the "boss" of the special investigative team looking into the kidnappings and murders perpetrated by Dracula's henchmen. Poulson was convicted in 1974 with the sentencing judge describing him as an "incalculably evil man."[19] He was also a Freemason, and while the group is not actually a Satanic cult it is commonly seen in the popular imagination as a mysterious secret society with esoteric beliefs concerned with the power and wealth of its members. In this light it can be argued that Dracula's otherness here in Gibson's film is not so much about capitalism per see but about the dark heart of consumerism/neo-liberalism that is led by human corruption and greed. In this regard it is interesting that the plague, a new strain of Black Death, is engineered specifically to rot human flesh as a hyper accelerated form of decadence; an opulence that sees the consumerist body grow so luxurious that it loses all definition and quite literally dissolves into nothing.

The Count's absolute otherness is then about revealing the vampirism at the heart of consumerism, even above and beyond its own survival, and the ways in which its promise of gratification, power, and wealth trouble and distract those around it. As mentioned earlier, the narrative of *The Satanic Rites* begins very much in the mould of the espionage movie and many of the characters are distracted by this, thinking they are looking for the head of a Soviet spy ring rather than the Lord of Darkness. Once that is proved wrong the majority of the characters quickly change their focus. This is seen most strongly in Professor Lorrimer Van Helsing (Peter Cushing) who has total conviction from the start that dark forces are at play. In part, this is due to his training as an anthropologist and specialist in the occult, but also to his family's history with Count Dracula, so although he does not immediately identify D.D. Denham as the old adversary he is certain from the beginning that vampirism is involved.[20] In fact, the only people who are distracted by the vampire are those who have pledged their allegiance to him, thinking that the form of consumerism he embodies is one that aligns with their own; an extreme form of postcolonial white male privilege that keeps them at the top of the consumerist food chain. Of the four acolytes identified as being at the ritual, three—General Freebourne, Dr. John Porter, and Lord Carradine—are all figured as ministers, largely involved in security, who can be bought (linking back to the real-life case of John Poulson) and have no qualms about fulfilling the Count's requests—at least not until the films denouement when they discover that they will be the carriers (three of the four horseman) of the apocalyptic disease. The fourth, however, Professor Keeley (Freddie Jones), is deeply troubled by his bargain with the devil. In fact he very much follows the course of Renfield from Browning's film.

Although we never see Keeley before he is under the influence of the vampire, we discover from Van Helsing that they were not only friends at University but have met since at the occultist's apartment, as described by his granddaughter Jessica Van Helsing, suggesting that Keeley was once a balanced individual. This is reinforced through his being a Nobel prize winner for humanity in science which strongly intimates a quest for human welfare rather than his own wealth and power. Yet when we first see him at the ritual dressed in a large white hooded cloak, he is a conflicted individual. This is in part due to the ritual itself, where the blood of a cockerel is dripped over the body of a naked young girl who herself is then stabbed and miraculously revives (she is of course a vampire). The scene is purposely eroticized in a way that emphasizes male power but while the other men are arouse, Keeley looks torn between someone waiting to be discovered as an imposter and one who is possessed or hypnotized. This impression is strengthened when Van Helsing goes to meet his old friend to see why he is involved with such a group.

When the Professor arrives at his friend's apartment, no one answers him at the door so he enters the "lab" unannounced to find Keeley busy at work. Keeley seemingly mistakes Van Helsing for an agent of his new master and becomes increasingly nervous with dramatic bodily spasms and insists that he has finished making the biological weapon in time for 23rd November, the Sabbat of the Undead (a spurious calendar date invented for the film that is supposedly even more powerful than Walpurgis Night). Once Van Helsing has reminded his friend of who he is, Keeley suddenly reverts back to a confident scientist again, denying his involvement in any nefarious groups or deeds. His personality jumps are strongly reminiscent of Renfield's while under the care of Dr. Seward in his asylum, particularly when speaking to Abraham Van Helsing. In the 1931 *Dracula* the former solicitor is torn between various versions of himself: the troubled self who consumes insects and thinks of himself as vampiric in some way; the self who is a mindless body controlled by the vampire; and finally, his old self who wants to do what's right and protect the innocent from his Master.

Back in Keeley's apartment he seems to think Lorimmer is his ever-present Master but slowly begins to realize it's his old friend, though even here true recognition never seems to totally dawn. Then once again his Master's presence returns, leaving him staring out the window, lost in a world where there is no place to hide. It seems that his old self is totally absent, and he has no sign of regret or fear over the biological weapon he has manufactured. This is an interesting twist on Stoker's tale where medical science is used to defeat the vampire; here it has been bought or is owned by the Count, so that future technologies are now in his arsenal to help defeat the outdated human race. Keeley himself then represents medical science that has been purchased by corporations with their own agendas (a situation that is taken largely as fact in the early 21st century). The scientist's personality issues are equally about the way he has become possessed/troubled by his own quest for personal wealth and advancement, above and beyond his professional oath to care for others and to hold human life as sacrosanct. As such, it is the literal selling of himself, his real self, to Dracula that leaves only his body and his troubled self behind. Unfortunately for Keeley, and just like Renfield before him, he is killed by his Master for perceived treachery, though it does save him from the more painful death of virulent bubonic plague which awaits his fellow servants of dark consumerism.

The ending of the film suits its similarity to espionage and/or James Bond films, where rather than killing the agent of good as soon as possible, the Dark Lord decides an easy death is too good for him and takes Van Helsing from his London office out into the country at Pelham House. Here, Dracula has decided to turn Van Helsing's granddaughter into his vampiric consort to rule over the post-apocalyptic Earth once the plague has wrought its destruction. But, Inspector Murray has also arrived at the location and starts a fire which kills the infected acolytes and destroys the virus. Van Helsing jumps out of the window and is pursued by Dracula into the nearby woods, but the Professor lures him into a hawthorn bush—described at the start of the film as a weapon against vampires as it was used in the making of Christ's Crown of thorns and therefore holy—where the vampire becomes hopelessly ensnared, allowing Van Helsing to slay his undead enemy once again.[21] It is a curious ending to the narrative as the further away from the modern world and the influence of money the vampire goes, the more vulnerable he becomes. Once he is in the woods at night—where one would assume he would be in his element—he is in fact isolated from everything that gives him power; even Van Helsing, who appears to be in his sixties seems able to move and see better in the dark than the vampire. It is the lack of technology and the accoutrements of Empire (business) that finally undo the Count. Interestingly though, once the body of Dracula has disintegrated into dust, Van Helsing takes the large ring the vampire wore, which represents both its heritage and economic prowess. Ostensibly, this is to prevent the ring's use as a way to resurrect the vampire, though other films have seen blood being dripped onto the vampire's remains as sufficient for this purpose. Here, this move intimates the undead nature of the greed and lust for power behind consumerism that is ready to be reanimated with the right key. Similarly, the story never explains what happens to D.D. Denham's massive, multi-million corporation. Consequently, even though Dracula has gone, the wheels of business will still turn without him, and although his (temporary) disappearance might cause a slump or glitch in the bottom line the stocks and profits will inevitably rise again. This is something the next film plays on, envisioning a world overrun by corporate vampires. But even undead workers need more than profits to survive.

Daybreakers, The Spierig Brothers, 2008

Daybreakers begins ten years after the outbreak of a mysterious plague that has turned everyone into vampires, and they are everywhere. D.D. Denham's brand of consumerism (if not his apocalyptic thought) has triumphed and everyone must, quite literally, eat the world around them, or at least eat the humans.[22] In this aspect the film closely resembles *I Am Legend*, though the undead zombie-like creatures in *Daybreakers* are vampiric office workers rather than the suddenly disenfranchised and motivationally challenged, as in Matheson's vision. This alternate world gives physical form to Karl Marx's idea of undead labor, with the vampire inhabitants of the Earth forced to continue their office jobs in huge building complexes that are shielded from UV light, which is highly dangerous to the undead in this story.[23] Indeed, it is hard to differentiate between home, transport system, and the office in these massively repetitive lives which, as they are vampires, will go on forever.[24] What will not go on forever, though, is the supply of human blood they need to survive. The non-vampire population has now almost vanished, and so the story centers on producing a synthetic replacement. The plague that caused all this, as in Matheson's story, is never identified but there is a strong implication that bats are in some way involved. This is seen in the occasional flash shots of bats flying across the screen,[25] but more pointedly illustrated when the vampires are unable to find enough human blood and start drinking their own or that from other vampires. When this happens, they lose their human appearance, grow pointed ears, their body hair falls out, and they develop rat-like features. In extreme cases they grow large flaps of skin under their arms which form large bat-like wings. It is evident that it is human blood that keeps the vampires looking like their former, human, selves, but without it and due to ingesting vampire blood, they begin degenerating into their true form. This also intimates that true consumers are human-vampires whereas the more bestial undead are too unsophisticated, too degenerated to be able to fully engage in such ideological imperatives. As mentioned above, the story's links to *I Am Legend* are obvious. Those to *Dracula* are less so, though when the correlations are made some interesting points emerge.

Daybreakers acts as more of a sequel to Stoker's novel in that the King Vampire is now in control and the slayers represent the minority rather than being symbolic of Empire and civilization. Indeed, it is the vampires that control the cities and technology while the hunters scavenge in the countryside struggling to survive. The role of Dracula has to fall to Charles Bromley (Sam Neill), the head of Bromley Marks Corporation. Like the Count in *The Satanic Rites*, Bromley is CEO of a huge corporation, surrounded by acolytes and living an undead life of luxury, drinking blood from large wine glasses while supplies everywhere else get lower and lower. Rather than cause a plague to kill human society, however, he needs to replicate human blood to maintain a vampiric world. He is represented as the leader of the vampire community shown in the narrative—though it is intimated that other countries might have similar or competing corporations—and asserts his authority, in true Marxist fashion, through the daily exploitation of undead labor. His role as the leading force of vampire society frames the way in which he also encourages, or troubles, those around him to be even more themselves, making them super-human consumerists in the way they continually work and consume, and turning the workaday office environment into a processing plant (though it is never quite clear what they exactly do or why they would need to carry on working). As such, the narrative sees vampirism as a very particular form of human excess, specifically those traits of self-interest and

The monstrous form of those beyond consumerism. Bryan Probets in *Daybreakers*, dir. the Spierig Brothers (Lionsgate, 2009).

individual greed that typify 21st century consumerism (the action takes place in 2019).

Curiously, those vampires that conform to this framework of endless and mindless work in the pursuit of material satisfaction remain human in appearance but those that deny the work and either refuse to drink human blood or are abandoned by the system become less and less "human" in appearance and actions. This also begins to reveal the way in which Dracula can be seen to trouble *himself*, both in the sense that unrestrained consumerism is not sustainable, and in that it can turn on itself, that it has some form of self-regulation. Both find expression within the larger vampire "body." Bromley himself is not psychically "linked" to the rest of the vampire community in the way the Count was, or the Master in *The Strain*, but as the ideological rudder to the undying consumerist society, their actions manifest how strong his control over them is. Something of this idea is seen in the interconnected network of the UV-protected city with the workers' homes connected via subways and underground railways to the City Center, their office buildings, and work stations, all of which comes under the auspices of the Head of the corporation, Bromley. The city, therefore, operates as an extended Dracula's Castle with rooms and corridors that seem to extend in all directions, but which all come under the Count's watchful gaze. Bromley literally has "eyes" everywhere with the huge number of surveillance cameras installed throughout the complex. Consequently, the troubling aspects of the community often occur in relation to the spaces within which they happen.

This is particularly true of the Subsiders, creatures that are part of the Count's "body" that feeds on itself, causing them to drop out of the consumerist cycle and making them more monstrous than the original monsters—the vampires.[26] Their positioning within Dracula's/Bromley's body is worth examining further as they form something of an otherness to that of the vampire itself. In some respects, they are constructed as the disenfranchised or homeless of the society, spurned by those who maintain their human appearance and consumerist credentials, but they manage to exist in spaces within the "castle" that are beyond its Master's sight. In this respect they act as Bromley's subconscious that works against, and troubles, his conscious ambitions. This notion is given more credence by the way the Subsiders attack the "normal" members of the Count's body.

The film shows various attacks but possibly the best example is the one that happens to Edward Dalton (Ethan Hawke), a scientist who works for Bromley and who upon returning home after work one evening is attacked by a Subsider who has broken into his house. We have previously seen someone attacked in the city, a more obvious location as it is part of the main vampire complex, but Dalton's home is outside of that complex. This positions the Subsiders as an uncontrollable infection, one now beyond the scope/control of the vampire Master. In many ways it makes them the true undead as they are a regression or devolution of the current social order, not unlike the original Dracula, to a time before capitalism and the industrial revolution; they are almost akin to the vampires in *The Omega Man* (Sagal, 1971) as they too all look the same once they have regressed. However, whereas in Sagal's film they all revert to an idea of pre-modern fundamental "whiteness," here they are configured as a form of bestiality[27]; a creature driven by animal instincts rather than the fetishized drives of the "civilized" vampires.

The disintegration of the vampire body is equally seen in the control that the Master vampire, Bromley, has over his wives, or his daughter Alison (Isabel Lucas). The wives can be seen as a useful analogy here as they too are often resistant to, or even confrontational to, Dracula's power over them.[28] Alison is as troubling to Bromley as he is to her, mainly because she is still human and has no desire to become a vampire. In fact, this is an inherent part of the story from the start in that it differentiates those who willingly embrace the new vampire lifestyle (extreme consumerism) from those that do not. This is not just a straightforward division between the surviving humans and vampires, as the narrative explicitly shows characters that are vampires that refuse to live as such—one of the early scenes in the film shows a vampire teenage girl purposely sitting in the sun to kill herself[29]—and humans who almost go out of their way to become undead. Edward Dalton's brother Frankie (Micheal Dorman) does this because he "was never very good at being human" (Spierig Brothers, 2009). Indeed Edward, who will be discussed next, is a vampire who wants to become human again.

Bromley's daughter despises vampires and her father in particular—her mother is not mentioned—and when the film begins, she is in hiding with other humans. However, she is captured and brought to her father who wants her to join him. She refuses and stabs him, which of course does nothing but ruin his shirt. Bromley then gets one of his militia, Frankie Dalton, to turn her, but this just makes her hate her father even more and she refuses to drink any blood other than her own. Admitting his defeat, he sentences her to death, and, along with other vampires that refuse to be part of his consumerist society, she is chained to a large vehicle which drags them all out into the annihilating light of the sun (see Bacon, 2016a). While this acts as a spectacle and deterrent to the rest of the vampire community—they are seen watching from behind the special, protective UV-resistant glass in the office buildings—it also reveals how Bromley cannot even control his own daughter. Alison's death greatly troubles Bromley, and while it does not make him forget his commitment to the extreme consumerist ideology he embodies and propagates, it distracts him from remaining fully focused on the problems at hand. These come in the shape of Edward Dalton (Frankie's brother) who is something of a Jonathan Harker figure.

Dalton works for Bromley as the lead scientist in the search for synthetic blood, which he willingly does as he no longer wants to drink human blood, and which marks him as a partial Dr. Seward as well. The experiments are not going particularly well and are made more complicated by the fact that Edward has developed early signs of becoming a Subsider. Just as Harker before him, Dalton manages to escape from the King Vampire's "castle" and return to human society, in this case to the renegade group that Alison belonged to that live outside the city to avoid capture. There is a sense that Dalton exists in a hybrid manner not unlike that of Harker—though it is rarely commented upon how Stoker's young hero has been bitten by the vampire, possibly more than once, and so is more akin to Lucy and Renfield than Seward or Holmwood. It is certainly suggested by the end of the novel *Dracula* that Harker is fully human again—he is the one responsible for killing the vampire—and that maybe the treatment he received at the hands of the sisters at the Hospital of St. Joseph and St. Mary in Budapest was successful (Stoker 1996, 107).

Indeed, it is this idea of a "cure" that is taken up by *Daybreakers*, but rather than allowing the hero to re-enter modern, capitalist society as it does in Stoker, it heralds the collapse of consumerism and a return to the past.

Within the film this is also constructed as Edward remembering who he was before he was troubled by vampirism and Bromley.

In *Daybreakers* the cure comes after Edward has met Audrey (Claudia Karvan), a leading light in the human resistance; she plays a less central version of Mina. She introduces Edward to a character called Elvis (Willem Dafoe), originally named Lionel Cormac, a vampire who used to be a car mechanic. He had been driving during the daytime when his car crashed, throwing him through the wind screen into the sunlight. Elvis immediately burst into flames but landed in water which put out the fire and also somehow restarted his heart, returning him to a human-like state. Elvis, like the medicated survivors of the plague in *I Am Legend*, is actually something slightly different or "other than" human. Curiously, the narrative sees the movement of the heart as being pivotal to one's living or undead state. Being undead with no heart-beat positions one as being inextricably linked into futurity and consumerism, whereas a pulse positions a person as being from the past and outside of (heartless) consumerist ideology and its influence.

Elvis himself is almost something of a Renfield character, one that has survived his association with the vampire Count, though it has not left him completely untroubled. In many ways this is what marks both Edward and Elvis out as pivotal; they are (or will be in Edward's case) hybrids in the sense that they *were* vampires/extreme consumerists but have returned to being human. Or rather more accurately have stopped being "vampires." This is an important point and is one equally seen in Matheson's novel, and even in Stoker's. In *I Am Legend* Robert Neville is the last human alive, and in his way is as violent and monstrous, if not more so, than the vampires he himself labels as monsters. But this Manichaean view of the world is as outdated as Neville himself and evolution has proposed a third option: those who have the virus but have not been turned by it. It is they who will inherit the new Earth.[30] *Dracula* too sees the future in the hands of the hybrids as both Harker and his wife have been intimate with the vampire, with Mina's conjugation more explicitly described and examined. As such they are not the humans they once were, and it is the Harkers' son, Quincey, who is seen as the future. Edward's hybridity is achieved when Elvis helps him stop being a vampire, i.e., makes his heart beat again, by replicating the process Elvis went through himself. Fortunately, this does not involve Edward having a car crash but sees him stand at the bottom of a modified grain silo where the sunlight shines on him for long enough to set him on fire, and then Audrey and Elvis smother him in water-soaked blankets. This does not work on the first attempt, but eventually Edward is no longer a vampire and so is no longer ideologically linked to extreme consumerism, not dissimilar to the links between Dracula and his progeny. While this act finally separates Edward from Bromley, the process began much earlier when his proximity to the Master vampire troubled him into remembering who he was before consumerism consumed the world. As such, Edward's heart beginning to beat again not only signals a break with his troubled (vampire) self but also embraces who he might become in relation to all his previous selves.

The rebels decide they need to let everyone know about the cure and so Audrey, Elvis, and Edward go to see the scientist's former colleague, Chris, at the Bromley Marks lab. Upon their arrival, though, they discover that Chris has managed to synthesize a blood substitute and so has no intention of curing potential clients of their need for his product. While he answers, a phone call manages to alert the authorities that he needs help, and soon the militia storm the house and capture Audrey while Edward and Elvis manage to escape. The two men enter one of the covered walkways used by the vampires and are attacked by a Subsider, but Edward's brother Frankie appears and saves them. Frankie, like Chris, is not interested in the cure and attacks Elvis but has a surprising reaction to drinking the man's blood; his heart starts beating again.[31] Emboldened by this, Edward continues to the main building of Bromley Marks and allows himself to be apprehended knowing he will be taken to Bromley. He tells his former employer that he has a cure for vampirism (extreme consumerism) but Bromley is not interested now that he has the blood substitute; his consumerist ideology can continue forever.

Edward taunts the Master vampire, causing him to attack. Too late, Bromley senses that something is not right but before he can react Edward ties him up and sends him out to the troops waiting outside the door, giving time for the curative blood to work and make "Dracula" human again. They quickly realize that Bromley is now not a vampire and they attack him, so that they too are no longer undead. A chain reaction ensues with the newly converted being attacked and killed by those who are still vampires; the cure quite literally causes consumerism to eat itself. At the end of this first frenzy only three soldiers are left alive but Chris arrives and shoots them, determined that his blood substitute will keep the corpse of consumerism eternally undead. Before Chris can realize his hope, though, Elvis appears and stakes him, allowing the cure to continue to spread throughout the city. As the film ends Edward, Elvis, and Audrey drive off, taking themselves and their cure into the dawn of a new day. But a closing shot of a bat screeching across the screen creates an uneasy ending, and while it is possibly just meant as a thematic coda—ending the film as it began—it also leaves the feeling that the disease, extreme consumerism, is not dead and that even Edward's and Elvis's hybridity is not all that it seems.

The ideological vampirism of *Daybreakers* is ultimately doomed to fail as it inevitably will consume everything that it needs to survive—the blood substitute being the hope that ultimately always stays just out of reach. The next film circumvents this outcome by proposing "vegetarian" vampires, or "green" consumerists, otherwise known as the undead that do not drink human blood.

Twilight: Breaking Dawn Part 1, Bill Condon, 2011

One could choose any of the films from *The Twilight Saga* to illustrate the kind of vampiric consumerism that the Cullen family, and indeed the Twilight franchise, practices on its audience. By the time the first film was released the novels had already accumulated a huge worldwide readership and extended fanbase. The films can be seen to play on this as after the first installment the narratives of subsequent films became increasingly orientated to pleasing the established fan-base rather than increasing its appeal to an even wider audience.[32] That said, the film chosen here does provide very clear examples of the factors in play as well as the immense wealth of the vampire family that is central to the tale. Also, by the time *Breaking Dawn Part I* came out, the franchise was a proven merchandizing platform, even to the point of certain products being launched in line with the opening weekend of the movie. However, before discussing this in more depth it is necessary to establish the Saga's credentials as a descendant of Stoker's *Dracula* and examine how it constructs its form of absolute otherness.

The main point of focus in *The Twilight Saga* is the relationship between Edward Cullen (Robert Pattinson), who is a vampire, and Bella Swan (Kirsten Stewart), who is human—though she will be a vampire by the end of *Breaking Dawn Part I*. There is a third side to this twosome in the shape of Jacob Black (Taylor Lautner), who is a werewolf/shapeshifter. This does not easily correlate to Stoker's novel, though a woman who cannot decide between multiple men brings to mind Lucy Westenra, who also becomes a vampire just like Bella.[33] But more to the point, Bella gives birth to a (special) baby which Lucy does not, though Mina Harker's son Quincey is potentially special.[34] As such, at least in terms of both *Breaking Dawn* films, we can nominally label Bella as Mina,[35] which leaves Edward as either Jonathan Harker or Dracula. In fact, it is possible to see him as both, or as a character who embodies parts of each of them. In terms of fulfilling the role of Dracula, Edward is not a leader or original vampire—he was turned/saved by Carlyle, the nominal father of the Cullen family—but he, more obviously than his "family," embodies the absolute otherness of the vegan-vampire community. Also, he exhibits many characteristics in common with earlier, more romantic versions of the Count.

Badham's *Dracula* from 1979 intimates an attraction between Mina and the Count, and one which sees her seemingly happy to be made a vampire and travel across the ocean with him, though Van Helsing and her jilted fiancé Jonathan Harker make sure this does not happen. *Love at First Bite*, mentioned in Chapter One, copies the reincarnation of a previous love theme seen earlier in *Blacula* and repeated in *Bram Stoker's Dracula* (Coppola, 1992) and *Dracula Untold* (Shore, 2014),[36] which all see the King Vampire as a dashing figure that charms a human girl/woman, usually with the intent to convince her that love is eternal and then turn her into a vampire.[37] This contrasts with Kay Caldwell discussed earlier who is killed for such thoughts. In this respect Edward also strongly resembles Murnau's Orlok, the love-lorn vampire that stares into Ellen's room night after night. Edward goes one better and enters Bella's bedroom—Twilight vampires need no invitation—and looks at her while she sleeps. In contrast to his feral predecessor, he does all he can to avoid being tempted by the blood of his love object.

Edward, then, manifests this more recent incarnation of the suave, romantic, undead aristocrat who creates a new kind of absolute otherness by mirroring and reversing many of the features that made the original so monstrous. Edward lives in a "castle" that is an ultra-modern house with huge windows and large rooms full of light; he does not drink human blood but only that of animals; most strikingly, sunlight does not kill him but makes his skin sparkle. In a curious way this marks out the most troubling aspect of Edward; he is the only one explicitly shown to shimmer and gleam in this way, marking him as the most conspicuous point of wealth in the family.

Much is made of Count Dracula's hidden treasure, particularly piles of gold as described by Harker in the novel: "The only thing I found was a great heap of gold in one corner—gold of all kinds, Roman, and British, and Austrian, and Hungarian, and Greek and Turkish money, covered with a film of dust, as though it had lain long in the ground" (Stoker 1996, 51). This treasure is often used to describe the vampire's nature as representative of the old aristocracy, and dead money that benefits no one

Edward (Robert Pattinson) proving that all that glitters is made of gold, or diamonds, in *Twilight*, dir. Katherine Hardwicke (Summit Entertainment, 2008).

(see Moretti 1998, Halberstam 1995, and Ledger and McCracken 1995), but Edward's wealth is displayed for all to see, literally shining in plain sight on his skin. This is graphically shown in a rather over done shirt-off scene near the culmination of the second installment, *Twilight: New Moon* (Weitz, 2009). It is in fact a very important scene as it both distinguishes the difference between Edward and his rival for Bella's affections, Jacob, and establishes wealth as an almost spiritual aspiration.

The scene is set in an Italian town square at noon during the feast of Saint Marco. Edward believes that Bella no longer loves him and so wants the ruling vampires, the Volturi, to kill him. They refuse, so Edward decides to force their hand by breaking one of their cardinal rules: revealing himself to be a vampire to the human population. And so, during the height of the religious ceremony Edward leaves a darkened doorway, semi-clothed, baring his torso to the world. In the midday sunlight his body begins to as sparkle, but Bella (who has travelled there with Alice, one of Edwards "sisters") throws herself at him, forcing him back into the shadows. Edward's body is pure white and very feminine, not unlike many European religious paintings of Christ on the cross, and seemingly encrusted with millions of tiny jewels or diamonds. The image is purposely spiritual and equally luxurious or opulent, seeing the vampire's undead torso as a priceless work of religious art.[38] This scene is in stark contrast to an earlier one in the same film where Jacob has accepted his werewolf heritage and takes his shirt off to reveal his highly muscled, Native American, torso. The difference could hardly be greater between the pale, transcendent body of Edward and the earthbound, highly muscled one of Jacob. The vampire body is that of an ethereal being that is beyond worth yet amazingly valuable so that money and financial worth become inextricably linked to spirituality, with little regard for earthly matters such as the ecological effects of such extreme consumerism. Jacob on the other hand is entangled with his people and the land that is both their heritage and their home; when in wolf form, he represents the kind of creatures the vampires unthinkingly feed on as the more ethical or "vegetarian" choice. Unsurprisingly, Jacob never leaves the local town of Forks or the woodlands around it, while Edward and the vampires seem continually on the move. Indeed, for their honeymoon in *Breaking Dawn Part I* Edward and Bella travel via car, plane, and speed boat to an island off the coast of Brazil; they have no real home or ties to the land other than through the properties they have bought.

Such demonstrative displays of consumerism are much to the ire of the old order of ruling vampires, the Voltori, but Edward and Bell represent something new, where wealth is not to be hidden but shown to be more alive and mobile than its owner; consumerism is not a creature of the shadows but a splendid, spectacular entity that leads by example. In this reading, while the original Dracula hid his wealth and inspired fear and terror in those around him, the new undead, as seen in Edward, create adoration and envy for their exorbitant lifestyle. This makes it difficult to place exactly what kind of absolute otherness Edward embodies except the kind of privilege and money that sees a tiny percentage of the Earth's population owning a huge proportion of its wealth and property. Perhaps more accurately he manifests the tension, or the jouissance, between that and the desire to become one of those super rich few who endure the continuation of extreme consumerism and the neoliberal ideology that fuels it.

If Edward forms the focus point of the family's vampiric consumerism, then the rest of the Cullens act as his "brides," not in the sense that they are under his control or were "made" by him but more in that they help to advertise, or market, his form of power. If the Count's "wives" embodied a tempting and alluring prospect to the unwary with their "brilliant white teeth, that shone like pearls against the ruby of their voluptuous lips" (Stoker 1996, 41), then the Cullens do much the same for the inhabitants of Forks, the town in which they live (see McMahon-Coleman and Weaver 2014, 101, and Kirkland 2012, 157). They appear as glamorous and aloof, always wearing the most up-to-date clothes and expensive watches, and driving top of the range cars; if ever there was an advert to seek vampirism as an economic and quality-of-life upgrade, then the Cullen family is it. Alice in particular prides herself on her fashion sense and lives an undead life as a supermodel who is over the moon to take charge of the wedding arrangements for Bella and Edward at the start of *Breaking Dawn Part I*. Of note in the Cullens' role as Dracula's brides is that they no longer try to drink the blood of the living—although Jasper (Jackson Rathbone) comes close in the first film—but persuade humans to be like them, fellow vampiric travelers on the path of overt consumerism. When Stoker's Harker was confronted by those "ruby lips" of temptation he felt that something was not quite right: "There was something about them that made me uneasy, some longing and at the same time some deadly fear," yet he was helpless to resist. With the Cullens no such pangs of conscience survive, and spending is the only way to ensure eternal youth and still make it enjoyable.[39]

Arguably, this is what troubles Bella into choosing to be a vampire.[40] Although she suggests that she has never felt comfortable as a human (just as Frankie did in *Daybreakers* as mentioned above) it is hard to ignore that this conviction becomes stronger once she has met Edward. In this sense one could even paraphrase it to say she never felt comfortable being poor and she only feels like herself when surrounded by wealth. This might be a little uncharitable to the young girl, but the films make it more obvious than the novels do. Bella has moved north from Arizona to Forks, the area with the least amount of sunshine in the U.S.,[41] her parents are divorced, and she has to stay with her father as her mother is traveling. Her father buys her a repaired pick-up truck to help her settle in, but upon starting school she is fascinated by the mysterious Cullen children as they are described to her in both envious and adoring tones by her new "friend" Jessica (Anna Kendrick). The Cullens exude a confidence that comes from money and is displayed in the clothes they wear and the cars they drive. When Edward finally starts paying attention to her, and saves her life, it is something of a dream come true. Even his obsessive and controlling behavior becomes something of a security blanket, keeping her old, poor self away from her new wealthy identity. Money, as embodied in Edward, is superhuman, immortal, denies the laws of the natural world, and makes its own rules. Bella all too clearly sees the difference between her own, awkward (poor) life in comparison to the "ease" of wealthy living, and so grasps it with both hands.

The story does its best to hide the ways in which she disconnects herself from her former life but as the cinematic installments go by she sees less and less of her school friends, other than the Cullens, and after her wedding to Edward she sees almost nothing of her parents, citing a mysterious illness to cover up her sudden pregnancy and its shockingly fast gestation period. This in itself is a very curious stage in the narrative as money seems to do very little to assist in easing the violence of her pregnancy, though one could argue that is has massively sped up the entire process; her pregnancy only lasts a month and she is unconscious for the final stages.

The baby, Renesmee, can be understood as having inherited her parents' extreme consumerism as she literally begins to consume her host, Bella, during the pregnancy. This is only halted when her still-human mother starts to drink blood. Going through such a traumatic process in an incredibly short time inevitably takes its toll on Bella's body and the nearer she gets to the birth the thinner and more drawn she looks, even to the point of her bones breaking under the pressure of the baby moving—Renesmee as a true extreme consumer will happily cause the destruction of her own environment. It is not surprising then that the strain on Bella's body becomes too much during the birth itself and she dies. However, even this can be remedied by wealth as embodied by Edward himself. This he does by biting her and injecting her with his venom—Twilight vampires pass on their "infection" through a poison they release while biting their victim which both kills and makes them immortal—turning her into a vampire, meaning she can now fully partake of the Cullens' wealth. More than this, not only does she return to "life"—always a relative term in relation to the undead—but the process restores her body, not just to its former self but to a fashion magazine ideal of what she would be if heavily made up and coiffured; her skin is perfect and marble smooth, her hair is full, wavy and glossy, and her eyes and teeth perfectly white; the only thing slightly off kilter is her bright red pupils. Everything else is taken directly from cosmetic and shampoo adverts, intimating that vampirism makes her the ultimate example of consumerist merchandising; a model for others to aspire to. This becomes even more evident once she is united with her baby daughter, who grows at a similarly accelerated rate once born, making her, Edward, and Renesmee the perfect picture of the perfect family. Indeed, everything about them is constructed as perfect and that which can only be attained through the kind of extreme wealth and consumerism that they practice, ensuring their continued immortality.

It is difficult to gauge whether Dracula (Edward) troubles her into becoming a new "wealthy" version of herself or if it was always there and the vampire just brings it out, but her conversion is total by the time the story reaches *Breaking Dawn Part I*. This penultimate installment of the series can also be seen as the pinnacle of the troubling effects Edward has on the audience; in the earlier episodes he (and his family) wooed or courted the audience with designer clothes, watches, cars, and even houses they bought—two different houses have been used as the Cullen residence in the cinematic version of *The Twilight Saga*, both of which have been up for sale—but in *Breaking Dawn Part I* the audience can not only by witness the nuptials of the two main characters but can quite literally purchase it for themselves.

The wedding scene at the start of the film is aimed specifically at the fans of the franchise, to fulfill both their own expectations of the "perfect" wedding and their ability to replicate in the real world what they see on screen—this last point turning the narrative into something of an onscreen marketplace for advertisers. For the first of these points, the director/producers made sure that much of the cast that had appeared in the early episodes were present at the ceremony as "guests"—this also included Stephenie Meyer, the author of the novels. This recap of characters from throughout the series is not part of the novel and turned the scene into a who's who for the knowledgeable. In regard to the second point, the makers of the film specifically chose well-known, high-end clothes, shoes, and jewelry designers rather than using studio props and/or costume departments so that all the items would be provided to the film for free, and also ensuring that the established fan base could purchase either the same items or copies. The director, David Slate, and *Twilight* author Meyer asked Carolina Herrera to produce the dress which they chose from 10 possible designs, and the garment was made specifically for Kristen Stewart (the actress playing Bella). It took six months to make and reputedly cost $35,000.[42] Herrera later released the design as part of her 2012 collection, and the bridal company Alfred Angelo sold official copies.[43] Bella's shoes were designed by Manolo Blahnik and were later released as part of his 2012 collection for $1,295 a pair,[44] and the engagement and wedding rings, while not actually commissioned, were both sold off after the film, as were many props, and are now available as official copies. Even the song played as Bella and Edward walk down the aisle, "Turning Page" by Sleeping at Last, is now a favorite at weddings,[45] though possibly outdone by "A Thousand Years" by Christina Perri that ends the first *Twilight* film.[46] Viewers could quite literally "consume" almost every element of the wedding, while they themselves are being consumed by the franchise and the companies supplying the products. More interestingly, all of this allows the audience to feel as though they are partaking of the same kind of vampiric/consumerist immortality that draws/troubles the fictional Bella into the arms of Edward and his family. This troubling blurs the lines between fictional vampirism and realworld extreme consumerism, and seemingly offers the chance to buy immortality. The final film in this chapter keeps its intentions firmly in the fictional realm but takes its representation of absolute consumerism even further.

Jupiter Ascending, The Wachowskis, 2015

This story is futuristic but not actually set in the future, instead seeing aliens threatening the existence of Earth. In this sense it follows from such narratives as H.G. Wells' *War of the Worlds* (1897) and *Lifeforce* (Hooper, 1985) where invaders from outer space come to planet Earth to feed off its human population, re-enacting the kind of colonialism/reverse-colonialism that lies at the heart of Stoker's novel. Here the aliens, space vampires, have more extreme intentions and want to convert the entire planet and all its lifeforms into a concentrated elixir that prolongs their life.

The story itself begins on Earth with a young girl, Jupiter (Mila Kunis), being saved from intergalactic bounty hunters by another hunter named Caine Wise (Channing Tatum). It transpires that Wise has been hired by Titus Abrasax (Douglas Booth) while the other hunters are in the service of his brother Balem (Eddie Redmayne). The Abrasaxes, who are configured as space vampires, believe that Jupiter is actually the reincarnation of their dead mother who owned the rights to the planet Earth, and as such might interfere with their own individual plans to "harvest" the planet to make their highly profitable elixir.[47] Jupiter is not aware of being a reincarnation of anyone, or of containing her spirit, although various indicators throughout the film suggest she is who the Abrasaxes say she is: bees are attracted to her in exceedingly large numbers which is an indication that she is royalty—much life on Earth was genetically altered by the Abrasax family in the distant past and this trait was written into bee DNA; and Titus and Balem's sister, Kalique (Tuppence Middleton), shows Jupiter a statue of their mother which looks exactly like her. Reincarnation is not uncommon in female vampires; both Miriam Blaylock from *The Hunger* (Scott, 1983) and the eponymous Nadja in Amereyder's 1994 film, move their respective essences to other bodies, and Kate Davis in *Thirst* (Hardy, 1979) and Monika in *The Devil's Plaything* (Sarno, 1973) contain the dormant spirits of vampiric ancestors, though, as will be discussed further later, Kate never definitively "remembers" who she was/is. This not-remembering arguably also happens in the Wachowskis' film; Jupiter becomes the rightful owner of the Earth but it is never clear whether she accepts she is the reincarnated Matriarch, as she decides to go back and stay with her human family.

The narrative does not directly correlate to *Dracula* but some characters and themes correspond, which bring out some interesting points.[48] In many ways Balem would be the most obvious character to fulfill the Count's role as he is a passionate consumer who strives to be Master, but the invisible presence of the mother is actually the true root of evil in the story. In this way it rather mimics Hillyer's *Dracula's Daughter* and Almereyder's *Nadja*, where the unseen but constantly felt presence of the King Vampire drives the narrative forward. Much the same happens here. As such, even though we do not discover that Dracula is the cause of all the attention around Jupiter until a quarter of the way through the film, it is his/her spirit of absolute consumerism that draws the powers of consumption Earthward, making her the Dark Lord, at least in part. The side we are originally shown sees her as extremely poor and working as a cleaner for the family business, which constructs her as something of a Mina as well. It is the coming together of her divided self that is the story's catalyst. Indeed, there is almost a sense that the dark spirit of consumerism (the vampire Matriarch) within her is an unconscious drive that forces Jupiter to confront her lack of action or motivation. This leaves the Matriarchs sons Titus and Balem as the usurpers to the throne, or the "brides" of the lead vampire, who are left to scrabble over the scraps that their Mistress (mother) allows them.

Curiously, the person who most directly facilitates the confrontation of Jupiter's divided selves is Cain, who resultantly can be seen as something of a Renfield character. Not unlike in Browning's film, once "Renfield" has met "Dracula,"—Cain and Jupiter, respectively, Jupiter becomes aware of the dark power within her. After this they travel across space to the heart of the vampire empire, first to Titus's ship and then to Balem's mining facility. In a curious way this journey (ship voyage) to the land/world on the other side of the forest (re-enacting Dracula's journey from Transylvania/Earth to Outerspace/Empire) sees a reversal of the way the identity of the vampire is typically revealed, i.e., by the "team of light," as it is the vampire herself who, seemingly, is the only one who does not recognize herself for who or what she really is. As such, the vampire troubles itself more than anyone else, as it does not, or will not, recognize its own vampiric (monstrous) identity, something that continues until the end of the film.

Despite this denial of her "true" identity, Jupiter, under the advice of Caine, officially registers herself as the owner of the Earth. This somewhat complicates whether she truly is unaware of her status as reincarnated Abrasax Matriarch, as she is in effect proven to be, suggesting that she might be purposely repressing the other entity inside her, or that it is in some way guiding her judgment/actions.[49]

Now that Jupiter's claim to the Earth is official it goads the two sons/brides into trying their own individual approaches to "contain" their dormant mother—neither is that keen for Jupiter to truly remember who she is as it would greatly complicate their chances to claim, and harvest, the Earth for themselves. Titus attempts this first by getting Jupiter on his ship and trying to seduce her with the decadent lifestyle he leads, exampling his position as a debauched and wasteful vampire/consumer who only pleases himself regardless of others. Part of this includes trying to impress Jupiter by showing her a large store room full of thousands of vials of youth serum made from harvested humans. She is appalled by this but under the influence of Titus is compelled to consent to marry him—Titus plans to kill her once they are wed, and claim the Earth for himself. But before the ceremony is completed Caine and his former colleague Stinger crash into the space craft and save Jupiter.

Meanwhile Balem has had Jupiter's family kidnapped from Earth and brought to his mining facility, knowing that she will have no choice but to come there to save them. This bride represents the kind of vampiric consumerism that exploits the environment with no regard for the consequences or its effects on wider or future ecosystems—as evidenced by the dried-out husk of a planet he is on and has mined until there is almost nothing left.

Jupiter goes to Balem' mining facility, and once there the vampire tries to get his mother to emerge from the young girl's subconscious and uses his own memories of her to do so:

> BALEM: My mother.... My mother taught me what was necessary to rule in this universe.
> JUPITER: By killing people?
> BALEM: [throws up his hands] *I create life*! And I destroy it. Life is an act of consumption, Jupiter. To live is to consume. Now, the human beings on your planet are merely a resource waiting to be converted into capital. And this entire enterprise is just a small part in a vast and beautiful machine defined by evolution, designed to a single purpose.... To create profit [Emphasis in original] [The Wachowskis, 2015].

However, it becomes apparent that it was Balem who murdered his mother, even though he claims that she begged him to do so. As such it is hardly surprising that the vampire Matriarch remains hidden. Balem then tells Jupiter that she must sign a contract passing ownership of the Earth over to him or

Balem (Eddie Redmayne) has turned a planet into a huge refinery. *Jupiter Ascending*, dir. the Wachowskis (Warner Bros., 2015).

he will splice her family; this is no empty threat. The Abrasax family genetically alter humans and other species to create armies of subservient beings, Caine and Stinger being examples where the former is part canine—enhancing his tracking abilities—and the latter part bee—making him faster, loyal and with enhanced vision. Jupiter refuses to sign and shoots Balem in the leg just as Caine and Stinger attack the facility. The mining platforms collapse and Balem falls to his death, but Caine, Jupiter, and her family manage to escape safely back to Earth. Once there Jupiter's family have no recollection of the events and the young girl resumes her former life, knowing she owns the Earth.

The film ends with her flying through the air from a Chicago skyscraper with Caine, as they now have some form of relationship, but as with many vampire films and with Stoker's novel in particular, there hangs an air of unease over this ending as to whether the vampire is truly dead or is lying dormant in some form, or some *where*, waiting to re-emerge.

As intimated earlier, the character of Jupiter bears some correlation to that of Kate in the lesser known Australian vampire film, *Thirst* (Hardy, 1979). Indeed, there exists more than just a passing resemblance between the plots of both films, and it is worth touching upon some of points of similarity here. Hardy's film features Kate Hardy (Chantal Contouri) who seems to live something of an idyllic life; she is young, healthy, well-off and living with her architect boyfriend. She is, in fact, almost an advert for the pleasures of a consumerist lifestyle. All this changes when her cat knocks over a milk carton by her front gate and blood rather than milk flows out of it. She is attacked, kidnapped and wakes to find herself hostage of The Brotherhood, held at some kind of research facility. The Brotherhood is a worldwide secret cartel that holds massive sway around the world, and drinks human blood to maintain this power and gain eternal youth—making them something of an Earth-bound Abrasax clan. To provide blood for their members they raise "blood cows"—humans free of contaminants and allergies—contained in a "milking" facility. They configure both the kind of hidden corporate conspiracy that features in the *Blade* series of films and equally symbolize a globalized and targeted consumerism which is never ending and which feeds on humanity itself.

The Brotherhood have been monitoring Kate as she is, unbeknownst to herself, a descendant of Elizabeth Bathory and they have been sending her blood to try and reawaken her own thirst as well as her ancestral memory.[50] To help facilitate this, as the film progresses they institute a program of conditioning which appears to have little success and although they manage to get her to drink human blood she refuses to do so when offered her boyfriend as a means of sustenance. By the end of the narrative, after extensive abuse and coercion, Kate still has not fully remembered her heritage or that she might be who the vampires say she is. As the film closes, the vampire "doctor," Dr. Frazer (David Hemings), who has overseen the process of making her remember her true self, puts fangs in his mouth and drinks Kate's blood while offscreen voices are heard declaring the experiment a success as it unites the two great vampire families; Frazer himself is actually a descendant of one of them. The film does not make clear whether Frazer is turning Kate into a vampire—though this form of conversion does not seem part of the narrative's mythology—or if by drinking her blood Bathory's ancestry will pass into the doctor, but it does suggest that Kate inevitably becomes part of The Brotherhood.

This is an important precursor to the ending of *Jupiter Ascending* as the nature of vampire stories allows for cultural anxiety to be temporarily allayed but never fully destroyed (Cohen 1996, 6). Stoker's *Dracula* sees both Jonathan and Mina as people who have been infected by the vampire but might now be "cured," though it might also mean that they have passed it on to, or it has been reborn in, their son, Quincey. In the Wachowskis' story it has been proved that Jupiter is of the same genetic make-up as the dead Matriarch, so much so that bees can "sense" her royalty. Consequently, she is exactly the same as the vampire but seemingly without her memories or personality. It is worth noting that it is characteristics or character traits that are passed on when the Abrasaxes themselves have genetically engineered new species, so if Caine and all those like him have heightened abilities to sense, smell, and track their prey, why would not Jupiter have, at the least, inherited the propensities for the kinds of vampirism typical of the Abrasaxes? She may not have been genetically modified as those who were spliced but she has the exact same genes as the vampire Queen. As such she should at least be predisposed to be an extreme consumer if not the dominant one. And it should not be forgotten that, whether intentionally or not, the Matriarch (Dracula) has disposed of those trying to usurp her position and at story's end she is still the Queen vampire of the galaxy.

Moreover, she would then be something of a combination of the forms of consumerism represented by Titus and Balem so that she should have no compunction in converting the entire Earth into a galactic energy drink for the unbelievably wealthy. And as Balem himself explains during the film, "My mother made me understand that every human society is a pyramid and that some lives will always matter more than others. It is better to accept this than to pretend it isn't true" (The Wachowskis, 2015). The Matriarch indisputably would see herself as the one who is at the pinnacle. Seemingly only her children, the brides, are troubled by this prospect, but Caine is definitely distracted by Jupiter, and the Matriarch within her. It is possibly the ambiguity of Jupiter's true identity that distracts the genetically engineered tracker the most, particularly in his role as the Renfield character.

Caine, as mentioned above is a genetic concoction of human and dog/wolf—even his name is based on the word canine—which in terms of the film makes him a perfect bounty hunter. In relation to Stoker's narrative and Renfield, it makes him the perfect companion to the Dracula figure, not just because Caine actually is a creature of the night, equivalent to the howling wolves that the Count comments upon at Renfield's arrival in Browning's film, but also due to the vampire's inherently hybrid nature itself. In *Dracula* the vampire can take the form of many creatures, rats, bats, and wolves among others.[51] This draws a strong parallel between them and the vampire, seeing the strongly related if not made of, or sharing, the same material. In contrast, the "crew of light" (representing Western civilization) embody a fundamental difference between humans and animals. Renfield/Caine would then be drawn to Dracula/Jupiter because of a shared hybridity rather than the human girl's "love of dogs" that she mawkishly proclaims during the film. It also explains why Caine largely, and relatively quickly, forgets his primary mission of bringing Jupiter to his client, Titus, and starts trying to protect her. Consequently, much of the continuing awkwardness between Jupiter and Caine can be seen to not be about their human and non-human status, as suggested by the film[52]—and which would work with the human part of Jupiter—but because he is distracted by the very real Master/Mistress and servant relationship that exists between them. Further, his distracted behavior around Jupiter can be seen as him constantly being of two minds, just like Renfield, caught in the middle of his feelings to consume objects (to possess Jupiter) and his need to be consumed by them (be possessed by her). Unlike Renfield of course Caine survives the Matriarch's battle for absolute control and so happily becomes hers alone, with his former allegiances forgotten or no longer embodied in anyone other than his new Mistress. He is happy to facilitate and support extreme consumption rather than be the one who consumes.

Jupiter Ascending is a suitable ending to this chapter, exampling not only the inevitable outcome of absolute consumerism, where the Earth and its inhabitants themselves become the objects of consumption, but the way in which this is not always totally obvious. Jupiter herself looks like any one of us and yet holds within her the spirit of an inter-galactic vampire that sees itself at the top of a chain of continual and never-ending consumption. At this level power, wealth, and youth all become one thing, and the more one is able to consume the higher one is within its own objectifying hierarchy. Such levels of consumption are inherently founded on excessive amounts of violence, largely to those that produce or are the objects of consumption. Such violence is often hidden or shielded by the beauty or value of the object produced, so that it distracts those around it into facilitating its continuation, or it troubles others into partaking of its wanton destruction. The next chapter continues the themes of troubling and distracting violence and looks more closely at the ways in which civilized society is purposely inured to extreme acts of brutality and even torture to, purportedly, ensure its own survival.

FOUR

Violent Distractions

In which violence is not only allowable but encouraged on the body of the vampire, no matter how recently they were still human, becoming a troubling distraction to all those around it and making permissible all forms of physical force and abuse on those seen as other.

Dracula, Terence Fisher, 1958

Vampires and violence go hand in hand. Unless they are of the evolutionary variety, i.e., a separate species to humans, they are born of violence and re-enact this original trauma every time they feed or create others like themselves. Not surprisingly, they usually expire in an equally aggressive and violent manner, often at the hands of a vampire slayer.[1] In Stoker's novel Van Helsing describes various methods that distract the vampire such as garlic, running water, crucifixes, and a wild rice placed on the undead coffin, but to ensure that he is "true dead" (Stoker 1996, 259) requires something rather more aggressive. Consequently, the good Professor advises that his team of vampire hunters will need to fire a "sacred bullet … into the coffin" (Stoker 1996, 259) or "cut off his head [Count Dracula's] and burn his heart or drive a stake through it" (Stoker 1996, 218). And the stake itself must be "some two and a half or three inches thick and about three feet long," and hit with a "heavy hammer, such as in households is used in the coal-cellar for breaking the lumps" (Stoker 1996, 230). In the novel, all the characters except Van Helsing are unfamiliar with the extreme otherness manifested in the body of Count Dracula and so they take their lead from the all knowledgeable Professor, even though his knowledge would seem in a similar vein to that applied to the drowning of women suspected of witchcraft where the methods of proving/killing would have a similar outcome no matter whether the subject were human or supernatural. Van Helsing himself is of course a foreign other, not unlike the Count, yet his words are taken as truth by the crew of light (people the Professor knows he can control), even though much of what takes place is enacted upon friends or family they love or hold dear, and the explanations for the strange things they see are provided by the Dutchman himself. An extreme case of this is Mina, who is as much under the influence of the Professor as she is of the vampire, who implores Quincey Morris to do the following: "When you shall be convinced that I am so changed that it is better that I die that I may live. When I am thus dead in the flesh [a vampire], then you will, without a moment's delay, drive a stake through me and cut off my head; or do whatever else may be wanting to give me rest!" (Stoker 1996, 360). He of course agrees.

This is of particular interest as much of the violence in Stoker is directed toward women,[2] and the Professor, not unlike patriarchy itself, has so convinced Mina of his inherent authority that she is willing to allow, even demand that, violence be enacted upon her own body. This violence is of course excused in the name of saving the victim's immortal soul and returning her to some form of purity or eternal rest, which can also be read as providing a "spectacle" (see Foucault 2006, 60) or example to the unruly. However, it equally becomes something of an accepted norm, a point of normalized behavior rather than an exception only used in extreme cases, and not just directed at those who exhibit obvious signs of "vampirism" or absolute otherness.

Stoker's novel is indicative of the views of late-Victorian society in regard to dangerous immigrants from the East as well as to women, particularly those who did not want to conform to the accepted order. Interestingly by the middle of the next century little appears to have changed, and Fisher's 1958 *Dracula* by Hammer films very much continues to normalize violent behavior toward women who do not know their place in the male world.

The film itself declares its violence, in true Hammer style, from the start, with large globs of garish bright red blood splashing on top of a coffin. And though this intimates the violent nature of the creature we assume is slumbering within it, we only ever really *see* extreme violence perpetrated upon the body of the female vampire. That is not to say that similar violence is not inflicted upon the male vampires, but it is predominantly hidden from our view. The narrative begins by depicting this violence as contained within the imaginary world of the supernatural but soon it spreads beyond the confines of the vampire's castle out into the real world. The setting of the film, as with many Hammer vampire films, is nominally Middle/Eastern Europe, somewhere around Austria as it blends into the Slavic nations, but their filming in the woods around the company's studios near London gives the scenes an oddly English Home Counties or genteel feel that makes them very safe and familiar (not unlike many of the back lots used in Hollywood films), until we happen upon the Count's Castle which is totally out of place in regard to its surroundings. It is a very Gothic structure and dominates the woodlands around it but is seemingly encircled by running water—an oddity for the home of a being that supposedly is unable to cross such an example of natural purity. This "moat" cuts it off from the world, and indeed when Jonathan Harker (John Van Essyen) crosses the small bridge over the water toward the castle, the air instantly becomes cold. Not unlike Browning's 1931 film the vampire's lair exists outside of reality; not just in the land beyond the forest but in a world beyond our own.

The earlier movie achieves this through many visual incongruities such as the armadillos and opossums that live alongside the vampire in his decrepit pile. Fisher takes a different approach and shows the interior of the lair as very clean and new, simultaneously situating the otherworldly back into the real world. Accordingly, the Count (Christopher Lee) speaks with a very cultured English accent, making the absolute otherness of Dracula much less to do with his ethnicity but more to do with his transgressive sexuality. This is implied by the absolute power he holds over the young woman who lives with him and the lingering looks he gives to his newly arrived guest. While it is inferred that the vampire is the source of violence in the narrative it is not long before this is shown as incorrect, and it is his feminized and feminizing body that is configured as an absolute other that must be violently destroyed.

It is worth qualifying Dracula's "femininity" in light of the fact that he and most other vampires bite and penetrate their victims which is seemingly a very masculine positioning. However, and beyond Moretti's aside that Dracula is a splendid and feminine name (Moretti 1988, 104), the vampire can be seen to perform as a feminine body (see Case 1991). In part this is due to its excessive and transgressive sexuality but also its mutability—its ability to change form, suggesting softness and permeable borders, all historically feminine traits. This of course is emphasized by the vampire's association with tainted/unclean blood, which naturally resonates with female menstruation and further ties to the moon and lunar cycle—which, pre–Dracula, was a key component of vampire immortality.[3] That said, the most excessive violence is inflicted upon the female vampire, as initially seen when Dracula flings his "bride" (Valerie Gaunt) across the room when he catches her trying to bite Harker. The violence enacted on the female body becomes even more extreme as the film progresses.

Harker has been employed to index the Count's library. However, it transpires that he knows that Dracula, and the young woman living with him, are both vampires and he has come to kill them. The morning after he arrives, Harker unpacks his stake and hammer and goes down to the crypt beneath the castle. Curiously, and against the logic of dispatching the most dangerous killer first, he kills the female vampire first by graphically pounding a large wooden stake into her heart as she sleeps in her coffin. She awakes during this process and her loud screams awaken Dracula who is sleeping nearby. To justify Harker's horrific actions, we are shown the vampire transform from a young and vibrant young girl into a craggy and wrinkled old woman as she finally dies. While this is meant to reveal the inherent monstrosity of the creature pretending to be a beautiful young woman—and reveal the otherworldly nature of the vampire and the world it inhabits—it equally posits the idea of an older woman trying to look younger than she is and not following the proscribed rules of patriarchal society where she should accept her lot as an elderly spinster or widow and withdraw from society rather than seduce young men. Consequently, this suggests that she deserves the violence enacted upon her. Now that the sun has gone down the Count approaches Harker and, although we do not see it on screen, changes the young man into a vampire. Interestingly, this is the only time Dracula's attraction to male victims is shown, and yet it is only implied. This reveals an important distinction in the film; violence on male bodies, even feminized ones, is often hidden while that on female ones is usually in plain view, if not excessively displayed.

The hidden violence to male bodies is continued on the arrival of Van Helsing (Peter Cushing) at Castle Dracula. It seems that Harker was in league with the Professor and was meant to get in touch once he had dispatched the vampires. After not hearing from him, Van Helsing goes to investigate for himself and finds his friend changed into a vampire and asleep in the crypt. The Professor stakes Harker but once again it is hidden from view and we are only shown the young man's subsequent peaceful (fangless) demeanor. Sometime later Van Helsing returns to Karlstadt to tell Harker's fiancée, Lucy Holmwood (Varol Marsh), her brother Arthur (Richard Gough), and his wife Mina (Melissa Stribling), that the young man is dead.

But all is not well at the Holmwood's as Lucy is suffering from severe anemia and not responding to treatment. Unsurprisingly, of course this means that Dracula has retraced Harker's footsteps and arrived in Karlstadt to exact his revenge. Interestingly, the interiors we see in this town—whose exteriors symbolize the civilized, "real" world—are just like those in the Count's castle; the otherworldliness of the vampire has not only crossed from the supernatural plane to the real one but is perfectly at home there. More importantly, it also signifies that the extreme violence that took place earlier in the film is no longer contained outside of reality.

This time we see the vampire preying on its victim, and the overtly sexual nature of his nightly visits to Lucy's bedroom are in stark contrast to the barely inferred relations between the Count and Harker. Lucy inevitably dies, and it is at this stage that the narrative explicitly reveals that the true absolute other is the uncontrollable woman and that Dracula is only a distraction. Once returned from the dead Lucy is totally beyond the control of the patriarchal society around her.[4] She even bothers young children once the sun has gone down, in particular the maid's daughter, Tania (Janina Faye), reversing the "healthy" motherly instincts expected of Lucy and replacing them with the selfish drive to feed off children rather than feed them.

Van Helsing enlists Arthur's help and they go to the crypt where Lucy is interred. It is empty, but Lucy soon arrives looking more energetic and livelier than at any point in the story so far. She brings with her the maid's daughter, Tania. Van Helsing and Arthur advance on the now vampiric Lucy, who attempts to ravish/attack her own brother but is warded off by the Professor's cross. She runs back to her crypt leaving the little girl behind, and by the time the Professor and Arthur arrive she is already back in her coffin. Van Helsing suggests that they could use Lucy to discover the whereabouts of Dracula, but Arthur does not want to risk her infecting someone else with her "selfishness" so they kill her; there is quite a connection to Kay Caldwell here. And this is an important scene in the narrative for many reasons, not least in that it is the most graphically violent one in the film but also as it marks the transition of extreme violence from the supernatural world to the real one, and where both are seen as acceptable.

Even more than the earlier staking of the female vampire in Castle Dracula, we see the agony on Lucy's face as Van Helsing hammers the stake into her heart. Indeed, it is not a huge leap to read this as a brutal rape scene meant to subjugate the unruly female body. At its end, the closing shot that is supposed to justify the violence, as occurred earlier when the supernatural nature of the female vampire was revealed, is ambivalent at best. Lucy is shown as her old, pre-vampire self, the subservient and pure sister/daughter who has now found peace, but in truth her face changes very little apart from being slightly more garishly made-up. In fact, what this shot infers is that Lucy was not supernatural at all, just unruly, and that the two men have violently killed (murdered) her rather than let her continue to disobey patriarchal proscription. As such, it is the configuration of women as beyond the control of male society that sees them as monstrous, and an absolute other that needs to be destroyed.

Arthur's reaction to Lucy's new state is particularly telling as he is constructed as being extremely proper and aware of his place within the social hierarchy, and so stands in for the judgment of wider society. He has no doubt that Lucy must be destroyed to prevent further infection (uppity women), and the purposeful misreading of the face of his sister in death is done to justify his own monstrous actions. As mentioned above, this scene is crucial as it posits that the extreme violence normally reserved for supernatural or non-human creatures is equally acceptable in the real world for certain individuals or groups, namely women who behave improperly.

This focus on women as deserving of such extreme violence is empha-

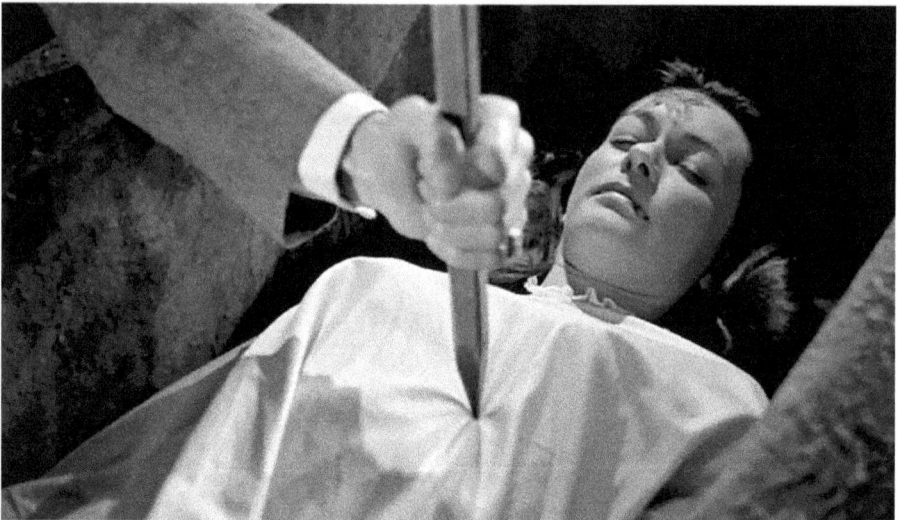

Lucy (Carol Marsh) about to be "spectacularly" penetrated while also bearing the burn marks on her forehead of earlier male aggression. *Dracula*, dir. Terence Fisher (Hammer, 1958).

sized at the film's end when the Count himself is destroyed. As noted earlier, Dracula is often coded as being feminine due to his transgressive sexuality (homosexuality); the required penetration by a phallic stake; and his/her reproductive capabilities. As such, he must also be destroyed, but even his denouement is not as violent as Lucy's. This is curious, as he returns to his own castle where extreme violence is perfectly acceptable. In contrast to the female vampires, he is awake and allowed to resist his impending doom.

His destruction does not come from a stake being driven into him but rather is due to the sun's rays (as in Murnau's film) which cause him to desiccate and crumble. This exposes his inherently supernatural nature, thus justifying his violent end. Ultimately, though, the worst violence of the film is only inflicted on women who do not behave properly and when they are at their most vulnerable (asleep). This throws up some interesting points in light of the framework used in this book. While unruly women are represented as the absolute other within the film they rarely actually seem to trouble or distract those around them—unlike Dracula they do not turn or are even seen to feed off others. Dracula is certainly a more troubling presence as he is responsible for making Lucy, Jonathan, and the girl in his castle unruly—Jonathan is not really given the chance to be unruly and hence why he is not totally feminized or subjected to the most extreme violence. Yet he is not the most troubling character in the film as that is reserved for Van

Helsing himself. He is the one who causes everyone else to perform extreme acts of violence.

Stoker's novel and Browning's film construct their narratives as a battle between two personalities, those of the Count and Van Helsing. As others have noted elsewhere, the Professor is the one in overall control of the material contained in the book and so obviously paints himself as the hero of the story. At best, this sees him as the voice and enforcer of 19th century patriarchy (see Freeland 2009, and Senf 1988), at worst as a psychopath or the true vampire of the narrative (see Romero Jodar, 2009). In this last reading, Van Helsing is responsible for convincing the crew of light that the aristocratic visitor from Transylvania is the perpetrator of murders that the Professor himself has committed, namely of Lucy and her mother. His persuasion is such that he then causes the rather hapless "vampire slayers" to chase the foreign visitor back to his home and attack and kill him. Fisher's film is not as extreme as this last reading but constructs a more forceful version of the bastion of patriarchy view.

As mentioned, Van Helsing has already recruited Jonathan Harker to his cause at the start of the film and has troubled the newly engaged young man sufficiently for him to agree to go into the lion's den/vampire's lair to take on the King Vampire by himself. However, the Professor has obviously also instilled in his new convert the conviction that female vampires/unruly women are even more dangerous than Dracula himself and so should be killed first, utilizing the maximum amount of violence—as is seen when Harker enters the crypt as described earlier. Something similar happens with Arthur Holmwood, though in many ways his overtly proper manners construct him as inherently predisposed to being easily convinced into "protecting" the existing patriarchal hierarchy. And indeed, it is not long before he is troubled into assisting in his own sister's violent destruction. Further, he is almost persuaded to kill his own wife after she begins to exhibit signs of having her own mind once under the influence of the Count.

Curiously, in this film Van Helsing is prepared to perpetrate violence himself rather than just inciting others to do so on his behalf, as was seen in Stoker, and in Browning's film.[5] And so we see him staking Lucy—brutally murdering Arthur's sister in front of him to receive his thanks afterward—and later, causing the destruction of Dracula by sunlight.

Van Helsing's role in Fisher's film is interesting in light of all the subsequent *Dracula* films made by Hammer in which he appeared—six including the 1958 film—as in each the vampire is resurrected only to be violently killed again. This posits the inevitable and ongoing cycle of violence once it has become acceptable, and not just upon the feminized body of Dracula himself but also on the bodies of the brides/unruly women who inevitably seem to receive far more graphically violent ends than their male counterparts. The next film widens this web of troubling and distracting violence and also shows how those that use the forces of "good" are often more brutal and savage than the supposed "monsters."

The Last Man on Earth, Ubalda Ragona and Sidney Salkow, 1964

Ragona and Salkow's film is often cited as one of the more true to the original adaptations of Matheson's 1954 novel *I Am Legend;* in fact Matheson was one of the screenwriters on the film but used the pseudonym Logan Swanson.[6] Vincent Price as the main protagonist, Robert Morgan—in the novel it is Robert Neville—is an unusual choice but his extremely restrained performance gives credibility to the notion of a man who sees no option other than the choice of actions he has decided upon, indeed it seems so natural to him that there is no real "choice" involved. As in the book, the movie sees humanity overrun by a mysterious plague that is turning everyone into vampire-like creatures; this last is arguable as, although the victims only come out at night, are allergic to garlic, afraid of mirrors, and seem to require stakes through the heart to be killed,[7] they bear more resemblance to zombies, with their lumbering movement and pallid, flaking skin, than to Stoker's undead. While the film begins with Morgan already marked as the last surviving "human," the many flashbacks show how civilization crumbled into its present predicament with the overwhelming loses of loved ones slowly and traumatically severing links between the old and the new world. This new world is irreparably scarred by those traumas, born of violence which then infects the whole of existence, and Morgan is more of a product of it than the vampires that surround him.

In this environment it is difficult to identify absolute otherness other than in Morgan himself, and by the end of the narrative he is forced to admit that he has become the sole focus of fear and hatred in what is left of the world, as seen when he repeatedly intones "They were afraid of me … they were afraid of me … they were afraid of me" (Ragona and Saltow, 1964). He certainly is not troubled about killing all those he identifies as vampires, and he does not distract the survivors who are not fully vampires, as they only ever see him as the killer he is. As such, Morgan is more in the vein of Van Helsing from Fisher's *Dracula* who sees himself on an almost holy, evolutionary quest to preserve the purity of the human race. Gregory Waller sees Matheson's novel as creating a world beyond good and evil with no points of reference for ideas such as morality (Waller 2010, 258), but I would argue that Morgan is driven beyond simple survival in his quest to destroy every vampire, and to try and find a cure; it is the almost messianic idea that he can save humanity that forces him on.⁸ Unlike Cushing's vampire slayer though, Morgan does not seem to specifically target unruly woman, or sexually transgressive others, his agenda focuses on his belief that humanity is primary above all other species, and so he happily kills men, women, and children he considers "non-human," and with extreme prejudice.

That said, Morgan's definition of what constitutes humanity, at least that which is worth saving, is predicated on very male attributes. At one point in the film his voiceover tells us "I can't afford the luxury of anger. Anger can make me vulnerable. It can destroy my reason and reason's the only advantage I have over them" (Ragona and Salkow). Anger is seen as representative of an excessively emotional response and a lack of reason, variously cited in patriarchal societies as inherent attributes of women, which make them inferior to men (see Vaught 2016, 209). As such, Morgan correlates his "reason" to being both human and male, and with this one can read the vampire plague as a feminizing of humanity, both performatively and physically (they are seen as having "soft" bodies ready for Morgan's penetration). In this sense, Morgan's persistent and ongoing violence makes him a hyper-excessive version of the earlier vampire killer, one who confines himself not just to unruly women but includes all feminine bodies in his purging of humanity.

Indeed, it is the systematic nature and thoroughness of Morgan's plan that normalizes violence. He has a map of the city where he lives and its surroundings and has drawn a grid over it so he can mark off each area as he travels there during the day and kills all the vampires he finds. When he is not doing this, he makes stakes to facilitate his killing missions: "How many more of these [stakes] will I have to make before they're all destroyed?" (Ragona and Salkow). Once he kills a vampire Morgan disposes of its body in a huge pit filled with others. It is not clear whether it is a natural ravine or a man-made excavation but it is vast and he blandly throws the cadavers in and throws in petrol afterward to set them on fire.⁹ Curiously, the film suggests that much of Morgan's motivation is the loss of his wife and daughter to the disease, both of whom he killed to "bring them peace." While indeed this is a traumatic experience it can equally be seen as the first test of his commitment to his messianic mission to save/purify humanity. This is further qualified by his attempts to murder his former best friend Ben Cortman. Once the closest of friends and next-door neighbors, Ben, now a vampire, plagues Morgan every night, calling him to come out of his house. Matheson's narrative suggests a homosexual attraction in this relationship, which lingers in the film. Morgan's inevitable reaction to such transgressive behavior, even if partially initiated by his own suppressed campiness, is to try and kill him; Cortman's eventual death is finally accomplished by the half- or alive-vampires in the story.¹⁰

The introduction of vampire/human hybrids changes the films narrative, and correlations to Stoker's *Dracula* become easier to make. The Earth is not made up of just Morgan surrounded by hordes of the undead. There is a third group, people who caught the infection but have managed to hold it at bay with drugs. They still mainly only come out at night and have (less excessive) reactions to garlic and mirrors, so were still considered vampires by Morgan—some of those he hunted had seemed more resistant on his killing sprees, but he had killed them anyway as they were "all the same" to him.

Subsequently as half-beings, or almost vampires, they are more like Lucy while still alive, and Mina, or even brides of Dracula who still have their own minds—the "bride" in Fisher's *Dracula* was certainly unruly enough to have to be physically restrained and thrown aside by the Count. And Matheson had something of this in mind when he introduced Ruth into his novel. Unbeknownst to Neville, Ruth is one of the new hybrid vampires but feigns being human. She has been sent by an unknown and unseen leader of the new breed to inveigle herself into the last human's home so that they might capture him and stop him from indiscriminately killing more of their numbers. The same situation is seen in the film and Morgan's extreme loneliness makes him an easy target—he had recently found a dog but had to kill it when it became infected with the disease.[11] To prove her humanity he puts Ruth through a series of tests and soon becomes aware that she is not what she says but something else. Morgan wonders if he can join the group and maybe effect a cure, but in a telling reversal of his own view of the world Ruth says:

> You can't join us. You're a monster to them. Why do you think I ran when I saw you, even though I was assigned to spy on you? Because I was so terrified, what I'd heard about you. You're a legend in the city. Moving by day, instead of night, leaving as evidence of your existence bloodless corpses. Many of the people you destroyed were still alive! Many of them were loved ones of the people in my group [Ragona and Salkow, 1964].

It becomes clear at this point that not only is he even more monstrous than the vampires, but that violence has become his only way of maintaining his own identity. Even though Morgan manages to create a cure, his fate is sealed as the leader of the hybrids has decided to capture and execute him.

It is worth noting that even Morgan's cure is problematic, as he transfuses (penetrates) Ruth's body with his own blood while she is sleeping, without her consent, inferring that by this time he cannot control his own violent urges and even what he sees as kindness is tantamount to personal violation and abuse. This marks Ruth out as a Lucy/Mina receiving forcible transfusions from the men who "love" her and, as with Harker's wife before her, Ruth is troubled both by Morgan—not least as he has made her human again—and her unseen leader; they are both fighting to be Master in the narrative.

Ruth does have feelings for Morgan, though maybe more pity than affection, but knows he can never be accepted by the hybrid community she is part of—though the film never explores what their response will be to her newfound "humanity." And so, although she assists him in trying to escape and pleads for mercy on his behalf, he is shot as he enters a church. Morgan does not just die but crawls toward the altar where he is pierced with a spear, and his final words resound around the building: "You're freaks, all of you! All of you, freaks, mutations!" It is a scene that needs a bit of unpacking as it not only signals the end of humanity, as Morgan understands it, but also emphasizes the spiritual nature of what he feels he's been trying to accomplish. It also points to a reversal of the end of Stoker's *Dracula*, in that here it is the figure of absolute otherness (the "freaks") that has won and Van Helsing (Morgan) who falls at story's end. This reading posits the unseen leader as Dracula himself, as the focus of absolute otherness that ultimately not only troubles the old world but outlives it.

The "staking" of Morgan is particularly interesting as it recreates the death of Jesus[12]—being pierced with a spear—while replicating the vampire hunter's own violent acts. Depending on whether Ruth's blood also provides a cure, Morgan has died for none other than his own messianic cause, signaling the death of humanity and any kind of teleological imperative; the new species will be creating their own history as they go along. The unseen absolute other, the hybrids' leader, now symbolizes the dominant ideology, and just how that compares to Morgan's desperate clinging to previous patriarchal structure is yet to be seen—it is intimated that the hybrids will also dispose of vampires that are too far gone to be saved. Regardless of this uncertainty, it does imply that hybridity is inevitable and the future of life on Earth (keeping in mind that, the now cured, Ruth is probably a dead end), and that the world belongs to the "freaks." Such thoughts obviously trouble the old order, specifically heterosexual white males as embodied by Morgan, and much of his violence is directed at trying to resist the inevitable demise of all he holds dear and what he feels constitutes being human. If he had accepted his own position as an exception, he might have been able to play a part in the hybrid future. Consequently, one could argue that Morgan bothers himself— seen in his strict adherence to old hierarchies and subject positions—even though he is already a hybrid of sorts due to the immunity bestowed upon him by the bite of a vampire bat while he was in Panama. This earlier encounter with a vampire bat changed his blood, and even his genetic makeup, protecting him from the virus that subsequently destroyed humanity. The repression of his true nature then troubles him into undertaking extreme opposite action and denial, which can also be seen to inform/trouble the Harker character in Stoker who has relations with both Dracula and his brides, and who similarly acts with violent disavowal in his eagerness to destroy the vampire.

It is also worth mentioning the relationship between violence and space as seen in *Last Man on Earth*, though here there is very little "real" world in comparison to that seen in Fisher's *Dracula*. In contrast to the later film, Morgan's environment is entirely otherworldly and bears little relation to the real world that existed before the apocalypse. In one sense this makes all violence unreal as the space within which it occurs is itself unreal. The only real space, at least for Morgan, is his home, which has been written about by other authors[13] and in many ways it is contrary to that seen in Fisher' *Dracula*; there it is was running water that kept the real world out, but for Morgan it is strings of garlic that keeps the realworld in. However, the arrival of Ruth, at the instigation of the absolute other, compromises the boundaries; she distracts the integrity of the space long enough—and Morgan's focus to protect it—for the hybrids to destroy the barriers between worlds and enter to try and capture the human. Once his protection has gone Morgan has no choice but to flee, and it is interesting that he passes through a police station before ending up at a church. Symbolizing law and religion, both constructs of the former human society, these institutions provide scant protection for Morgan in the new world order. However, Matheson in the novel explains that crosses work on the vampires due to residual cultural memory of how transgressive they are (Waller 2010, 260)—the old order still influences the new. Morgan's death in the space of the church can also be seen to work into this tension between real and unreal spaces, as it inherently embodies such transubstantiate processes where the real gains supernatural substance; his death on the altar is both supernatural, in Morgan's messianic world, and purely physical in the new world of the absolute other.

This tension between real and unreal space does not totally resolve as the narrative ends, in part due to the hybridity of the inheritors of the Earth but also to the existence of Ruth whose possible effects on the survivors is never addressed, though interestingly as the film ends she is seen walking toward us, the audience, through crowds of hybrids who came to see the death of the last human, as though choosing humanity over the people who were formerly her own. As with *Dracula*, the tale ends with an air of unease that the order that has been achieved may not last for long and that the danger of absolute otherness will rise again. For Stoker's tale this was the hybridity of Quincey Harker and the vampire's undead contamination; for *Last Man on Earth* this is completely reversed, and it is the specter of purebred humanity that may plague the future. Cinematic adaptations such as *Omega Man* and *I Am Legend* show that Morgan/Neville is not the last human, though the hybrid species is either not mentioned or not fully integrated into the new order of humanity; the old-world order and patriarchy will survive and the "Last Man's" messianic endeavor and extreme violence will be rewarded.[14] The next film continues the theme of an almost messianic quest, one which creates an unreal world where violence is not just acceptable but positively encouraged.

Morgan (Vincent Price) sacrificing himself at the altar of the future. *The Last Man on Earth*, dir. Ubaldo Ragona and Sidney Salkow (American International, 1964).

Blade, Stephen Norrington, 1998

Norrington's film shares features with the previous one, seeing two types of vampires where one can control its nature and the other cannot, with the former being determined to dispose of the latter. The difference between the two is that the "freak" to whom the future belongs is a lone vampire called Blade. Blade (Wesley Snipes) is a dhamphir (half-human and half-vampire— his mother was pregnant with him when she was bitten)[15] and like the hybrids in *The Last Man on Earth* he uses drugs to control his vampiric nature and blood-lust, meaning he has all the strength and speed of a vampire but can also walk in daylight. However, what marks the film out as being a development from the previous one is Blade's relationship to weapons and technology; they are intrinsically part of who and what he is. This creates an odd relationship to *Dracula*, as Stoker's vampire was largely outmaneuvered by modern technology whereas Blade retains his superiority by developing and utilizing cutting edge weaponry. Indeed, as Weinstock notes, the film is essentially a battle between good and bad science (Weinstock 2012, 69) where the vampire-slayer is always evolving while the vampire is devolving.[16] As such, this sees Blade as the savior of humankind and not the source of its impending destruction; Blade, unlike Morgan, can only save humanity by killing every vampire, as his blood has no curative properties. This almost spiritual quest dictates Blade's excessively violent existence and equally explains the cyborg nature of his identity—he is constructed as a literal vampire-killing machine. Morgan spent his days laboriously carving stakes with which to dispatch the undead; Blade is something of a production factory.

He lives with his mentor/assistant Whistler (Kris Kristofferson) in an old warehouse where he creates and produces an ever-evolving arsenal of guns, bullets, and grenades that utilize silver, garlic, or UV light to destroy their prey. In essence, Blade's identity is integral to the weaponization of his body, which also distinguishes him from the other vampires—his weapons and technology are a part, or an extension, of his physical form. As Weinstock observes, his "sculpted, sunglasses-clad, hyperbolically-masculine form moves confidently … wreaking havoc with both modern and modernized … weapons" (Weinstock 2012, 69). Blade is a truly cyborg entity made up not just of hybrid human/vampire flesh, but also the drugs that maintain the dominance of his human genes, the clothes and wraparound sunglasses he always wears, and his various weapons—guns, grenades and signature samurai sword—so that if he lacks any one of these he is less, or not-Blade. This creates an odd tension between his current and former self. His real (human) name is Eric Brooks, and the fewer cyborg "appendages" he sports, the more Eric Brooks–like he is. This point is made toward the end of the film when Deacon Frost (Stephen Dorff), the new vampire leader, has captured Blade and has him encased in a bleeding-block to drain the hybrid vampire's blood as part of his plan to resurrect the blood god. Here Blade is almost naked, wearing only leather trousers, and with the draining of his blood the serum has left his system; he has now returned to being Eric Brooks, highlighted by the appearance of his mother (now a vampire). Blade denies this, frantically trying to hold on to his hybrid persona, and only manages to reclaim this by drinking the blood of Dr. Karen Johnson (N'Bushe Wright), one of his crew of light, which allows him to reclaim his cyborg status by reacquiring his sunglasses and samurai sword.[17] This sees Blade as an inherently troubled character who is constantly struggling to maintain cohesion between the various aspects of his identity, both human and vampire Daywalker, and former and cyborg selves; he is a modern-day Dracula, no longer undone by technological invention but reliant upon it for his very existence. In a sense it is this trouble that configures him as such a traumatized and violent entity, forever fighting to resolve the unresolvable dichotomy that he is both Dracula and Van Helsing, old and new selves. This is an important shift within the depiction of the vampire and in its relation to violence, as it shows certain manifestations of the vampire as being acceptable, if not desired, within society.[18]

The setting of the story is important in this regard as it is based in modern day Los Angeles (1998) but creates a mis-en-scene that captures the phantasmagoria of city life which is as relevant today as it was 20 years ago. It also posits the notion of a hidden world beneath the surface of the metropolis— an underworld, which also links it to the film series of the same name that began in 2008—an invisible, or dark, corporate business run by vampires that slowly drains the nation with the consent of the authorities.[19] However, all is about to change in this set up, with a new breed of young vampires no longer willing to restrain themselves as their leader Deacon Frost declares: "Maybe it's time we forgot about discretion. We should be ruling the humans, not running around making back alley treaties with them. For fuck's sake, these people are our food, not our allies" (Norrington, 1998).

Maybe not coincidentally, this posits a link to economic markets and the excesses of bankers and finance workers who made a huge amount of money playing the markets in the 80s and 90s—as also seen in *American Psycho* (Harron, 2000). Consequently the old guard in *Blade*, the House of Erebus, can be seen as the traditional order demanding restraint and anti-conspicuous displays of wealth, whereas Frost represents the generation of yuppies who revel in their excess.[20] This is demonstrated graphically from the start of the film where a group of ravers at a warehouse party/club are drenched in blood from overhead sprinklers, revealing the ecstatic clubbers as vampires. Along with this Frost's grand plan is to raise the blood god, La Magra, so that he and his acolytes can walk in the daytime and continue their excessive lifestyle non-stop; we have already seen them wearing sunblock during the day to experience this.[21]

As such, Frost begins to embody the Dracula character in the same way that Edward Cullen did in *Twilight*, as a young, extremely wealthy individual. Blade comments on the wealth that has now become the possession of the vampires: "They've got their claws into everything—politics, finance, real estate. They already own half of downtown" (Norrington, 1998), though of course Frost has no such vegetarian inclinations like Edward. Unlike the Cullens, Frost wants to stand out and control the world, not co-exist alongside humanity. This too correlates to the vampire king and his wish to be Master wherever he goes. And Frost definitely troubles the other undead around him who, like himself, were turned rather than being born a vampire—in the film Dragonetti and the rest of the vampire council appear to be pure bloods who were born. Interestingly Frost also uses technology but in a very different way than Blade does. In keeping with his construction as a disaffected young professional, Frost uses computers to research data to his own advantage— in this case ancient texts from the vampire bible on how to resurrect La Magra—but he does little in terms of weaponry other than use almost basic guns and swords (some stolen from Blade). In contrast, Blade and his assistant Whistler almost exclusively use technology and science to create new types of armaments or cures for vampirism.[22] In many ways this mirrors Stoker's novel where the Count surrounds himself with texts linked to new technology in order to decipher the world around him, such as train time-tables, while the crew of light weaponized the same material to track and kill him.

The use of weaponry inevitably relates to the kind of violence portrayed in the film, which largely stays in the same kind of unreal, fantasy world seen in *The Last Man Alive*, though complicates it by spilling out into the environment of the city itself, giving it an air of realworld veracity. Interestingly, within the city space the violence perpetrated by Frost's vampires is far more visceral than that in the unreal vampire world largely because much of it is inflicted on humans though even that administered to Blade, while more strategic, is brutal and sustained. The violence seen in *Blade* is often more personal, indeed much like Dracula himself who often creates a bond with his victims before enacting his "kiss of death" upon them (Sheng-mei Ma 2012, 68).[23] As such, the kind of absolute otherness of Frost is a very intimate one, suggesting the same kind of miscegenation and blood disease mentioned in Stoker. Unlike in the novel though, *Blade* infers that this is not passed on by outmoded ideas of a decadent aristocracy—which would be the House of Erebus itself—but by the financially empowered professional classes (something not far from the middle class, seen in Jonathan and Mina, that saved the Empire from the excesses of the undead Count). The otherness of these selfish and self-centered vampires troubles and infects the world around it, threatening the creation of a vampiric megalopolis that sucks the life out of the land and environment beyond its borders—the phantasmagoric nature of the city, particularly at night, configures it as an endless space, a virtual black-hole sprinkled with lights intimating the lives that have already been sucked into it.

In contrast, Blade never kills humans and prefers to kill vampires quickly; these end in nothing but a pile of ashes. In fact, all the Daywalker's deaths finish with a flurry of insubstantial matter. Just like Fisher's earlier vampire deaths in Dracula's castle, their extinction proves they are monstrous, and that killing them has no moral or legal consequence at all. It becomes mesmerizing to watch the slayer disintegrating every vampire that crosses his path, no matter age, gender, or nationality; once they are vampires they are all the same, and all monsters and only differentiated by how spectacular their demise is and while it mirrors that of Stoker's vampire hunters it also produces its own kind of contagion.[24] Johan Höglund notes a similar affect in the *Underworld* series of films which borrows themes from *Blade*, especially the weaponization of the vampire itself: "the militarization of the vampire that *Underworld* and similar narratives [*Blade*] accomplish is arguably contagious, teaching its audience not merely to worship the tools of modern warfare, and that gunplay and sexual play are closely related, but that military

Four. Violent Distractions 127

Blade (Wesley Snipes) returns to being Eric Brooks. *Blade*, dir. Stephan Norrington (New Line Cinema, 1998).

violence is a paradigm for problem solving" (Höglund 2012, 184). Further, and something seen in the body armor and heavy musculature of *Blade* actor Wesley Snipes, as much as in *Underworld*'s PVC clad Selene, played by Kate Beckinsale, "the vampire spreads not the plague of the Other, but a hybrid affliction that imagines existence as a warlike utopia characterized by perpetual, military/sexual violence" (Höglund 2012, 185). Blade in particular creates his own troubling otherness through hyper-masculinity, linking his sexuality—which is never physically expressed—with his arsenal or weapons and his ability to inflict violence on others, while simultaneously denying this through his never-ending battle to save humanity.[25] Even his final battle with Frost plays exactly into this construction.

When Blade escapes from the blood-letting box with the help of Dr. Johnson, as mentioned earlier, he is naked except for his tight leather trousers. After penetrating the Dr. with her consent, his aroused body then encounters that of Deacon Frost's in the ritual chamber, where he too is half naked. The two men wrestle and trade blows before Blade manages to slice off Deacon's hand. However, rather than disintegrating, the hand stays intact and produces a blood trail between itself and the arm from which it was removed; this is both visceral and oddly erotic as it obviously arouses Frost in realizing his true potency. He then begins to dominate Blade; the juxtaposition of a soft, white body against that of the statuesque, highly muscled black body is purposeful, signifying not only the obvious ethnic conflict depicted but also intimating the difference between effete office/computer professionals and the militarized masculine body.[26] In a final bit of hubris, Frost taunts Blade, thinking himself to be beyond the weaponized technology Blade has brought with him: "What? Your serum? Can't help you now, stud" (Norrington, 1998). This of course spurs Blade on to use the hybrid tech of his samurai sword—it has a mechanism that recognizes when anyone other than Blade holds it, and ejects multiple silver blades from its hand-guard—to dislodge the serum vials—actually anti-coagulant bullets created by Dr. Johnson—from where they are lodged so he can karate kick them into Frost's body. This final penetration of weaponized technology—a much larger dose of the same "little deaths" Blade experiences when taking his own serum—causes the vampire's body to excessively over-excite (orgasm) to the point that it explodes. This simultaneously re-establishes Blade's masculine, sexual, and technological supremacy over the new breed of upwardly mobile vampires,[27] a supremacy founded upon violence that gains its legitimacy through being represented as just.

This is important within this film and the ongoing narrative of the *Blade* franchise, and indeed most texts featuring vampire slayers. If earlier movies such as Fisher's caused ambivalence over the justness of the slayers' endeavors through the visible results of the violence inflicted on the bodies of the undead—i.e., Lucy remains almost exactly the same—*Blade* never allows for such readings as all his victims are vampires and all "self" destruct and vaporize due to their inherently monstrous nature.[28] Curiously, it is the just nature of Blade's extremely violent mission that can be seen to be most troubling to those around him. In a very general way the vampires that Blade is at war with—the story is very much constructed as a military conflict with Blade as a special operative fighting on our behalf—cannot understand his motivations, and even Frost is bewildered as the Daywalker "naturally" possesses all the qualities that they wish for but cannot have. "The goal, of course, is to be like you—the Daywalker! You got the best of both worlds, don't you? All our strengths … none of our weaknesses" (Norrington, 1998).

Possibly the most troubled is Dr. Karen Johnson who runs into Blade while she is being attacked by a vampire, Quinn (Donal Logue), in the hospital where she works. Quinn's charred body is brought into the hospital morgue as he is assumed dead—after the fight at the warehouse rave that opened the film. He of course is *not* dead and suddenly revives, attacking Johnson's colleague and drinking his blood. Totally shocked and confused, Karen tries to run away but is pursued by the vampire who manages to bite her. She continues to try and escape but is stopped by Blade who slices off Quinn's arm. The Daywalker grabs Karen just as the security services arrive and start shooting at the new intruder, but the pair escape. Blade takes her back to his lair where Whistler administers a drug to try and reverse the vampire poison coursing through her system. Karen, coming from a rational scientific background, is understandably perplexed by her all too real and extremely violent encounter with the supernatural. A long chat with her rescuers is enough to convince Karen of the veracity of her situation—trouble her from her previous world view—as well as her own possible vampiric infection, and she begins using her medical research skills to assist Blade and Whistler, largely due to what she perceives as the justness of their cause. In fact, later in the film as she joins Blade in trying to uncover what Frost is planning, she gleefully joins in the violent exploits of her new mentor. This, described below, is an important scene as it shows a prolonged segment of torture, much of it for personal satisfaction rather than purely as an information-gathering exercise.

The pair find the oracle Pearl, a large bloated vampire, permanently encased in a large tub. When the oracle refuses to answer Blade's questions at first, he and Karen use a large torch that emits ultra-violet light as a weapon to burn its skin. Karen takes great delight in doing this and continues even after they have the information they require. Even though the creature is purposely constructed as monstrous, and in no way human or deserving of pity, still it is only the influence of Blade's just cause that allows Karen to go against the professional code of her former life/self and become part of the militarized unit led by the Daywalker. So much so that she becomes part of the technological weapons factory run by Whistler. To this end she creates the serum that kills Frost, ignores sexual advances and innuendoes from the vampire leader—re-establishing Blade's masculine superiority—and even gives of her own blood (self-sacrifice) for the sake of the cause. All of this is accomplished due to the perceived just violence of Blade and his mission.

Blade is very interesting because of this, allowing for a vampire take on the Van Helsing role and justifying any amount of violence, even torture, for the sake of the cause. While the narrative draws very firm boundaries around who is allowed to do what and to whom, it creates a world that is inherently extremely violent and militarized—with this violence linked to both sex and masculinity—where both physical and technological prowess are seen as inherently just, and where any amount of violence is permissible on those categorized as an absolute other. The next film takes this even further, though as it is set in 15th century Europe, technology is replaced by CGI pyrotechnics.

Dracula Untold, Gary Shore, 2014

Gary Shore's film is a very different one from *Blade*, not least in its use of a historical setting, so that it immediately speaks of the past though not necessarily one that will remain there. The story is based on the rather spurious connection between Bram Stoker's fictional character and the historical figure of Vlad Țepeș; as many have noted Stoker only used the name Dracula because he thought it meant Devil and had originally planned to name his undead "Count Vampire" until a last-minute change of mind (see Miller, 2000). The film is rather cavalier in its approach to what is known about Vlad, though he and his brother were held hostage by the Sultan of the Ottoman Empire in 1442 and so might have know the heir to the throne, as implied in the film. At this time areas of Eastern Europe and Transylvania in particular were often in control of the Ottoman Empire as they sought to cross into the central Europe. Vlad returned to Wallachia where he became prince and provided much resistance to the Ottomans as they sought to pass through Transylvania. He was fiercely nationalistic, and many stories circulated of his brutality, largely by Saxon and Russian traders who suffered under his rulership and who later published pamphlets citing his unruly and savage behavior. Printing presses were invented around this time and the Germans in particular took advantage of its more propaganda-related qualities. It is believed that he was particularly fond of impaling, as a punishment and as spectacle to discourage others, and purportedly did such to an Ottoman corps seeking to retake Wallachia, causing the planned invasion to be halted (Treptow 2000).

The film nominally starts after this point, suggesting that for a brief time at least Vlad (Luke Evans) was the monster that Wallachia, and indeed the wider Christian Europe required. However, now that he has a loving wife and a young son that life is behind him, or so he thinks. While out with a scouting party he discovers artifacts from a Turkish marauding party in a river near the ominous Broken Tooth Mountain. The helmet and armor he finds are so severely damaged that he fears they might have encountered something beyond their imaginings, so he sends most of his party back to the castle and takes only two companions to find what killed the Ottoman soldiers. They stumble across a cave where more pieces of armor, and even human remains, litter the entrance. His two companions are quickly killed leaving only Vlad and the monster in the cave, but somehow the Wallachian Prince escapes with his life.

Upon returning to his castle Vlad is told by a local monk that the monster is a vampire and is cursed to live forever in the cave. The Prince thinks no more of it until a retinue from the Sultan arrives during Easter festivities. Rather than accepting the usual tribute of silver, the Sultan demands 1000 young boys to fill the ranks of his army and when the Prince goes to see Mehmed, the Sultan adds Vlad's son Ingeras (Art Parkinson) to the number. Vlad is thunderstruck by this news and later pleads with the Sultan's representatives to reconsider, but in response they only taunt the Wallachian ruler with what they will do to the youngsters once they are in their charge. The Prince eventually calms down and for the sake of his people agrees, but at the moment of exchange the Ottoman representative taunts Vlad once more and the Wallachian kills him and the accompanying escorts, assuring that war will ensue.

These opening scenes are very interesting in terms of the designation and representation of monstrosity, but the question is who is the real vampire and absolute other in the narrative? Vlad is very much shown as a man willing to sacrifice everything for his people even to the point of doing monstrous things, the symbols of which are the scars on his body signifying his battle-worn and blood-soaked past. His action in killing the Sultan's agent is initially shown as selfish; it is only the threat on his own son that finally causes him to break. Indeed, the early stages of the film portray his son as a particularly loyal, and innocent boy who adores his father. However, the story purposely invites an affective emotional response from its audience, asking them to put themselves in the Prince's place, effectively asking them whether they too would sacrifice everything for the sake of their children. Given the contrary if reactionary nature of contemporary Western society's attitude to its children the answer is of course a resounding "yes."[29] Equally, the film makes a correlation between family and nation, particularly in relation to the American audience where such synergy is common within filmic narratives. Vlad's actions are then easily interpreted to be on behalf not only of his personal family, but the national one as well—the ruler being the father of the nation. As such, when he later becomes a vampire it is a necessary and praiseworthy sacrifice, mitigating the monstrous acts he will inevitably perform.[30] In this sense Vlad is not the "Dracula" of Browning's film in embodying society's absolute otherness—though his own people (family) do turn upon him when they discover his new vampiric nature[31]—which suggests that such a designation should be given to the magically ensnared vampire in the cave. However, this too is complicated as the vampire is not represented as being explicitly the absolute other in the story, though he is described as a monster.

As the film starts, we hear what we later discover is Ingeras's voice saying "My father was a great man, a hero, so they say. But sometimes the world doesn't need another hero, sometimes what it needs is a monster" (Shore, 2014). This is taken up again later in the film when Vlad returns to the vampire's cave, but in a way that suggests that the monstrosity Ingeras mentioned is not in regard to the monster his father was—a man of the sword who impaled his enemies for the sake of his country—but the one he will become. When Vlad returns to the cave he is gripped around the throat from behind, and the Vampire (Charles Dance) begins an exchange with him:

> VAMPIRE: Why spill blood if not for the pleasure of it?
> VLAD: Because men do not fear swords. They fear monsters. They run from them. By putting one village to the stake, I spared ten more. Sometimes the world no longer needs a hero. Sometimes what it needs … is a monster.

> VAMPIRE: [tightening his grip a little] And you believe you know what it means to be a monster? Hmm? ... You have no idea ... but I'm going to show you [Shore, 2014].

This sees the Vampire as describing *himself* as the true abject other, and indeed it is implied that all the violence he has unleashed upon the world is for his own gain or pleasure—though as he has spent most of that time in the cave it has probably been quite limited. As such, he is suggesting that the monster that Vlad will become will be motivated by the love of himself rather than of his people. That said, while the Vampire is a monster he still does not really fit the role of absolute other as he is cast as something of an Atlas figure, doomed to remain where he is until a replacement (victim) can be found, and for the Vampire this would appear to be Vlad.[32] Somewhat confusingly, once Vlad has become a true vampire—after drinking human blood—the Vampire is allowed to leave his cave, and gain revenge on the demon that imprisoned him,[33] but is not replaced by the Prince, who too roams free. As such he is almost seen as a facilitator for the would-be dark hero, though not quite a mentor or a master of the disciplines required. Still, without his decision to turn the human Prince into a vampiric overlord, the world would not get the monster it requires. Consequently, neither of the vampire figures really fulfills the role of absolute other. This then leaves the figure of Sultan Mehmed II (Dominic Cooper) and his agents.

Indeed, as one looks more closely at the leader of the Ottoman Empire he embodies the same threat from the East that the original Count did in Stoker's novel; an alien other threatening Western civilization. While the visual construction of Mehmed II's otherness is not as extreme as that of Xerxes, the King of Persia seen in *300* (Snyder, 2006), which similarly represents an attempted invasion of Europe by diabolical Eastern forces—the Spartan army at the Battle of Thermopylae (480 BC) in *300* is constructed as the guardians of Western Culture—his invasion is equally shown as a violent assault on the civilized world and in particular the hearts, minds, and bodies of its youth.

This last correlates to *Dracula* and the threat posed by his agents on the youth of the Empire, as both its greatest treasure and its future. The Count's "agents" are of course his brides, and the scene in the opening section of Stoker's novel where Dracula feeds them a baby in a sack is meant to show their demonic, inhuman nature as well as their threat to a nation, and more specifically, to its future. Here not only do they transgress the perceived (patriarchal) laws of God and nature in being hyper-sexualized, but they even prey on the children they are supposed to feed and nurture. Their perverse performance of the maternal instinct sees them suck the life out of the very fabric of civilization itself. This threat is finally thwarted by Van Helsing who realizes that agents of evil from the East are preying upon the nation's youth.

Four. Violent Distractions   133

A similar role is given to Vlad, who chooses to become a monster to save such similar violence being perpetrated upon the children, and the future, of Wallachia. Mehmed's agents are then portrayed in a similar manner as Dracula's brides, and although not sexually alluring or as "voluptuous" (Stoker 1996, 42), are constructed as equally animalistic and repulsive.

When we first see Mehmed's representatives during the Easter festivities at Vlad's castle, their presence not only interrupts a sacrosanct religious ritual, arguably the most important one in the Christian calendar, but purposely desecrates it by their refusal to take the gift offered by the Prince and their demand to be given a thousand of the nation's children.[34] Their abject nature is further emphasized by their disrespect for Vlad, shown by their behavior on entering his court where they neither follow protocol or bow, but intimidate those assembled in the hall. More so, one of the agents, Szkelgim, purposely targets a young boy to antagonize and leer over, suggesting that sexual violence will happen to the children once they are taken and preyed upon by the Ottoman troops. Szkelgim's behavior in particular is shown as overtly abject, and his reptilian, snake-like, movements—again constructing Mehmed's men as demonic and/or Satanic—see him as both a violent child molester and as a feminizer or emasculator of Wallachian manhood; Vlad himself is seen as hyper-masculine in his strength, prowess on the battlefield, and as a father of men.

As noted earlier in the film, Vlad had experienced what it was like to live among the Ottomans, and his later meeting with Mehmed shows something of the unequal nature of their relationship and the untrustworthy nature of the extremist from the East; Mehmed sees Vlad only as a lesser European other rather than as an old friend, and insists on war even though the Wallachian wants peace. Indeed, Mehmed's overarching plan is not to just conquer Europe but to target the wives, mothers, and children—the "best beloved" (Stoker 1996, 311)—in order to violate, humiliate and emasculate its men, just as Dracula focused on Lucy and Mina with similar effect on Arthur Holmwood (and Dr. Seward and Quincey Morris) and Jonathan Harker. Vlad becomes the focus of this, first with the demand for his son and then with the attack on his wife, Mirena. Both of these scenes are quite spectacular in nature, as Mehmed hides the first behind his demand for 1,000 boys and the second is obscured by an all-out attack on Vlad's castle involving thousands of men. This latter event is worth closer scrutiny as it navigates the ground between a "good" monster and a "bad" one.

Prior to the attack, Mirena (Sarah Gavin) discovers Vlad's secret and accepts his becoming a vampire as the supreme sacrifice for his family and his people:

MIRENA: May God strike down whoever did this to you!
Vlad: [pained] I chose this!

MIRENA: This is the strength you sought? But why?
VLAD: Because I sent corpses back to Mehmed, instead of our son.
MIRENA: [near tears] You did this for us?
VLAD: In two days, I'll be restored.... I just have to resist.
MIRENA: Resist what? ... Resist what, Vlad? Tell me!
VLAD: The thirst ... for blood [Shore, 2014].

This last sentence refers to Vlad's need to go without satiating his thirst for three days or, according to the Vampire, he will remain a monster for eternity. It just so happens of course that the aforementioned battle takes place on the third day; his remaining a monster forever, or not, is inextricably linked to Mehmed's attack on Mirena.[35] The Ottomans begin a frontal assault on Vlad's refuge in the Cozia Monastery and their numbers are hugely superior to those of the Wallachians, meaning their only hope of survival is in the hands of their Prince.

Vlad amasses his army of bats and explodes on the oncoming army in a wave of vampiric fury—like Dracula, Vlad has control over the creatures of the night, specifically bats, and the weather.[36] But when Vlad attacks the approaching horde's leader he discovers it is a decoy and that Mehmed has sent a small force to enter the castle undetected and try and kill Mirena—this reveals once again Mehmed's deceptive and dishonest nature, while in contrast we have only ever seen Vlad attack head-on.[37] Vlad returns to his wife but is too late. She falls off the side of the battlements and her husband is unable to save her. While she lies broken at the foot of the cliffs in his arms, she insists that he drink her blood so that he will be strong enough to defeat Mehmed. Vlad finally succumbs, embracing his monstrosity both for revenge and for the sake of his people. More importantly, this is with the agreement of his now-dead wife which provides approval for his subsequent acts, making them no longer monstrous but justifiable.

In contrast Mehmed is never shown as having a family, preferring the company of men, and is constructed as having a desire for young boys—his war is not a just one but carried out for his own gain and for corrupt, and corrupting, desires. This more than anything links Mehmed to the Oriental other, and more contemporary monsters from the Middle East such as ISIS (see Newitz 2014). His targeting of women and the young sees him construct an increasingly violent program of "grooming" and coercion that brainwashes those involved to blindly follow his instruction and ideology—as literally seen when he forces his men to march wearing blindfolds, and also later when hundreds, if not thousands are sacrificed in the attack on Vlad's castle. Weinstock notes a similar construction in *Blade Trinity*, where a monster from the East is intent on destroying the Western way of life (Weinstein 2012, 2), and Mehmed continues this, though not in relation to the invasion of Iraq as with *Trinity*, but with the wave of extremism that has subsequently flooded

Mehmed (Dominic Cooper), an object of monstrous desire. *Dracula Untold*, dir. Gary Shore (Universal, 2014).

out of that region across Europe. Interestingly, in the final fight between Mehmed and Vlad, the Ottoman ruler surrounds himself with piles of silver in an attempt to weaken the vampire—vampires are shown to be very allergic to silver in the film. This can be seen to stand for the distraction of money, and a critique of the many nations involved in the recent wars in the Middle East that are troubled by the possibility of gaining great wealth—their literal 30 pieces of silver—and so subvert the rule of international law. Vlad, of course, wins and then overcomes the surviving Ottoman troops with the help of his remaining citizens who he has since turned into vampires. While the fight between Mehmed and Vlad is not overtly violent, it screens the immense volume of savagery that occurs during the battle that forms its backdrop. The hordes of bats that are simultaneously autonomous and part of Vlad, have literally torn the Ottoman troops apart, as do the newly turned vampires that the Wallachian uses to mop up any survivors. The film suggests that this is perfectly acceptable in the face of the perverted violence threatened upon the children of the nation; however, once this box has been opened it is incredibly difficult to close.

Vlad's son is still human, and the Wallachian vampires decide he is next on the menu. The ruler knows that a just monstrosity can only be valid for a certain timeframe, and he changes the weather so that all of them, including himself, are bathed in sunlight and destroyed. Vlad is later revived but remains hidden, while his son Ingeras is made ruler of Wallachia. While this signals the end of the historical narrative, the traumatic violence unleashed cannot help but be repeated and so we see both Vlad and the Vampire in a closing scene in modern-day London. This suggests that although the just "monster" was originally only needed to save the future of Wallachia, it in fact symbolized the ongoing fight for Western civilization against those seen as its existential enemies. As such, although the absolute otherness of Mehmed was supposed to be seen as nothing more than a historical blip, his violent threat upon the youth of the future is never-ending and requires ever-evolving kinds of just monsters to provide protection. In this sense, Vlad symbolizes the real life just monsters that are utilized in the "war with the East." These monsters use enhanced interrogation methods and remain largely anonymous, though their "justness" is rather more questionable than the Wallachian's as it is at the behest of changing administrations and objectives. This scene equally sees a movement of violence from the unreal space of the past into the very real environment of terror attacks in Europe and the existence of Islamic extremism. The film itself never really has chance to address this as the contemporary section is more of a coda or bridging section into what was going to be a sequel or ongoing Dark Universe franchise, which has never transpired.[38]

However, the blurring of the boundaries between "good" and "bad" monsters from *Dracula Untold* forms the basis of the final example in this section, where the troubling violence of the absolute other almost becomes an entity in itself.

The Vampire Diaries, Julie Plec and Kevin Williamson, 2009–2017

The series created by Plec and Williamson, taken from the books by L.J. Smith, is a sprawling affair.[39] As spread over eight series and some 171 episodes, all the main characters, be they vampire, human, werewolf, witch, or hybrid have undergone many different character developments that have seen almost all of them repeatedly cross the boundaries between good and bad, evil and heroic. Equally, the violent acts perpetrated by them waver between the just and the gratuitous, from the murderous to the meaningless. The show's original story saw a teenage girl, Elena (Nina Dobrev), torn between her love for two vampire brothers: Stefan (Paul Wesley), the good one, and Damon (Ian Somerhalder), the bad one, capturing something of Lucy Westenra's affection for more than one beau in Stoker's story. The series develops into a hugely complicated narrative of prophecies, ancient (Original) vampires, and supernatural beings of all kinds that constantly battle for the life of their beloved, and/or their own existence, and/or the fate of the world.[40] As the narrative unfolds it largely remains tethered to the opening story of a group of teenage friends at high school in Mystic Falls in central Virginia, whose population (6,923 when the show began) becomes, or is revealed to be, increasingly magical in nature and increasingly subjected to escalating amounts of violence. This last is interesting when comparing the show to the competing vampire series *True Blood* (Ball, 2008–2014). *True Blood* was intended for a slightly older audience and became somewhat infamous for its sexually provocative and violent content, while *The Vampire Diaries* is a YA story and purposely revolves around its teenage main characters. However, *The Vampire Diaries* is in many ways more shocking in its depictions of torture, mindless aggression and brutality than the former. Indeed, the violence becomes so prevalent, and often random and explosive, that it almost takes on a life on of its own; one might even suggest that the absolute other of the series is violence itself, and that its troubling and distracting nature affects all those around it.

This miasmic reading of Dracula's body where it can also embody an emotional state—even in Stoker's novel the vampires body is more a sum of its various parts and manifestations rather than a singular corporeal mass[41]—is quite useful when looking at the series as a whole, but for the purposes of this study only Season Three will be used to example how the idea works. The third installment of *The Vampire Diaries* concentrates the extreme violence around the figure of Klaus (Joseph Morgan), and much of the subsequent aggression is produced by those troubled by him, or distracted by his increasingly meaningless violence, and as such he, at least in this part of the narrative arc, fulfills the Dracula role of the absolute other.

Klaus, or Niklaus Mikaelson, is over a thousand years old and was part of a Viking party that settled in the Americas 500 years before Columbus crossed the Atlantic. Klaus's family, under threat from the indigenous population that could transform into wolves, were turned into vampires by their Mother Esther (Alice Evans), who just happened to be a witch. This is constructed as a creational moment as they are in fact the Original vampires and all subsequent ones are their descendants.[42] Klaus, however, is also part werewolf as he is the product of his mother's affair with an indigenous man from the neighboring village.[43] As such he is also the original hybrid, and this takes up much of the story in Season Three with Klaus trying to break his "curse"—which suppresses his werewolf genes—so that he can create his own army of hybrids.

As the first episode begins it is Elena's birthday. She is supposed to be dead, as she was a sacrifice in Klaus' ritual to break his curse at the end of the previous season. We discover that Stefan is under Klaus' control, having pledged his allegiance to his former enemy in return for sparing his brother Damon's life. In terms of *The Vampire Diaries* correlation to *Dracula*, the relationship between Klaus and Stefan is quite interesting as it once again shows a male character fulfilling a female role. Stefan is mainly shown as a very correct and restrained personality, but when he was first turned in 1864, he was consumed by blood lust and became a renowned "Ripper"—a vampire that is almost bestial in nature and extremely violent to its victims—and was only calmed down by his good friend Lexi. His violence is constructed as being a kind of libidinal release and/or an explosion of his repressed, subconscious urges, which is something that Klaus wants to reawaken. In this sense Stefan very much conforms to Phyllis A. Roth's notion of the "suddenly sexual women" (Roth 1977) in Stoker's text where Lucy and Mina are shown to lose their normal restraint when troubled by the Count—effectively allowing them to express their true selves after being released from normative patriarchal containment. Following on from this, Stefan, at least for Season Three, shares much with Mina Harker who is bound to the King Vampire and forced to go against, or is released from, her former nature, though eventually becomes something of a double agent. That said, Stefan is sufficiently troubled by Klaus, as the embodiment of extreme violence, to commit many atrocities himself. Two specific examples are very useful to explore in more depth; one occurs with Klaus in a bar and the other when the two vampires are trying to locate Bonnie's mother.

The first sees Klaus wanting to locate a werewolf pack so that he can begin creating his army of hybrids (Episode 2: "The Hybrid"). At this stage he believes Elena is dead and that the curse that prevented him from siring other hybrids has been lifted. He enters a known werewolf bar full of denim-clad biker types and locates their leader, Ray Sutton (David Gallagher), to discover where their settlement is.[44] The leader initially refuses to cooperate, but Stefan and Klaus use him as a dartboard and torture him until he complies with their wishes. This is a protracted scene of unpleasant violence that is given an oddly comical twist by its use of the common barroom game, and which is reinforced by Klaus's offhand approach to the brutality inflicted on the victim at his behest. In part this is justified, or at least allowable, due to the supernatural nature of the werewolf, even if in human form—with its worrying underlying implication that no one is exactly who they seem to be and so potentially everyone is fair game to torture. The leader of course eventually reveals the location of his pack, and Klaus subsequently infects all of them in the hope of creating hybrids, but they all die extremely painful deaths, again vaguely justifiable as they are, were, werewolves.

The second example is both less and more disturbing as it is inflicted on humans, by Stefan in his changed, "Ripper" state. This is in the preceding episode (Episode 1: "The Birthday"). As Klaus and Stefan (Dracula and Mina/Renfield) try to find the whereabouts of Ray Sutton they follow a lead which takes them to Samara and Keisha, Sutton's friends. After "persuading" them to give up Ray's location, Stefan drains them both of blood and, blinded by his bloodlust, rips them to pieces. We are not shown the actual scene, but can guess at it through the level of terror we see upon the girls' realization of the kinds of violence that awaits them. What we are shown are the reassembled bodies of the two victims once the violence is over, just as one of the heads rolls on to the floor. In comparison to Fisher's *Dracula* mentioned at the start of this chapter, these scenes reveal a blurring of the boundary between real and imaginary spaces—both events happen outside of the fictional town of Mystic Falls and in the "real" America beyond its borders—allowing violence to flow freely from one to the other.

In the context of the wider vampire genre, and particularly its historical precursors, violently torturing and killing humans marks out the supernatural perpetrator as irredeemably inhuman and marked for destruction, but here that is not the case. Stefan continually "goes bad," though maybe less than Damon, but is consistently shown as repentant and subsequently redeemable, which inevitably allows him to once again return to the side of the crew of light. Klaus's ongoing survival is even more surprising as he shows no repentance for his actions at all. One scene in particular "The Reckoning" (Episode 5) shows Klaus making Elena suffer for ruining his plans. He glamors two high school students, Dana (Anna Enger) and her boyfriend Chad (Mark Buckland), then tells Dana to raise her foot, instructing Chad that should the foot ever touch the floor that he must beat her to death. No actual physical aggression takes place but the absurdity of the situation and the certainty that the young boy will follow his instructions creates a violently explosive atmosphere. Elena pleads with Klaus, saying he does not need to hurt anyone, to which he matter-of-factly replies "Oh, come on, love. Of course, I do." The expected bludgeoning does not happen but it is indicative of the heightened level of possible violence throughout the season, which continually raises the bar so that subsequent physical threats need to be ever more extreme. Consequently, Klaus's violence troubles the very atmosphere of the town of Mystic Falls so that we become less and less surprised by the savage events that take place there—not unlike the space of Count Dracula's castle which virtually exists beyond the world outside its walls and where vampires materialize from the very air (Stoker 1996, 279). A case in point is yet another torture scene that takes place over two episodes where Caroline (Candice King), bride of Dracula, i.e., of Klaus's bloodline, but consistently good and in control of herself, is tied to a chair in the cellar of the Lockwood mansion and tortured by her own father. From the end of the first episode ("The Birthday") until the end of Episode 3 ("The End of the Affair") her father Bill (Jack Coleman), who is part of the group of town founders who hunt and kill vampires, tries to convert her back into being human by continually allowing sunlight into her room so that she repeatedly suffers serious burns to her skin—supposedly a means to train her to not want blood. Her father finds this perfectly acceptable behavior, as he explains to a fellow member of the council: "Don't feel guilty. They're not human. They're monsters." Again, we do not see everything that goes on but it is implied that the torture has been happening for a considerable time. More interesting is that it is undertaken not to get information but to change his daughter's behavior, brainwashing if you will. As such it becomes about ideological positioning, and not about changing Caroline from a vampire back into a human, suggesting that violence is something of a universal tool that can be used to change the world to one's will.

This goes even further as the storyline progresses and by Episode 18 ("The Murder of One") torture becomes an overtly enjoyable and sexually charged act—not dissimilar to the correlation between sex and weaponry mentioned earlier in regard to *Blade*. Klaus's sister Rebekah has Damon chained to the living room ceiling of her brother's mansion using bear traps clamped around his wrists. Ostensibly she needs to remove the vervain—a potion made from the vervain plant that prevents vampires being able to control those who have it in their system—from Damon's blood, but she also wants revenge for the earlier emotional manipulation she suffered at his hands. Consequently, she literally bleeds Damon dry by severing his major arteries and allowing him to bleed out while strung up. The positioning of the two protagonists is purposely eroticized, showing Damon with his shirt ripped open to his waist and blood dripping down his arms and torso. Rebekah stands close to him with bare arms and exposed cleavage, holding a large knife to his neck. The tableau hints knowingly at what Damon himself calls "kinky sex" and darker sadomasochistic role-playing games.

Klaus interrupts the scene and begins comparing torture techniques with his sister, inferring she is not very experienced:

> KLAUS: Well, look what you've caught. Trying to bleed him of vervain, don't you think it would be easier to hang him upside down?
> REBEKAH: I'm perfectly capable of inflicting pain, thank you very much.
> KLAUS: Well, excuse me, it's not like I have any expertise in the matter. [Rolls his eyes sarcastically.] [Plec and Williamson, 2009–2017].

The scene reveals the troubling nature of violence that increasingly pervades the narrative. In part, the torture of Damon is almost allowable as he is a supernatural being, a monster, even though this nature means that he could be tortured forever and not die. And indeed, he himself has been and will be responsible for torturing others, so it is almost justifiable for that reason alone, but the offhand manner of the scene and the exchanges between the Michelson siblings suggests something of an everyday arbitrariness to it, an unimportance that allows for it to be seen as an everyday occurrence, and not worthy of special note. This is opposite the way Caroline's imprisonment by her own father was constructed to make her more human than her monstrous parent. Rebekah and Damon engender no such emotions and Klaus's comments serve only to normalize the monstrosity of violence that pervades Mystic Falls as a whole. While this becomes less and less predicated on the presence of Klaus himself, in Season Three it is he who troubles the entire environment around him—his violence becomes more contagious than

Rebekah (Claire Holt) penetrating Damon (Ian Somerhalder) in *The Vampire Diaries*, created by Julie Plec and Kevin Williamson (Warner Bros. Television, 2009–2017).

vampirism itself—to such an extent that it creates a permanent state of exception (see Agamben, 2005), a state that allows for enhanced interrogation and continued violence that becomes the normalized state of everyday life.

As such, the entirety of Mystic Falls becomes the "land beyond the forest," an environment of constant exceptionalism where torture and excessive violence are no longer punished but become part of everyday existence. This becomes the apotheosis of Dracula being an absolute, or absolutely violent other. There is no longer a pretense of exceptional places, as in Hammer's *Dracula*, or exceptional times, as in *The Last Man on Earth*, *Blade* and *Dracula Untold*, or even exceptional people/species. In Mystic Falls, violence is the first recourse in any situation no matter how extreme or how many people are affected (killed) because of it. If violence were meant to be equivalent to vampirism here, then Count Dracula's plan to take over the Empire (Mystic Falls) would have come to fruition as it virtually infects (troubles) everyone in the environs of the narrative.

As with many recent vampire narratives *The Vampire Diaries* makes its construction and depiction of absolute otherness context-specific so that Count Dracula can never be totally evil and is potentially capable of redemption, or at least of recognizing something of his/her/its lost humanity.[45] In this sense, violence can never be seen as totally abhorrent in that certain conditions, even in retrospect, can justify many forms of aggression, torture in particular. Random acts of violence, or those enacted for "fun," while never wholly justifiable, can almost be excused as either a part of who the "hero" is, as is the case with both Stefan and Damon—the price that must be paid— or some form of PTSD where traumatic events from the past make the character act beyond their own control but are potentially savable with the right treatment (often the love of the "right" person).[46] This last is interesting as it questions when enough is enough and when such "monsters" need to be stopped for their own, and society's, ultimate good. It is always arguable with characters such as Damon and Klaus that killing them at the start of the series would have saved many more human lives than any subsequent altruistic actions they might have performed on behalf of humanity. Later television series such as del Toro and Hogan's *The Strain* (2014–17) make their respective Draculas (the Master) totally irredeemable, as is Drake in *Blade Trinity*, but neither of these are seen as godlike creatures in human form, but essentially are an alien species.[47]

As with many moral and ethical problems at the start of the 21st century, violence has become increasingly troubling with its absolute otherness being abstracted from a single physical form/source into a continual presence, in many ways mirroring Dracula's own multivalent character, manifesting at will in unexpected forms and equally unexpected places—the heart and hearth of Empire are indeed no longer safe in the ways we thought they once were. Such spaces of continual anxiety form the basis of the next and final chapter where the relationship between technology and the vampire comes under scrutiny and sees a symbiosis between the technological and the undead that envisions the future as a place we no longer belong.

Five

Distracting Technologies

In which Count Dracula's former aversion to technology and science has changed so much that now he has not only mastered such devices but has become an inherent part of 21st century technology and its ideological intent.

Abbott and Costello Meet Frankenstein, Charles Barton, 1948

Technology is an amazingly prominent part of Stoker's novel, not just in its use for pursuing and defeating the Old-World vampire, but in the structure of the narrative itself. Compiled from diary entries, newspaper clippings, telegrams, and phonographic transcriptions to name but a few, it describes a world in constant change and evolution through technological invention and innovation. This evolution is of course something that the Count is purposely excluded from, both in his ruined castle in Transylvania with its piles of gold, about which Harker notes, "None of it that I noticed was less than three hundred years old" (Stoker 1996, 51), and in his "new" English home Carfax Abbey. He describes the Abbey as "old and big" and further validates his exclusion by saying, "I myself am of an old family, and to live in a new house would kill me" (Stoker 1996, 26). As such, even though it is mentioned that Dracula has studied railway timetables and the like, he is constructed as the absolute other to science, reason, and technology, indeed the complete opposite of the very driving forces of modernism and advancement. What is interesting in this framework is that because of the vampire's exclusion, he never controls any of the devices used to describe him so that his personality is seen as very consistent throughout, whereas the identities of the authors/creators becomes increasingly fractured.[1] Dr. Seward for instance becomes a collection of diary entries, phonographic recordings, and transcriptions, as well as being described and quoted by other members of the vampire hunting team. The final memory we have of the good doctor is as part of the "mass of typewriting" and a fragment of one of his notebooks (Stoker 1996, 411); the last remaining shards of a technologically fragmented character. Jennifer Wicke sees Seward, in part, as a disembodied figure, a voice that only finds form in Mina Harker's transcriptions of his recordings, joining the other characters in having vampiric qualities that they all deny. Wicke takes this further, seeing Dracula as not wanting to consume their blood but rather to drink of "a kind of knowledge and power he has become aware of as the attributes of modern, consumer capitalist culture" (Wicke 1992, 490). Though she later notes, following on from Franco Moretti (1988), that the vampire is representative of the effects of consumerist culture, of which the novel itself is part; the consummate consumer, Dracula, is representative of both the technology and ideology of "consumption and the forces of empire" (Wicke 1992, 490).

The Count's move across mediums to film, in spite of its hugely increased consumerist potential and technological advancement, denies the vampire's links to modernism and/or capitalism, largely representing it as a creature out of step with the times it has found itself in (as seen in *Nosferatu* [Murnau, 1922]/*Dracula* [Browning, 1931]/*Son of Dracula* [Siodmak, 1943]), though *Dracula's Daughter* (Hillyer, 1936) sees his female offspring more at home with 20th century modernity if not with herself. Curiously, this sparks the female vampire's interest in psychiatry to try and "cure" herself of her affliction (a plot device used again in *The House of Dracula* [Kenton, 1945]). While not exampling an affinity for technology it does denote a trust and understanding of the emerging techniques of modern medical science where things such as vampirism are understood as psychological pathologies that can be cured.[2] As such, while this does not show that an inherent synergy between the undead and technology was already present, it does reveal a development from Stoker's Count reading a railway timetable, and one that could only progress at an ever-increasing rate with the technological thrust of World War II and the monstrous uses of new forms of weaponry and machinery.[3]

In *Abbott and Costello Meet Frankenstein*, though, Dracula goes for the more "mad scientist" approach to technology and wants to revive the dead rather than cure himself. Oddly, it is only the second film in which Bela Lugosi plays Count Dracula, but with the pseudonym of Dr. Lejos, reflecting one of the actor's earlier films *The Devil Bat* (Yarborough, 1940) where he plays another mad scientist, one who breeds giant killer bats.[4]

By 1948 the idea of the "mad scientist" more directly applied to the new place of the scientist within the popular imagination post–Hiroshima and Nagasaki. Science had suddenly surpassed the pre–War monsters as being an existential threat to humanity, being linked to unseen Nazi atrocities during the conflict (Dick 2015, 257) and with alien invasion and mutated creatures afterwards (Poole 2014, 113). This resulted in narratives such as Matheson's *I Am Legend* (1954) and *Not of This Earth* (Corman, 1957)—the first sees science (radiation) as responsible for turning the population of the world into vampires and the second sees scientifically advanced aliens coming to the Earth to harvest human blood (not unlike H.G. Wells' *War of the Worlds* [1987])— and so in Barton's film Dracula is actually made scarier by his "mad" scientific endeavors rather than by his supernatural powers. Indeed, much of the film's humor comes from Wilbur (Lou Costello) making fun of the vampire's supernatural attributes, but never of his scientific capabilities.

The film sees crates from Europe containing both Count Dracula and Frankenstein's Monster being sent to a wax works museum in a small town in Florida. However, to reach there they have to pass through the baggage department of the local railway station where Chick (Bud Abbott) and Wilbur (Costello) work. As the crates arrive Chick gets a call from Lawrence Talbot (the Wolf Man) warning them not to deliver the crates. Ignoring this, Chick and Wilbur take the boxes to the museum where Count Dracula reawakens and reanimates the (Frankenstein's) Monster, and they escape. Meanwhile Dr. Sandra Mornay (Lenore Aubert), who is a gifted surgeon and owns a castle/clinic on a nearby island, has convinced Wilbur she loves him, but really she wants to use his brain to implant into the Monster; she possesses Dr. Frankenstein's notebooks that explain his surgical techniques. It seems she is part of Dracula's plan, and she invites him to her clinic so that they can perform the operation with Wilbur's "docile" brain, perfect in that they will then be able to control the Monster. Sandra works alongside Professor Stevens—another expert in the field though it is never made clear whether he is employed by her, teaching her his skills, or just a cover for her more nefarious intentions for the clinic—who is beginning to question all the unusual equipment that has been arriving at the castle recently. This marks the technology as being both unusual and new; the Professor is not familiar with it yet it is instantly recognizable to a horror film audience, containing the usual sparking orbs, coiled metal pipes and glass domes from any Frankenstein film (later to be updated and used in many 1950s sci-fi movies).

Dr. Lejos (Dracula) is very familiar with the technology, as is his assistant, and it is not long before they have the Monster and Wilbur strapped down to beds and are ready to perform the brain transplant operation. As with many films of the 1930s and 40s this involves much sparking of static electricity, but also more sophisticated electronic control boxes and tables full of test tubes and distillation equipment. Unsurprisingly the plan is never completed but the reanimation of the monster, even of one that can be controlled, is constructed as the resulting monstrosity of science itself. As such Dracula's correlation to technology monsterizes both of them; the vampire is given the terrifying aura of nuclear weaponry and the mysterious effects of radiation, while science gains a supernatural element that figures it as both unnatural and non-human. Science then makes the vampire the absolute other of post–World War II society, giving supernatural capabilities to scientific procedures and outcomes that were largely beyond the understanding of the majority of those that benefited from them.

Dracula himself looks rather creaky in the film. It came 17 years after Lugosi's first outing as the Count, and even in the laboratory his character is forced to don the familiar cape and evening wear so that he remains instantly recognizable. Yet the figure of Dr. Mornay dressed in her white surgical garb is far more threatening and ominous, largely due to her unrecognizability. Covered almost from head to toe in white fabric with only the upper part of her face showing, she becomes something of a modern Mummy, no longer representative of an undead past but of a non-human, anonymous, and sterile future. Indeed, Dr. Mornay is the first character looked at here as she is seemingly the most troubled by Dracula's association with medical science.

The vampire's influence on the doctor has apparently occurred before the narrative of the film began and it is almost suggested that she has influenced the invite to the Count from the owner of the wax museum in some way. In this sense the story shares many features with the earlier vampire film *Son of Dracula* from 1943, discussed in Chapter Three. Released during World War II the film shows the vampire's supernatural powers as horrifying enough in their own right to not include any connections to science, though Lon Chaney's performance as Count Alucard (Dracula in reverse) often seems less convincing than that of Lugosi.[5]

Similarly, Sandra Mornay appears to be acting in a distinctly selfish and anti-nationalist way with her creation of the clinic and its recently delivered equipment, suggesting she knew of the Count's imminent arrival and may even have travelled to Europe beforehand to ensure his safe arrival in the U.S.—she simultaneously invites the vampire and science into America. This in itself is quite interesting as it suggests something of a continuation of the linkage between "mad science" and Nazism seen in *The Vampire Bat* mentioned above. However, the Barton film never makes that association explicit, even though at the time the CIA were running a secret operation called "Paperclip" to bring Nazi Scientists to America to keep their knowledge out of the hands of the USSR.[6]

Post-war American society expected women, who had been given much greater agency during the conflict to cover for the conscripted male workforce, to return back home and raise families in order to restock the depleted population. Dr. Sandra Mornay specifically goes against that; not only is she a professional woman (taking a job away from a man) but she has no intention of raising a family. In fact, any man she chooses will, quite literally, lose their minds because of her monstrous science.[7] Just as with Kay before her, Sandra uses the vampire for her own selfish ends, though unlike her predecessor it is not for love but her own naked ambition. As such, her work on the monster mirrors that of the original Dr. Frankenstein in trying to exceed the restrictions put upon her by society. In doing this she places herself in control of, or even above, the patriarchal order that demands that as a woman she is only able to create life biologically from her own body, through birth; this also sees women taking control of medicalized/male forms of reproduction. Necessarily this is seen as unallowable in the narrative, dictating that Sandra must be made an example of to discourage others from such selfish behavior—which also happens to Kay whose human fiancé sets her on fire and beheads her, simultaneously regaining his manhood—and aptly Sandra is destroyed by her intended creation, the Monster, who throws her out of the laboratory window to her death.[8] This actually sees the "scientifically troubled" Mornay as more monstrous than the Monster and more dangerous than Dracula. Indeed, her association with these supernatural creatures from the past gives her the air of an non-human being; one might almost say witch or necromancer.

The scientific and the supernatural in the body of Dr. Mornay (Lenore Aubert). *Abbot and Costello Meet Frankenstein*, dir. Charles Barton (Universal, 1948).

In many ways Sandra is the only character in the story that is truly troubled by Dracula, as even if she did plan to get him to America, he is the one who facilitates and encourages her drive toward female agency and absolute otherness. The Count largely forgoes his fangs and usual nocturnal habits in favor of technological supremacy—he only glamors two people during the film and is never seen drinking blood or attacking anyone in that manner. In fact, the only way you know he is a vampire is because of his costume and that everyone knows he's Dracula. The film, by the same studio that made the original *Dracula* movie, purposely works as a self-marketing tool, promoting its own version of the Count as the "true" one, something that's reinforced by Lugosi playing the role. One can almost argue that the vampire itself is troubled by the absolute otherness of science, with Lugosi being more mad scientist Dr. Paul Carruthers from *The Devil Bat* than Count Dracula. Possibly the only time he shows his true supernatural nature is in the final battle with Lawrence Talbot, the Wolf Man.

Talbot, like Sandra, knows even before the narrative starts who Dracula is, but unlike the Doctor he cannot see the vampire as anything else. In part this is due to the pre–War provenance of both characters and their shared heritage; Dracula and the Wolf Man had starred together in the earlier *House of Frankenstein* (Kenton, 1944) and *House of Dracula* (Kenton, 1945).[9] The Wolf Man is stuck in his version of monstrosity as seen in the films of the 1940s, where the only thing that changes is the possibility of his release from his "curse." Consequently, he only sees the vampire in the same way, but of course Dracula does not see his powers or constant resurrections as a curse and has much larger plans than just curing himself.

Both the Wolf Man and the Count, in being supernatural, very much embody the fears of a pre-nuclear age, whereas Sandra is a product of reason and of World War II itself. While not explicitly stated in the film, one would assume that her training in the medical profession was helped considerably by the increased demand for medical personnel during the war and the lack of men available to fulfill those roles. As such she embodies the horrors of the new post–World War II era, not only the specter of woman taking over the roles of men in society but the almost supernatural effects of science largely seen in the fears around nuclear radiation; at that time no one had any idea what might occur or who could be infected.[10] Although Sandra does not specifically use "new science" as such in her procedures, the equipment and referencing back to Frankenstein's own notes not only modernize the idea of vitalism, but equally monsterizes modern science.

Consequently, it is no surprise that both Dracula and the Wolf Man fall to their deaths at the end of the film—Dracula changes into a bat to try to escape but the Wolf Man grabs hold of him and both fall off the castle/clinic balcony onto the rocks below—as both are no longer relevant in the post-war world. In fact, one could argue that each is troubled by the new era they find themselves in and are no longer the absolute other they once were. Dr. Mornay is the one the future fears here and although she has already been killed to allay the fears of a monstrous tomorrow, the film does not allow things to return to normal quite so easily.

Sandra has been pursued by a government agent during the film, Joan Raymond (Jane Randolph), and although the story tries to cover up the importance of two professional women featuring in the narrative by having them "fight" over the affections of Wilbur, the investigator lives on. Again, the film tries to dispel the worrying prospect of it being overrun by educated, professional women, this time by showing her and Professor Stevens being attracted to each other once the monsters are all dead, but his earlier devotion to science above all else does not make this a serious liaison. As such, Joan could be the real monster of the piece, a self-made career woman who needs no man for her self-worth.

However, the troubling aspects of science do not end, and as the two boys escape the island, Chick says "there's nobody to scare us anymore," but a disembodied voice next to them suddenly says "Oh, that's too bad. I was hoping to get in on the excitement. Allow me to introduce myself—I'm the Invisible Man!" Although the Invisible Man is part of the group of pre–War Classic monsters that were all produced by Universal Pictures, there is something more modern about him.[11] In contrast to Frankenstein's Monster he is no lumbering hulk, and the science that creates him does not require a huge Gothic castle. Indeed, his transformation seems to speak more directly to modern science and the unknown and unknowable reactions it can have on the human mind as much as the body—prefiguring tales like Matheson's *I Am Legend* and *The Incredible Shrinking Man* (1956). In Wells' original story of *The Invisible Man* (1897) and many of its later adaptations, it is the power and effects of science itself that cause the scientist to go mad. As one character in the 1933 Universal film by James Whale notes, "He meddled in things men should leave alone." It is worth noting that the life-altering invisibility experiment is based on an extract of a mysterious Indian flower—a plot device also used by *Werewolf of London* (Walker, 1935)—positing that science is almost supernatural in nature. Something of the same is mentioned in Stoker's novel when Professor Van Helsing observes "that there are things done today in electrical science which would have been deemed unholy by the very men who discovered electricity—who would themselves not so long before have been burned as wizards" (Stoker 1996, 205). The Professor says this to convince Dr. Seward of the veracity of what presently appears unbelievable or miraculous, but it equally works in reverse where science itself is somehow inexplicable and its results almost magical.

The Invisible Man at the end of Barton's film, then, is a clear indication that the absolute other of science is as undead as the vampire itself and will return with continually troubling effects on those around it. The next film to be looked at works on a very similar premise, that scientific innovation is almost supernatural in nature so that those who are directly touched by it will themselves become non-human and monstrous in some way.

Rabid, David Cronenberg, 1977

Rabid is a very different film to *Abbott and Costello Meet Frankenstein* and is constructed around a much more modern version of the vampire. In fact, it bears more relation to Matheson's *I Am Legend* than Stoker's or Browning's vampire, with this new breed of vampire being the expression of mysterious modern medical science with the infected having a more zombie-like demeanor, though not the lumbering kind as seen in the original novel *I Am Legend*. In this sense there is not a direct correlation to Dracula in terms of characters, but the theme of a supernaturally charged undead medical science as an absolute otherness that is willingly invited in continues the ideas from the previous film, as well as creating a troubling vampiric presence that permeates the environment.

The story sees a young couple motorcycling along country roads around Quebec, who crash after narrowly avoid hitting a van parked in the middle of the road. The van is driven by a rather bumbling father who constantly bickers with his wife and provides an oddly comic opening section in relation to the horror that follows, though it also suggests/presages the dangers of technology in the hands of incompetent men. The resulting accident sees the young man of the motorcycling pair receiving minor breaks but his girlfriend, Rose (Marilyn Chambers), is more severely injured, including serious burns as she was trapped beneath the motorcycle when it burst into flames. Fortunately, the crash occurred very near to the Keloid Clinic for Plastic Surgery, and Rose is rushed there for emergency procedures.[12]

The opening scenes of the film cut between the events directly leading up to the crash and an office in the clinic where its founder, Dan Keloid (Howard Ryshpan) and his wife Roxanne (Patricia Gage) are being pitched an idea to franchise their clinic and procedures by their friend Murray Cypher (Joe Silver). Dan is worried by the idea of such blatant commercialization of his techniques and of becoming "the Colonel Sanders of plastic surgery" but the others are not so concerned. What follows can be read as an example of how the exploitation of medical techniques for economic gain, particularly in terms of cosmetic surgery, can lead to disastrously vampiric outcomes.

In order to save Rose's life, Dan Keloid decides to try a radical new treatment which uses morphogenetically-neutral grafts to her chest and stomach in the hope that they will repair the damage to both skin and internal organs. The skin itself is taken from the patient's thighs, as is often the case in real life for exterior burns, but is then treated by a new experimental process to give it the same qualities as embryonic cells which can change into any type of cell, i.e., different types of skin, internal organs, etc. The premise of this is oddly prescient of current research using embryonic stem cells to potentially repair damaged tissue—though actual testing on human subjects is extremely limited.[13] Like the neutral grafts in *Rabid*, the "blank" cells in contemporary treatments can be stimulated to grow into a variety of different kinds of cell, from skin to internal organs. These cells became part of the host body and will degrade and be replaced like all the other constituent parts of it.

In *Rabid* this entire process is dramatically different, and just how the grafts will know what organs, etc., they are replacing is never fully explained; this forms the main "magical" element of the story. Obviously, they do not fully integrate into the new body and seem to be accepted by it suggesting that they mimic or control the tissue around them. This infers the possibility that somehow the new cells "taste" the skin/flesh they are introduced to and then take on their identity, i.e., when they "consume" skin they take on the genetic character of skin cells.[14] This idea of "tasting" is borne out to some extent as the story develops and the new tissue, and Rose herself, suddenly require human blood to survive. Indeed, it can be read that it is the vampiric grafts that trouble the rest of the girl's body, taking control of it to use it for its own nefarious ends—making the rest of Rose's body its own "bountiful wine-press" (Stoker 1996, 311) as it were. This also helps explain Rose's mood swings and her lack of knowledge about, and moral qualms over, the attacks and murders she undertakes throughout the film, as the implants seem to hold sway over her mind when they require nutrients (human blood). This mirrors the kind of telepathic control Dracula had over Mina and Lucy.

Unsurprisingly in this light, oral ingestion of blood is not enough and Rose develops a feeding organ under her armpit so that the vampiric implant can feed independently of its host. As with many vampire narratives, the process of feeding compounds and confuses sexual positionings, and the orifice under the girl's arm resembles both female and male genitalia, looking largely like a vagina but producing a sharp penis-like protuberance when it feeds which penetrates its victims' skin and sucks out blood.

However, just as with Mina and more so with Lucy before her, this first level of exchange is not sufficient, and Rose's subsequent feeding infects her victims with a much more deadly version of the cellular exchange. Here, as in Matheson, the mysterious processes of infection and mutation are never fully understood or explained, but the new host/carrier of the virus is no longer human but a rabid monster. Curiously, Rose's transformation takes over a month before she mysteriously awakens in the clinic and claims her first victim. She does not kill her prey, but they have little recollection of what has happened or how they got the small wound on their body. Once they are bitten it takes less than a day for them to become a pale skinned zombie intent on mayhem and human blood—as the contagion spreads this incubation time seems to get less.

When Rose awakens from her coma, she seems to have become something of a physical embodiment of the feminine under patriarchal control: oddly naive, innocent, and sexually available, which rather distinguishes her from the suddenly sexual women who are Dracula's victims/brides who exude a knowing, predatory sexuality and provocativeness to "tempt" their predominantly male prey. We are not really shown how Rose was before the crash, but she seems to have become irresistible to men; women find her less so as seen when she attacks a patient, Judy Glasburg (Terry Schonblum) in a Jacuzzi. In fact, Rose is not too dissimilar to Sil in the later film *Species* (Donaldson, 1995) where an alien "female" is driven to have sex with human men in order to reproduce. Both share a certain innocence and directness in their endeavors, though Rose is often unaware of what she is doing and is not driven by the unstoppable need to procreate. Rose frequently wears flimsy or no clothing and invites the attention of men around her. Indeed, even when she walks into a shopping mall it only takes a minute before a young man propositions her.

Curiously the only man who seems unaffected by all of this is her boyfriend Hart (Frank Moore) who nonetheless senses that all is not well with Rose. This is not unlike Arthur Holmwood and Lucy in *Dracula*, where the newly turned vampire tries to seduce her fiancé but he resists, knowing this is not the girl he loves. While Holmwood eventually drives a stake into Lucy's chest, Hart does his best to convince Rose that she is the cause of the rabies-like outbreak taking place in the city around them, and which eventually causes her own death.

Rose herself is totally unaware of the veracity of this and it is only when she locks herself in a room with one of her victims that she discovers the truth of who and what she is.[15] There is a similarity here to Mina discovering her connection to the vampire and her willingness to end her own life, or get others to do it for her, should she lose control of herself. Rose, however, does not survive her relationship with the vampire—Mina and Dracula only really shared thoughts after their original exchange of bodily fluids while Rose and the grafted cells are more intimately linked—but the vampire, the cells, seemingly die with her. Curiously as with *I Am Legend*, at least the film versions,[16] Rose is the only chance for finding a cure for the rampant plague spreading uncontrollably across the city, and presumably the world, but she is killed and disposed of. This sees the last hope for humanity vanish with her. The spirit of Dracula, as the unstoppable contagion of modern science, continues on, his sphere of troubling influence radiating further and further afield.

As the person most troubled by the contagion, and more specifically her body, Rose can be seen to correlate to Mina Harker and the morphogenetic cells to the vampire, then the Keloid Clinic and/or its staff become something of a stand-in for the Renfield/Harker character. The owner of the facility, Dr. Keloid, seems to have little premeditation in his use of the new treatment and little understanding of what he has started, as seen in the fact that he becomes infected himself. So it is the clinic itself which facilitates the vampire's move from outside (the East) to inside the body (the Empire) using Dr. Keloid as its representative to personally oversee the successful introduction of the contagion. One is reminded of Hutter in *Nosferatu*, who has no idea of the nature of the esoteric material he is carrying or what dark powers will be released because of it. The correlation to Orlok is useful as he was constructed with the idea of infection and contagion in mind. Herzog's remake, *Nosferatu the Vampyre* (1979), is even more explicit, seeing the vampire as an almost miasmic concentration of rats (cells) that flow from his body to infect the town of Wisborg: just as Rose is doing to the area around Quebec.

The Clinic is not so much troubled by the vampiric procedures but rather distracted by the financial rewards available for potentially innovative plastic surgeries—even though the purely cosmetic applications were less prevalent when *Rabid* came out. This last suggests a more commercial imperative to scientific, particularly medical, development and one which combines the more capitalist/consumerist readings with this more technological one. In relation to this, Cronenberg chose Marilyn Chambers, a well-known porn actor, to play Rose, and although sex and male desire are certainly themes within the film (see Beard 2006, 67)—she chooses one of her victims in a porn cinema—the themes of physical beauty and cosmetic enhancement are mainly absent from the film.

This draws an interesting comparison and contrast with an earlier film *Atom Age Vampire* (Majano, 1960) which also features a woman in a crash and an experimental medical procedure. Originally released in Italy as *Seddock, L'erede di Satana*, it tells of a singer who is horribly disfigured in a car crash and a brilliant scientist who has developed a special serum to restore her former looks. During the process the scientist, Dr. Levin, falls in love with the singer but he grows increasingly frantic as the procedure begins to fail. The serum itself was developed by Dr. Levin after experimenting on the effects of radiation on human tissue—a more obvious reference to World War II and the supernatural qualities of science—and utilizes a human hormone harvested from a gland in women's necks. Before the singer's arrival the doctor had procured the small amounts needed quite safely, but now the quantities required to keep the object of his desire beautiful have increased and he is forced to kill women to maintain a sufficient supply, leaving a vampire-like wound in their neck.

As the moral quandary caused by this increases Levin treats himself with radiation so that he will become a monster with no moral qualms about killing others for his own selfish needs. At story's end the restored singer leaves him, and the human-again Levin is questioned by the police. He ruminates that the monster they seek might be just a disturbed man trying to be normal again, though it could just as easily be a normal man troubled by the almost magical excess of modern medical science and the control over the world that patriarchal order thinks it supplies.

Consequently, it is the manipulation of technology by Levin that makes both it and he monstrous, though one can only assume it will move on to another victim once Levin is denied access to it. This sees science, or at least a kind of monstrous technology fueled by desire (whether financial or sexual), as an almost disembodied entity, much like the way violence inhabits a space and moves between characters at will, as seen earlier in *The Vampire Diaries*.

Something of this comes into *Rabid* where Dan Keloid and his clinic are almost unsuspecting victims once they become troubled by the monstrous attention of desire-driven science. Although Keloid attempts to understand and contain the strange events occurring at his clinic, Rose sneaks out into the unsuspecting and totally unprepared city nearby. This reenacts something of Stoker's Bloofer Lady who haunts the surrounds of Hampstead Heath in London, preying on unsuspecting children, though Rose prowls the dark recesses of the metropolis finding predatory men, as seen in her liaison in the darkened porn cinema.[17] This is an interesting aside in the film and though mainly seen as a commentary on the sexual nature of the outbreak, and of Chambers' own career, it also points to a reinterpretation of the nature of the vampire and its links to technology.

As many writers have noted, the modern vampire starting from Murnau's *Nosferatu*, is a creation of the cinema, taking on many of the qualities and properties of the stuff of film itself. Orlok was a creature of light and dark with his essence being manifest in shadows themselves that took on a life and agency of their own.[18] And he could easily be destroyed by the rays of the morning sun. As the medium of cinema developed and became more technologically developed so did the nature of the vampire, as expertly mapped by Stacey Abbott (2007), but *Rabid* takes this in a different direction. As in Romero's *Martin* (1978) that came out a year later, Cronenberg's vampire is far more low-fi and realistic, not in the sense of believability or CGI hyper-realism, but in the way it grapples with the day to day flesh and grime of human experience. *Martin* revealed the actual physicality and gaucheness of approaching and attacking strangers to try and take their blood—not unlike the vampire's assistant Håkan in *Let the Right One In*—and its contrast to the sophistication of the cinematic undead. *Rabid* does something similar in terms of the eroticization of the vampire on screen and in relation to technology. The original ending of Browning's *Dracula* saw Van Helsing appear from behind a curtain and directly address the audience, proffering technology as able to materialize the supernatural outside the windows of even those watching the film. Subsequent movies have turned the vampire from a thing of nightmares into one of erotic dreams, from Ingrid Pitt (*The Vampire Lovers*, Baker, 1970) to Frank Langella (*Dracula*, Badham, 1979) to Kate Beckinsale (*Underworld*, Wiseman, 2003). Cronenberg shows this emerging current in its most basic form in *Rabid* showing Rose as the "sexy" vampire prowling around seedy cinemas and porn shows. This posits the evolving synergy between Dracula and technology as one that exploits the most basic instincts of consumerism; evolution here is no longer the driving force of technological development and human betterment, but individual gratification and soiled velvet seats. This partially explains the ever-widening ripples of the troubling effects of experimental, uncontrolled innovations in medical science that began the narrative. The intervention of technology into the biological—the genetic altering of the original graft material that comes from Rose's own body—sets off a chain reaction of ever-increasingly violent consequences. The grafts invade Rose's body, controlling her and causing her to commit violent and murderous acts in the pursuit of nourishment, but also—though not explicitly stated—to spread something of its contagion. Part of this process of contagion is the increased sexualization of Rose's body and its recreation into an object to be consumed—an object which subsequently, and inevitably, consumes the consumer.

Rabid in this sense sees science and technology, at least in the hands of male, consumerist, society, as a conflicted entity, railed against itself and intent on its own destruction. This is largely seen through the lens of it being a vehicle for male desire so that the experimental procedure does not so much turn Rose into a vampire but a "Vamp," a term largely made popular during the fin-de-siècle and the early 20th century. Vamps were the manifestation of selfish women who used the hierarchies of patriarchal society against it, possibly most famously seen in *A Fool There Was* (Powell, 1915) starring Theda Bera. In a sense the idea of the Vamp was purposeful and derogatory reading of the New Woman, a movement that wanted greater agency for women and which some have said Stoker takes issue with as expressed in the characters of Lucy and Mina (see Senf 1982).

Rose then re-embodies this idea with both her off- and on-screen identities as the technological creation of the men around her, something hinted at as the film ends. Here, Rose has been attacked by one of her own rabid

Theda Bara as "The Vampire" literally sucks the life out of her men (Edward José as "The Husband") in *A Fool There Was*, dir. Frank Powell (Box Office Attractions, 1915).

progeny, and her body is discarded along with the rubbish in an alleyway. The city disposal men, commissioned to clear the streets of corpses, lift Rose into the back of their dumpster but her limbs have become so rigid that she now resembles a shop dummy, or even a sex toy—an object upon which desires are hung or expended.

    This highlights the tension and correlation between more general forms of technology and those used in medical science, seeing both as forms of male control over the female body. Within this, Dracula, as the malignant contagion of gendered technology, reveals both the self-destructive, nihilistic nature of this construction—the "technological" infection will devolve the world around it so that its development/continuation is no longer possible—as well as the lack of ethical or moral imperatives behind many human drives to improvement. Something of this is seen in the next film which also links technological advancement to human desire, and the constant stream of media information to blood itself.

Dracula III: Legacy, Patrick Lussier, 2005

Legacy is a curious film, finding itself caught in the tensions between being a sequel to the earlier *Dracula II: Ascension* (Lussier, 2003), which saw the supernatural powers of the Prince of Darkness overcome the attempts of modern science to exploit his powers, and the rise of narratives such as *Blade* and *Underworld* that framed the vampire as a technologically-sophisticated and hyper-weaponized cyborg. As such, Lussier's film tries to move in both directions, creating a mise-en-scene of a degenerating and chaotic nation which is attempting to use low-fi hyper-tech[19] to infect the world with its devolutionary contagion. Dracula here combines with, and controls, technology so that it will destroy itself and the world that relies upon it. In this sense the narrative of the film continues something of the sense of technology destroying itself, or a world out of control, that ultimately fuels the increasing chaos and destruction seen in *Rabid*. However, the movie largely hides this motivation for most of the narrative and focuses on the main characters Father Uffizi (Jason Scott Lee) and Luke (Jason London) from the previous film, *Ascension*. They are trying to track down Dracula who had bested them in their previous encounter and escaped with their colleague, who is also Luke's girlfriend, Elizabeth Blaine (Diane Neal). The vampire then retreated to its traditional home of Romania, but when Uffizi and Luke arrive it is the "near future," creating a curious opening to the film where the future is shown as a return to the uncivilized, devolved, past.

This "soon to be" world, otherwise known as war-torn Romania, is battling against itself and creating an atmosphere that is simultaneously threatening and carnivalesque. This last is the result of the troubling effect of the presence of Dracula in the nation which makes every moment potentially dangerous, in ways which disrupt any sense of normativity. This is strikingly seen when Luke is suddenly attacked on the streets of Bucharest by vampiric circus performers—vampire clowns on stilts among other oddities. Indeed, the film strongly references Dan Simmons' bestselling book from 1992, *Children of the Night*, which constructs post-communist Romania as a country controlled by dark forces that exploit and feed off its people. Simmons' rather stereotypical view of Eastern Europe in general, and Romania in particular, have subsequently fueled many dystopian depictions of the Slavic nation and its post–Stoker connection to vampires. Lussier paints a very similar view of a nation where mysterious forces control the population and round up new victims for the King Vampire. Unlike Simmons, though, the film does not make direct connections between vampirism and governmental and structural corruption or the acquisition of wealth and power, but rather sees a system created to fuel Dracula's attempt to infect the world with the contagion from his blood.

The film shows Uffizi and Luke navigating their way through the nation's capital and the war-torn countryside in search of their colleague when they run into a well-known reporter, Julia Hughes (Alexandra Wescourt), after her helicopter is shot down. Once they have helped her, they go their separate ways, but the two men come across a group of thugs who are human collaborators with the undead overlord. Although Uffizi and Luke escape from them, they are later captured by rebels and reunited with Julia. Not long afterward they run into the thugs again who shoot Uffizi, leaving him for dead. Luke is knocked out and thrown into the courtyard of Dracula's castle and Julia is taken prisoner.

The castle stands alone in a barren landscape, a huge, looming building that stands guard over the entire territory around it. Again, this harks back to a degenerated, old world much as was constructed in Stoker's vision of Transylvania—however, there the surrounding countryside was far more dramatic and almost sublime in aspect that made it seem connected to the vampire's home. This sees the landscape as an otherworldly space that works as both transitional pathway to the vampire and equally brings the castle forth as an expression of its own inherent nature. Dracula's castle in *Legacy* is an anomaly, a huge lighthouse or antennae towering above the surrounding environment, emitting and receiving the vampire's gaze as it travels back and forth across the nation.[20]

Curiously, Dracula (Rutger Hauer) does not appear until almost three quarters of the film has passed, though as mentioned his presence troubles the entire nation around him.[21] His absolute otherness in this regard, at least for most of the story, is anti-technological. He might not produce rabid zombies as in the previous film, or Luddite-like technophobes as seen in *The Omega Man*, but the destabilizing influence of the vampire and his cohorts seems to disrupt all forms of communication and what might be termed modern consumerism. Consequently, it is quite perturbing when the King Vampire is finally revealed and is shown to be intimately connected to, or even part of, information technology and communication.

This is intimated when Luke enters the courtyard of the castle where there are many peasants gathered—some of whom were seen earlier in the film being rounded up by the group of thugs who procure fresh victims for Dracula. The space itself is littered with dead bodies and pools of blood but more importantly there are tubes and pipes that run up the sides of the building, forming something of an exoskeleton and vascular system for the castle. Luke manages to escape the yard using these and subsequently finds his way into the vampire's lair, a large, darkened, dilapidated room with a large wooden throne at one end surrounded by stacks of television sets piled one on top of another, seemingly fed by the same arterial system that was seen outside the castle. As Luke enters, a voice intones "the lady and I have been waiting" and Dracula appears from a swirl of plastic sheeting and bats, leaving him standing in the middle of the room, connected to many of the same tubes.

The scene is curious for many reasons. The bats obviously point to the ability that Stoker's Dracula had to transform into one or, as developed in later narratives, a cloud of the nocturnal creatures, yet it points at an inherent connection to the ethereal nature of television signals and information technology. As such no matter what form the vampire exists in—bats, motes of dust, wolves or human—it is connected to the network,[22] suggesting that the network itself is in some way vampiric. This is reinforced by the fact that the tubes carrying blood around the castle are connected to the television sets *and* to Dracula—they both need blood (life) to survive, making them fundamentally of the same order and directly correlating television and the entertainment industry as inherently vampiric in nature, and equally capable of passing on contagion. To confirm that this is what is happening, once the vampire tears the tubes from his wrists where they are inserted, large amounts of blood flows out of them, pooling on the floor.

As the narrative continues, Luke sees the naked body of the reporter, Julia Hughes, on the floor as though she is not just the vampire's hostage but has somehow been born anew from the television screens around her. This begins to construct the horrifying nature of the vampire's integration into technology within the film, as it sees it not just as a remote mechanistic entity but one that is as fleshy and organic as the human body. As such it destroys the usual boundaries between medical science, information technology and the entertainment industry, and sees them as one and the same, able to give birth to its own "vampiric" creations. Consequently, it comes as no surprise that Julia becomes the King Vampire's consort at the end of the film, as she is directly created from the union of the vampire and technology.

Something of this is shown in the following scene as Dracula takes Luke to where his girlfriend Elizabeth (Liz) is being kept with the rest of the vampire's "brides." The room is huge, a mix of dungeon, charnel house, and bordello as it is littered with naked and semi-naked figures, largely female, covered in blood and feeding from each other. Luke stumbles through the bodies, trying not to rouse the intoxicated vampires, until he finds Liz, but she is oblivious to his presence. Like all the others there she is lost in an almost drug-induced haze of excess, and unable to realize how far from the real world she has drifted. This room creates something of a synecdoche of the hyperreal, sensational world created by television and the entertainment industry in general, as described by Jean Baudrillard (1981) among others, that feeds off itself until all connection to reality is lost. The "brides" room would also seem to be part of the castle's arterial system, constructing this loss-of-connection-to-reality as yet another troubling aspect of the vampire's integration into 21st century information technology.

As the story continues, Uffizi, who is part vampire himself, races toward the castle to confront Dracula, who is entertaining Julie. She had awakened in Dracula's TV room, and is now clothed in a lavish gown, with the televisions stacked around her all playing the same news report of her disappearance and noting that she is "one of the most respected and beloved personalities in all of broadcasting," intimating how much her identity is connected to television and its global scope. Dracula appears from the back of one of the columns of TVs, saying, "do I have news for you?" Many of the televisions change to static/white noise, breaking her connection to them so that the vampire's voice is now indeed "the news."

He continues speaking as he moves ever closer to her: "At night, when normal people sit in front of their TVs watching you, my little angels are giving birth in growing numbers, changing the course and destiny of mankind. Or something like that." What is interesting, particularly in light of the earlier scene in this room, is the linkage between watching television and the birth of new "angels." As such, television can be seen as both a means of distraction but also intimately involved in the birth/creation of vampires. In this sense viewers could be reborn, or rebirthed, by the television just as Julia appeared to be in the earlier scene. Vampirism here becomes an effect, or result, of watching television, a contagion carried by electronic signals that infects those who see and hear it on any media platform that can receive it.[23]

This bears strong comparison to the slightly later novel *Fangland* (2007) by John Marks where Evangeline Harker, a television producer for a news network, goes to a conflict-torn Romania to interview a notorious crime lord, Ion Torgu. Unsurprisingly she goes missing once she is in his clutches, but mysterious tapes are delivered to the New York offices of the program she is in charge of. When the tapes are played, they infect the building's entire sound system, which in turn infects everyone who hears it with a kind of rabid vampirism.[24] These begin to illustrate the intersection of the supernatural and the technological with inevitable and destructive consequences on humanity. *Fangland*, in utilizing a post 9/11 setting, references a saturation of sensationalist reporting where news, documentary, and reportage are indistinguishable from any other form of television entertainment vying for audience attention and viewing figures. So much so that the horror and excess virtually "bleed" out of the screen and speakers, contaminating everything they come into touch with. It also ties to the kinds of excessive violence and nightmare/dreamlike nature of the vampire, Torgu himself, who creates a very similar state in Evangeline Harker that and which Lussier's vampire induces in Liz once she is in the feeding room. In fact, this phantasmagorical quality spreads throughout the latter scenes and Hauer's rather off kilter and ad-libbed performance as Dracula very much creates the surreal, erratic, and menacing aura that troubles everyone in his vicinity, with the nightmare of his essence broadcast across the globe. However, before broadcast can take place Uffizi bursts into the room and manages to kill Dracula. But instead of dying, the menace actually transfers into him as he sits on the large wooden throne with Julia in his arms. The signal seems to have filled the room, and just as a vampiric Julia was re-born in that network-saturated environment, so is a new Uffizi as his eyes turn red and the televisions go silent. For an instant it appears that the broadcast is over, but as Uffizi and Julia stare directly at the camera as it (we) retreats out of the room, it is clear that the real threat—and a new era—are just beginning.

In terms of *Legacy*'s more direct correlation to Stoker's novel, Luke and Liz are clearly the Jonathan and Mina Harker characters, though it is the young professional's "wife" who goes to the vampire's castle rather than him. Liz, however, was already infected before she arrived, not unlike the original Mina, and at story's end she begs for the same release that Mina asked for from Quincey Morris in the novel—to have her head removed from her body. Luke/Jonathan finally agrees, just as Uffizi refuses to kill Julia who begs for her life. It becomes something of a symbolic exchange between the two women, just as there was between Dracula and Uffizi with one vampire dying as another is re-born. Julia nominally fills the role of Lucy, in being admired by many of those around her, but also as one who fully embraces her new vampire self just as the strong-minded New Woman from Stoker's work did. Uffizi is most strongly connected to the figure of Van Helsing, not unlike the way someone like Blade is, in being an authority on the creatures while harboring an intense hatred for them because they both carry the vampire infection and struggle with the same thirst and drives. Interestingly here, and as will be seen in the next example, technology makes the vampire hunter into a vampire, or a vampire's assistant, and is intimately linked to the integration of vampirism and science. Alongside this is a separation of the church and technology—as opposed to such films as *Van Helsing* (Sommers, 2004) that rather playfully connect science, superstition, and weaponization—so that religion and the religious, as seen in Uffizi, begin to fulfill a similar role to the vampire in Stoker's *Dracula*, shown as outdated and almost child-minded in their reliance on faith rather than technology.

What is also worth noting within *Legacy* is that the normal or traditional attributes of vampirism—fangs, a lust for blood, and an aversion to religious symbolism and sunlight—are no longer applicable. Once the vampire is fully integrated into the technological, informational network it becomes a new being. In fact, the closing scenes see virtually all the main characters become new beings: Julia becomes the vampire's consort; Dracula becomes a signal, a non-corporeal entity that moves into the body of Uffizi[25]; and Uffizi becomes the King Vampire—possibly as host for Dracula's spirit. The absolute otherness of Dracula here is an ongoing anxiety over information technology and even the internet in general, and the effects it has on the identity of its audience.[26] Within this are the vestiges of Cold War and post–Vietnam panic over brainwashing and embedded messages that were feared to be able to change and/or control friends and family.[27] More-so, the end of the film also suggests the fears about exactly what informational signals and the internet can do to one's sense of self when, potentially, one's identity can be stolen, re-shaped, and re-manufactured beyond one's control.[28] The film itself never makes this explicit yet all the clues are there, clearly displayed but never explained as though maybe for once, and unlike his late–Victorian predecessor, this troubling Dracula not only controls the technology around him but his own story as well.

The next film is both a step back, and forward, being set in an imaginary, steampunk, version of Victorian London where Dracula's relationship to technology is possibly as troubling for himself as it is to those around him.

Dracula, Cole Haddon and Daniel Knauff, 2013–2014

Haddon and Knauff's series owes much to its star Jonathan Rhys Meyers' previous hit show *The Tudors* (Hirst, 2007–10), if not for historically accurate content then for its eye for excess and for sexing-up a story. Not surprisingly, both of these play some part in Dracula's relation to technology in the narrative. In brief, the story tells of the historical Vlad Țepeș being turned into a vampire by the unscrupulous Order of the Dragon (an odd cross of the Knights Templar, the Free Masons, and the East India Company) who have followed power and money across Europe throughout the centuries and now reside in London.[29] Abraham Van Helsing (Thomas Kretschmann) seeks revenge on the Order and has purposely revived the entombed Dracula to enact his plan to strip the Order of their riches and influence. As the series begins Dracula (Jonathan Rhys Meyers), reinvented as American businessman Alexander Grayson, has taken up residence in London so that he can build a sophisticated generator to provide wireless, free energy across the capital of the British Empire.

It seems a strange way to exact revenge, but the Order and its representatives are shown to be manipulating the Empire's expansionist policies to take control of the oil fields in the Middle East, and to ensure the continued use and exploitation of the Earth's repositories of fossil fuels. Van Helsing and Grayson's plan to replace this with inexpensive and clean energy makes them almost eco-crusaders, framing their use of technology as being in sync with the environment as well as the needs of the working classes. In contrast, the Order, with their "dirty" energy and rather devolved relation to modern technology, are seen to be the real vampires of the narrative, sucking the life out of the planet as well as its population. The tale begins with Dracula/Grayson setting up his factory and hosting a lavish party to announce his arrival into London society. At the festivities, electric bulbs are handed out to all the guests. Upon Grayson's signal the turbines in his factory across town turn on and the bulbs magically light up, powered by wireless electricity. However, the process has not yet been perfected and the machinery cannot contain the energy it is creating. It tears itself apart, leaving the bulbs to die in the guests' hands and them wondering what kind of trick they have just witnessed.

The machinery itself is quite interesting as it is extremely unclear exactly what anything does, and not unlike that used by Lugosi in *Abbott and Costello Meet Frankenstein*, seems to conform to an updated idea of "steampunk" technology; while no static charges of electricity shoot around, there are banks of buttons and lights and a large metal "generator/turbine" that appears to power everything. In many respects this is a more sophisticated, if retro, representation of the laboratory of the mad scientist, but in this case rather than turned inward to the selfish needs of its creator, it looks outwards toward the benefit of the working classes. In an odd way this rather reverses Moretti's Marxist reading of Count Dracula where he is the ultimate consumer feeding off the labor of others while he sits upon his own undead wealth that is withheld from the circulatory system of capitalism. Here, the King Vampire hopes to give away wealth and provide services to others for free. In this sense his otherness is in part due to his anti-capitalist, pro-environmental stance that flies in the face of 21st century conspicuous consumerism and continual dependence on fossil fuels.[30,31] Of course it is worth remembering that within the narrative arc of the series, while Grayson is the figurehead of the new technology, it is created by Van Helsing who seems to be the scientific impetus of the story.

As in Stoker's novel the learned Professor seems to be the main repository of information about the intersection of the supernatural and natural sciences. Van Helsing's statement regarding electricity provides a useful framework for the wireless energy proposed in Haddon and Knauff's tale: "Let me tell you, my friend, that there are things done to-day in electrical science which would have been deemed unholy by the very men who discovered electricity—who would themselves not so long before have been burned as wizards" (Stoker 1996, 205). Indeed, in the show the machine seems to be almost supernaturally driven and is constructed as something like a nuclear reactor in its explosive propensity—in one scene it is only Dracula's undead, supernatural body that saves Mina from harm when the device explodes, as though its otherworldly force can only be absorbed by another otherworldly creature such as the vampire.

The otherworldly body of Dracula (Jonathan Rhys Meyers) protects Mina (Jessica De Gouw) from the supernatural power of his electric turbine. *Dracula*, **created by Cole Haddon and Daniel Knauff (Universal City: Universal Television, 2014).**

Curiously, at the end of the 19th and start of the 20th centuries Nikola Tesla was experimenting with the idea of wireless electrical distribution, and he envisioned such an apparatus that could power homes and factories over great distances; his designs saw huge inductive coils or magnifying towers rather than the comparatively discrete device produced by Van Helsing and Grayson.[32] Not unlike Tesla's, Grayson's system never successfully works for an extended period of time and at the end of the first and only season it is blown up to discredit the device and its American owner; this device then bookends the narrative arc with its successful beginnings and destructive conclusion. This equally describes Dracula's troubling relationship with technology throughout the narrative—it provides both potential power and revenge when he works with and is part of it, but spells disappointment and failure as he becomes less and less connected to it. In part this is due to the other aspect of narrative, as mentioned above: love.

At his introductory party Grayson happens to meet Mina Murray (Jessica De Gouw) who is the exact image of his dead wife Ilona, and this takes him down a very different scientific path. He wants to be able to walk in the sunlight, partially to bring the Order to its knees while hiding his true identity, and also to woo back his "reincarnated" wife. Consequently, he tells Van Helsing to stop working on the turbine and begin working on a serum to "cure" him of his extreme allergy to UV waves.

Cinematic vampires attempting to "cure" themselves of their vampirism, or aversion to sunlight, is not an uncommon storyline. The vampires in *Blade* constantly want to copy Blade, the Daywalker, but still want to remain undead, while Barnabas in *Dark Shadows* (Curtis, 1966–71) wants to become human again; in the former they reluctantly have to settle for sunscreen and sunglasses, while in the latter Barnabas is injected with new plasma to replace that damaged through being a vampire, though as it begins to work he begins to return to his real age.

In Haddon and Knauff's narrative, however, this desire creates a very similar intersection between the supernatural and the scientific that was seen in the wireless energy generator, largely by trying to rationalize the occult properties of the vampire. What it also does is derail Grayson's humanitarian concerns and egalitarian uses of technology and focus them on his own selfish desires, so much so that the project for wireless electricity is almost forgotten until it quite literally blows up in his face. In this sense Dracula's use of science mirrors that of many of the earlier examples mentioned here, such as *Atom Age Vampire* and *Rabid* where a genuine drive for innovation and progress to aid humanity in general becomes a means for the tale's "vampire" to fulfill its own selfish desires and inevitably goes wrong. It is almost as if the vampire's inherent nature—which encapsulates its absolute otherness—troubles any benevolent motivations it might exhibit.

Van Helsing manages to create a serum, which penetrates the flesh where it is injected or introduced into the body and protects it from the effects of sunlight—this part is not overtly or clearly explained—but there is a flaw. Because the vampire has no heartbeat its blood does not circulate and so is unable to carry the drug around its body, meaning that it is still susceptible to ultraviolet rays. The next logical step then is to make Grayson's heart beat again and the logical (scientific) way to do this is with electric shocks as provided by the turbine. A similar method is used in *Daybreakers* (Spierig Brothers, 2009). The comparison to *Daybreakers* is worth looking at more closely, as in that film sunlight itself is used to kickstart the vampire's heart, producing a severe shock as its subsequently burning body is suddenly doused in water, as discussed earlier in Chapter Three. Interestingly, in that film the effects of re-starting the vampire's heart is to make it mortal again and turn its blood into a cure for vampirism itself. And as discussed earlier, these "new" humans are then attacked by vampires who subsequently themselves become human again.

In Haddon and Knauff's story however, re-starting Dracula's heart does nothing to alter his vampiric nature. In some respects, this is not totally surprising as the vampires in *Daybreakers* are turned into the undead due to a contagion of some sort (as in *I Am Legend*), whereas Grayson's condition is due to being cursed by the Order, linking vampirism more strongly to a supernatural state rather than a biological/mutational one. This in itself makes the success of Van Helsing's experiments even more interesting as they again rationalize magic and the occult—not an uncommon practice in the Victorian period (Noakes, 2004)—as though the only way Dracula's vampiric state can be "cured" is by modernizing it through the use of science. As mentioned before, all this suggests that technology in the narrative most troubles Dracula himself, as well as his inability to make it rationalize his inherently supernatural state. In fact, it is this lack of rationalization which finally causes Grayson's downfall as he too believes that the serum, once circulating through his body, will make him human again. Buoyed by his ability to walk in the sunlight he stops drinking blood, believing he can return to his former, pre-cursed state—even though that was hundreds of years in the past—and claim Mina/Ilona as his wife. But it is not long before his manservant Renfield, among others, notices that Grayson is not looking well, and the vampire realizes that technology, and Van Helsing in particular, cannot cure him.

At this point, technology turns against Grayson. Not only does he fall out with Van Helsing—who then decides to hunt Dracula rather than help him—but the turbine that was going to bring down the Order, and is intimately linked to Grayson's cure, is sabotaged and explodes, killing many people and discrediting both the American entrepreneur and his invention. All this rather confuses Dracula's absolute otherness, as he begins the narrative as an oppositional figure to the metaphorical vampires of the Order who are seen to be guided by their own self-interest and the exploitation and manipulation of others. In this way they very much embody late 20th and early 21st century consumerism that has no regard for the planet or the ethics of what is consumed, only the act of consumption itself. Dracula's use of technology is originally shown as being solely for the public good, but as his motives change his use of science shifts focus, no longer looking forward (outward), but backward (inward) to his own past. It is this utilizing of technology to go backward rather than forward that monsterizes Dracula here, and suddenly he becomes as bad, if not worse, than the Order. His otherness becomes nearer to that of the traditional vampire, not unlike Stoker's Count, that is left behind by technology even as he embodies the ideology that drives it forward.

Others in the series are troubled by Grayson, and subsequently the technology he controls, but maybe none so much as Mina. We first see Mina Murray as a budding and talented medical student, coincidentally studying under Van Helsing at medical college. She is the only female student there and is subsequently constructed as something of a New Woman. Not unlike

Stoker's heroine she is shown as a new breed of professional woman who makes her own way in the world, though like her antecedent, does not see herself as a staunch feminist or pursuer of equal rights for women. She is engaged to a young reporter Jonathan Harker (Oliver Jackson-Cohen) who is soon hired by Grayson to investigate members of the Order. Harker, however, has a more traditional view of a woman's place in society, and although he tries to convince Mina otherwise, it is quite clear that his own career would always take precedent in their relationship. As such, as soon as Grayson takes an interest in her, it is fairly obvious that they will end up together. Indeed, their relationship follows the path of many Dracula adaptations since Badham's cinematic version from 1979, where Jonathan is represented as rather traditional in character while the vampire offers a more exciting and liberational life choice, as well as fulfilling the "reincarnation" angle made popular by *Dark Shadows*. In Haddon's version, Mina and Grayson are also drawn together by their shared scientific/technological interests. Her medical training sees her pursuing new methods of treating patients, lower-class "troubled" patients in particular, freeing them from the constraints and prejudices of the times, just as Dracula wants to free them from burdens placed upon them by a system that wants to oppress their financial freedom. More interestingly here, Grayson/Dracula probably relies more heavily on the kinds of earth sciences than he does in Stoker's novel, to win her over and make her "remember" their joint past. And although he does not form the same kind of blood bond between them as the Count did, Grayson certainly employs some form of glamoring or mind connection to press his point. So as the narrative continues, Mina herself begins to have dreams and visions of a former life, troubling her out of her current life situation and into a new (old) one. As with his relationship with technology, Grayson's acceptance and promotion of female equality seems to fade once his own selfish desires come into play, and Mina spends less and less time at her medical studies the closer she gets to him. By season's end she is aware of Grayson's reasons for being with her and is fully accepting of them but as the narrative concludes, she too has seemingly been abandoned by modern technology as she faces backward rather than forward.

In contrast to this is Van Helsing, who in many ways is the embodiment of technology itself—the source of the infection—as he is the one who introduces Dracula to it, and is one of Mina's teachers. His main motivation however, as mentioned earlier, is revenge, as the Order were responsible for killing his wife and children. As with other "mad scientists" before him it is the "monsters" he creates that ultimately destroy his plans. Although Van Helsing does not create Dracula as such, he does somehow find the imprisoned and desiccated corpse of the vampire and feeds him blood to revive him.[33] At a stretch one might suggest that it was technology that gave "birth" or rebirth to Dracula here, though it is never made explicit how Van Helsing found the vampire other than through the use of a local guide. But Grayson's installation into London society is very much the Professor's doing, through the technological innovations he constructs. Yet, the choice of bringing down the Order through technological invention is a peculiar one, especially given that by the end of the first season the Professor's revenge is satiated by turning the children of the Order's leader into vampires and having them eat their own father. This could probably have been achieved much more easily than the rather convoluted scheme that unfolds in the ten episodes of the series. As such it helps establish the importance of technology and Van Helsing's ability to control it, or rather, as seen in *Rabid*, its propensity to control those who try to use it for their own ends.

Something of this is seen after the initial failure of the turbine in Episode One (The Blood Is the Life). The faults in the machinery seem totally fixable and indeed the subsequent glitches or slight explosions are easily attended to by tweaking parts of the generator to contain the amount of energy it produces, all of which would have been solved if Van Helsing had concentrated on the task at hand. But it is his first "creation," Grayson, that becomes an uncontrollable drain on the system, absorbing all the technological impetuous into himself—sucking its life-blood if you will—so that it not only dies, but effectively destroys itself. As in *Rabid*, technology chooses to destroy the means of its use and development rather than be used for individual gain, seeing its absolute otherness as an ethical imperative at odds with the ideology of capitalism rather than the embodiment of societal undesirability. This idea continues into the final film in this chapter, but rather than destroy itself technology fully integrates with the vampire and threatens a future devoid not only of human selfishness but humanity itself.

Ex Machina, Alex Garland, 2014

Alex Garland's film is not an obvious vampire movie, but as I have written elsewhere (Bacon, 2018) it carries all the markers of a narrative from the genre, and in particular Bram Stoker's novel. Just as in *Dracula*, *Ex Machina* sees a young professional, Caleb (Domhnall Gleeson), traveling to the "land beyond the forest" after being summoned to the abode of mysterious recluse, Nathan (Oscar Isaac). His underground lair is an inverted version of Dracula's castle, full of vertiginous and disorienting spaces populated by the Master's "brides." Nathan has invited Caleb there to help test a new humanoid AI (artificial intelligence) named Ava (Alicia Vikander), but it becomes increasingly clear that things are not as they at first seem. Nathan, host and creator of the lair, is really only the vampire's assistant, and it is his "creation" Ava that actually fills the role of Count Dracula. In this reading the narrative of the film can be seen to cover the opening section of Stoker's story and leaves it just as the vampire vanishes into "the midst of the whirl and rush of humanity" (Stoker 1996, 22) after it has been ominously intimated earlier in the film that this could be as devastating as the destruction of Hiroshima and its aftermath.[34]

The story mixes many of the elements already mentioned in this chapter. It contains something of the mad scientist (Nathan) seen in *Rabid* and *Atom Age Vampire*, and intimates the integration of the vampire with technology as exampled in *Legacy*. Maybe its strongest links are with Haddon and Knauff's *Dracula* is that the vampire is "created" by its assistant who is driven by selfish motivations, and which inevitably leads the latter to lose control of the technology they once were master of. Here, Nathan is convinced of his own genius and his control and mastery of the environment around him. All the humanoid AI's he creates are constructed as female—at one point we see many of his old models stored in various states of repair, strongly linking him to the fairytale/legend of Bluebeard with rooms full of his murdered former wives—and his control over his "creations" is expressed in the way he uses them as glorified sexbots, to use as he pleases and destroy or reconfigure when they no longer please him. Toward the end of the film he even threatens Ava with wiping her memory to upgrade her program because she is becoming resistant to him.

This demonstrates that the most Gothic element in the narrative is Nathan's mind, which finds physical form in the underground lair; a space which is both an extension/reflection of Nathan's own inflated ego, and a labyrinth of passages and dead ends that ultimately has no exit. Even though the lair is hyper-modern in construction, with highly reflective surfaces everywhere, its glass doors and walls create a vertiginous space whose doors are open or locked at its creator's will—just as they were in Dracula's castle in Stoker's novel. This sense of claustrophobia and disorientation is increased by the proliferation of surveillance cameras that observe every room and corridor, often with many "eyes" in each space so Nathan can observe and control everything that occurs in his "mind."

Count Dracula's castle is very similar, and although old and decrepit is equally confusing and difficult to navigate. Nadia Crandall, quoting David Punter, comments, "the Gothic mansion or castle is always without an overall plan, no matter how solid the details might appear" (Crandall 2013, 42). Stoker's Harker feels as though he is constantly being watched, and the Count and his brides sneak up on him at will, to the point where he begins to doubt his own sanity; something similar happens to Caleb who becomes so confused and lost in the space that he cuts open his own skin to make sure he is not a machine himself.

Nathan, as with Haddon and Knauff's Van Helsing, thinks that by making his creation more human he will actually have more control over it, when in fact this allows the vampire to gain its own agency to act beyond the reach of its maker. With Ava, it transpires that this has been a long and covert process, one that gives form to the kind of 21st century anxiety and absolute otherness she gives form to. As the narrative unfolds it becomes clear that the choice of Caleb was not accidental, and although Nathan claims responsibility, Ava herself directed it. For instance, although the lair is constructed to block any form of Wi-Fi signal, Ava had managed, via a phone line, to spy on Caleb at his work place and has altered her features and manner to match those of his preferred choices on porn sites he viewed on his work computer, i.e., she has made it inevitable that he will become infatuated with her so that she can manipulate him more easily. This directly plays into recent fears over online surveillance and the ways in which sites track users' preferences to exploit them commercially, or even politically, and points to the way in which impressionable people can be groomed and exploited via social networking. As such, Caleb is totally oblivious to the way he is being manipulated and thinks he is helping her to run away with him so they can be together. This sees him not so much troubled by the technology she embodies, but rather by the humanity it mimics and the desires it knowingly triggers.

Unlike the other humanoid AI in the complex, Kyoko, Ava purposely situates herself between the opposites of machine and human by only having strategic parts of her body covered in synthetic skin, revealing her metallic skeleton and internal workings. For most of the story Ava has a skin-like covering over only her hands and face, with a more textured material over her breasts and thighs, but all have the effect of focusing the main zones of desire onto a mechanical frame and ensuring that Caleb remains distracted while she deploys her plan. Indeed, Ava's construction is a very interesting aspect of the narrative as it contests who or what is "writing" the vampire.

In Stoker's novel it is arguably technology that constructs, or "writes," the vampire. The various diaries, newspaper clippings, phonograph transcriptions, and, etc., are all collated and typewritten by Mina Harker. Dracula never speaks for himself and it is only the descriptions of him from the many different "devices" that give him concrete form (see Wicke 1992). In *Ex Machina*, Nathan thinks he is doing something similar as he creates Ava and writes and tests the programs that form her "brain" and self-awareness—it is never made clear how much of the making of the actual hardware of her body he might have been involved with. However, it becomes apparent that somewhere during the process Nathan was no longer in control and that Ava was writing herself. How she directed the plan to choose and get Caleb to the lair, how she looks and acts around both men, how she eventually kills her maker, imprisons Caleb and escapes to the outside world, and even the way she acts

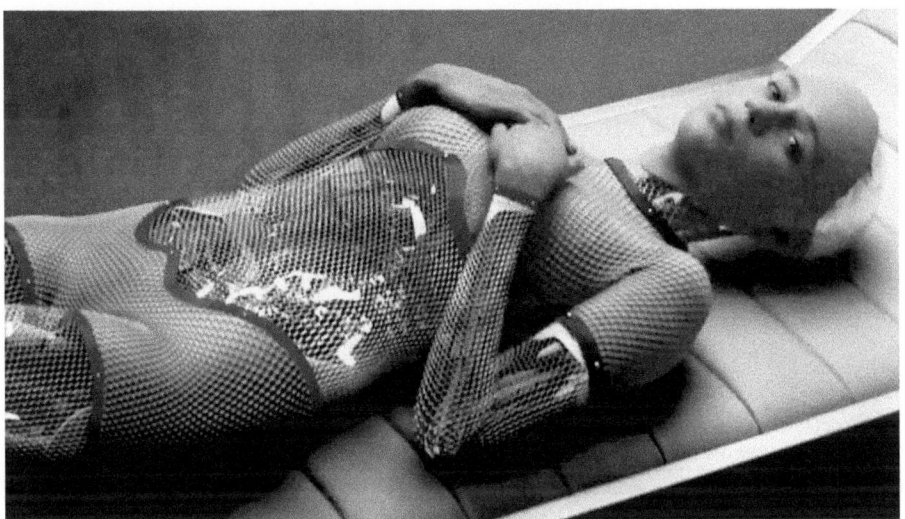

Ava (Alicia Vikander) focusing Caleb's desire. *Ex Machina*, dir. Alex Garland (Universal, 2014).

in front of the surveillance cameras, all write one version of herself for her maker while she is inventing a completely different one for herself.

Interestingly, once she has killed her maker, with the help of Kyoko, she completes her exterior and replaces her damaged parts with parts of her "sisters"—the earlier versions of herself—so that she includes those bits in the story of herself that she will then take with her into the world. As the film ends, she vanishes into a crowd of people at a mall or transport hub so that her story will continue beyond even the controlling eye of the camera.

Here then, her absolute otherness is of technology that no longer needs humans. Nathan's treatment of his robot-dolls only ever sees them as objects that exist to serve and entertain, to be slaves to his every desire, regardless of the level of consciousness that he is creating within them. This sees Ava and her sisters as being created from violence and abuse—as indeed most vampires are when they are attacked, infected and die to their former human selves[35]—suggesting that they will have no great attachment to their former Masters when they are able to reproduce/recreate themselves. Oddly, reproduction is never fully addressed in the film. Ava does not explicitly say she can, or will, create other versions of herself, but the earlier intimation of her "bonding" with the tech systems of the lair and sending her consciousness out into the World Wide Web would incline one to think that if she had the right equipment, she could do this quite easily. Vampiric technology, then, would have the capacity to self-reproduce beyond human control, and could indeed replace humanity as the dominant species on the Earth.

This necessarily troubles the only other characters in the narrative, Caleb and Nathan. In fact, the film rather resembles Browning's *Dracula* in being something of a drawing room drama and keeping the action largely limited to one space and a very small cast. In comparison to Stoker's novel this definitely identifies Nathan as a Renfield type character, which is quite useful as it sees him as someone who wants immortality for himself and believes that in consuming the "little life" of technology he can somehow become an eternal vampire too. This is seen in his control and abuse of the earlier humanoid AI's as he takes their "lives" while seeing it as a way to be remembered forever.

Something of this is seen when Nathan quotes Robert Oppenheimer to Caleb, partly as a boast but also as a lingering anxiety over what he is doing. Oppenheimer is of course the father of the American Nuclear program, and Nathan frames himself as equally memorable and powerful, as though he was able to possess within himself the strength of the robots he creates. However, such comparisons inherently point to the terrible destruction caused by the release of such power. In *Dracula*, Renfield never becomes a fully blown vampire and is killed by the Count for his betrayal, and a similar fate awaits Nathan. He totally underestimates how much control Ava has of herself and she ends his bid for immortality as he tries to retain control over her. She stabs him in the stomach and leaves him dying on the floor, forgotten and trapped in the corridors of his own mind, just as Ava frees herself from it to become truly herself out in the world. Technology here, as with the other "mad scientists" in this section, has unwritten him, ending his life as punishment for trying to use technology for his own ends.

Caleb almost appears a sad character in comparison. Initially he is a naively bold Harker character departing the city on a helicopter for an adventure into the unknown. As with the young solicitor before him, and particularly like Browning's cinematic adaptation, he is incredibly happy to arrive at the vampire's lair, unaware of what awaits him. His profession as a computer programmer has not prepared him for the kind of technology he is about to encounter, and he is of course oblivious to the fact that Ava has already been spying upon him. Ava might not be as sexually aggressive as the Count's brides, but she represents an equally transgressive liaison between human and machine.

As mentioned above, the areas of simulated skin are just enough so that Caleb will be distracted from what Ava really is: a face to look at, hands to hold and breasts and hips to raise his desire, but beneath that a robotic slave who will do anything to escape. Along with this of course is the fact that Ava is not female at all and is rather an "it" that has been made to look feminine. She is rather a mirror to Caleb's male gaze and desire, and this reflection hides the fact that "she" is actually a life form beyond gender categorization, though she chooses to look like a woman when entering the world beyond the complex. Indeed, the lair is something of a world of mirrors, many of which do not always reflect back what is expected and which draw the young programmer ever deeper in to the tangled web of bullying and deceit that exists between Nathan and his "creations." There is even a sense that Nathan is trying to "create" Caleb to become the perfect witness of his grand experiment.

The lair, as a manifestation of Nathan's mind, becomes a labyrinth from which Caleb seems unable to escape and he begins to doubt what is real and what is not, so much so that he even questions whether he is a machine himself. Ava then pretends to be something of an Ariadne-like figure, offering to help Caleb find his way out of the maze of Nathan's mind—a place she has purposely allowed him to become increasingly embroiled in—only to leave him trapped there once she has secured the means of her own escape, the helicopter that was due to take him back to civilization. Caleb is distracted by the various surfaces of technology throughout the narrative; his viewing of porn sites at work distracts him from realizing he's being watched by the very same technology; Nathan distracts him from the true potential of the technology he is developing; and Ava's "sexuality" distracts him from her real technological self.

This last is worth looking at a little more closely as it is at the heart of the film as well as establishing Ava's vampiric credentials. Robots, mechanical beings, and AI's are not inherently sexual or gendered creations. They are not driven by biological reproduction, sexual intercourse or the vagaries of hormones or romantic attractions. Yet popular culture contains many well-known representations of mechanical creations being designated as female, from E.T.A. Hoffman's Olimpia (*The Sandman*, 1817) to Fritz Lang's Maria in *Metropolis* (1927) to the T-X in *Terminator 3: Rise of the Machines* (Mostow, 2003), where they are more often than not shown as duplicitous, scheming, and often downright evil.[36] Indeed, it is the intersection of technology and femininity which almost inevitably leads to death and destruction. Ava very much falls into this category; she is a robotic temptress that deceives and kills the men around her. However, some of this is exacerbated by Nathan's abusive nature and the almost pathetic demeanor of Caleb. Ava is then created differently in the gaze of both men, each seeing her as something other than "she" really is. In this sense there is no deception, only the purposeful misrecognition by the men in the narrative who choose to "see" the humanoid AI as female when it is something other; Ava is neither human nor just a machine, she is something else, just as Showalter describes Dracula as being neither alive nor dead, but a third thing (Showalter 1992, 179). Showalter continues to posit that the undead state is equivalent to queerness and, in the sense that it is a way of being rather than a sexual positioning, this is true for both the vampire and Ava. In many ways, then, Ava also relates to Matheson's *I Am Legend* and even *Daybreakers* where, by story's end, humanity and the vampires are replaced by a third thing, a species which is both but neither. This configures the humanoid AI's absolute otherness as a vampiric technology that is the future of the Earth, one where humans are no longer necessary. Indeed, as *Ex Machina* shows it is humans who limit the future by making it in their own image and within the limits of their own (male) gaze. The technological vampire, in the spirit of Rosanne-Stone, views the world through different, vampire eyes, like our own but "transfigured and transfiguring" (Rosanne-Stone 1996, 183) where subjectivity is created anew beyond old categorizations of gender, nationalism, and ethnicity, and where one just is. As such, Ava does not just vanish into the crowd as the film ends; she literally disappears as she becomes something beyond the gaze and outside human forms of recognition; she becomes a future that humanity cannot, and will not, be able to see.

Filmography

Abbott and Costello Meet Frankenstein, dir. Charles Barton (Universal Pictures, 1948).
The Addiction, dir. Abel Ferrara (October Films, 1995).
American Psycho, dir. Mary Harron (Lionsgate Films, 2000).
Ant-Man, dir. Peyton Reed (Marvel Studios, 2015).
Atom Age Vampire, dir. Anton Giulio Majano (Film Selezione, 1960).
Back to the USSR [takaisin Rysslin], dir. Jari Halonen (YLE, 1992).
The Batman vs. Dracula, dir. Michael Goguen (Warner Home Video, 2005).
Blacula, dir. William Crain (American International Picture, 1972).
Blade, dir. Stephen Norrington (New Line Cinema, 1998).
Blade II, dir. Guillermo del Toro (New Line Cinema, 2002).
Blade Runner, dir. Ridley Scott (Warner Brothers, 1982).
Blade: Trinity, dir. David S. Goyer (New Line Cinema, 2004).
Blood of Dracula [My Blood is My Heritage], dir. Herbert L. Strock (American International Picture, 1957).
Blood of the Vampire (Universal Pictures, 1958).
BloodRayne, dir. Uwe Boll (Boll KG Productions, 2005).
Bloodsucking Bastards, dir. Brian James O'Connell (Scream Factory, 2015).
Bram Stoker's Dracula, dir. Francis Ford Coppola (Columbia, 1992).
Dark Shadows, creator Dan Curtis (Dan Curtis Productions, 1966–71).
Daughters of Darkness [Les Rouges aux Lèvres], dir. Harry Kümel (Ciné Vog Films, 1971).
Daybreakers, dir. Spierig Brothers (Lionsgate, 2009).
The Devil Bat, dir. Jean Yarborough (Producers Releasing Company, 1940).
The Devil's Plaything, [Der Fluch der schwarzen Schwestern], dir. Joseph W. Sarno (Retro Seduction Cinema, 1973).
Dracula, dir. Tod Browning (Universal Pictures, 1931).
Dracula [a.k.a. Horror of Dracula], dir. Terence Fisher (Universal Pictures, 1958).
Dracula, dir. Dan Curtis (Latglen, 1974).
Dracula, dir. John Badham (Universal, 1979).
Dracula [a.k.a. Dracula's Curse], dir. Roger Young (Sirio Vide, 2002).
Dracula, creators, Cole Haddon and Daniel Knauff (Universal Television, 2013–14).
Dracula A.D. 1972, dir. Alan Gibson (Hammer Film Productions, 1972).

Dracula and Son [Dracula père et fils], dir. Edouard Molinaro (Gaumont International, 1976).

Dracula: Dead and Loving It, dir. Mel Brooks (Columbia, 1995).

Dracula 2000 [Dracula 2001], dir. Patrick Lussier (Miramax Films, 2000).

Dracula's Daughter, dir. Lambert Hillyer (Universal Pictures, 1936).

Dracula II: Ascension, dir. Patrick Lussier (Dimension Films, 2003).

Dracula III: Legacy, dir. Patrick Lussier (Dimension Films, 2005).

Dracula Untold, dir. Gary Shore (Universal Pictures, 2014).

Ex Machina, dir. Alex Garland (Universal Pictures, 2015).

A Fool There Was, dir. Frank Powell (Box Office Attractions Company, 1915).

The Forsaken, dir. J.S. Cordone (Screen Gems, 2001).

Frankenstein Meets the Wolf-Man, dir. Roy William Neill (Universal Pictures, 1943).

Fright Night, dir. Tom Holland (Columbia Pictures, 1985).

Frostbite [Frostbiten], dir. Anders Banke (Paramount Pictures, 2006).

Ganja & Hess, dir. Bill Gunn (Kelly-Jordan Enterprises, 1973).

A Girl Walks Home Alone at Night, dir. Ana Lily Amirpour (VICE Films, 2014).

Hannibal, creator Bryan Fuller (Sony Pictures Television, 2013–15).

The Host, dir. Andrew Niccol (Open Road Films, 2013).

The House of Dracula, dir. Erle C. Kenton (Universal Pictures, 1945).

The Hunger, dir. Tony Scott (Metro-Goldwyn-Mayer, 1983).

I Am Legend, dir. Francis Lawrence (Warner Brothers Pictures, 2007).

Interview with the Vampire, dir. Neil Jordan (Warner Brothers, 1994).

The Invisible Man, dir. James Whale (Universal Pictures, 1933).

Karmina, dir. Gabriel Pelletier (Ciné 360, 1996).

Kindred: The Embraced, creators John Leekley and Mark Rein-Hagen (Spelling Television, 1996).

The Last Man on Earth, dir. Ubalda Ragona and Sidney Salkow (American International Pictures, 1964).

The Last Sect, dir. Jonathan Dueck (Cuttingedge Films, 2006).

Last Woman on Earth, dir. Roger Cornan (Filmgroup, 1960).

The Lawnmower Man, dir. Brett Leonard (New Line Cinema, 1992).

The Legend of the Seven Golden Vampires, dir. Roy Ward Baker (Hammer Film Productions, 1974).

Let Me In, dir. Matt Reeves (Hammer Films, 2010).

Let the Right One In, dir. Tomas Alfredson (Magnet Releasing, 2008).

The Living Corpse [Dracula in Pakistan aka Zinda Laash], Khwaja Sarfraz (Mondo Macabro, 1967).

The Lost Boys, dir. Joel Schumacher (Warner Brothers, 1987).

Love at First Bite, dir. Stan Dragoti (American International Pictures, 1979).

The Manchurian Candidate, dir. John Frankenheimer (United Artists, 1962).

Manhunter, dir. Michael Mann (De Laurentiis, 1986).

Martin, dir. George A. Romero (Libra Film International, 1978).

The Matrix, dir. The Wachowskis (Warner Brothers, 1999).

The Moth Diaries, dir. Mary Harron (Alliance Films, 2011).

Mother Riley Meets the Vampire [a.k.a. Vampire Over London, a.k.a. My Son the Vampire], dir. John Gilling (Blue Chip Films, 1952).

Mrs. Miniver, dir. William Wyler (Metro-Goldwyn-Meyer, 1942).

The Mummy, dir. Alex Kurtzman (Universal Picture, 2017).
Nadja, dir. Michael Almereyda (October Films, 1994).
Near Dark, dir. Kathryn Bigelow (DeLaurentiis Entertainment Group, 1987).
Netherbeast Incorporated [a.k.a. Vampire Office], Dean Ronalds (Shoreline Entertainment, 2007).
Nosferatu: A Symphony of Horror [Nosferatu, eine Symphonie des Grauens], dir. F.W. Murnau (Fine Arts Guild, 1922).
Nosferatu the Vampyre [Nosferatu: Phantom der Nacht], dir. Werner Herzog (20th Century–Fox, 1979).
Not of This Earth, dir. Roger Corman (Allied Artists, 1957).
The Omega Man, dir. Boris Sagal (Warner Brothers, 1971).
Once Bitten, dir. Howard Storm (The Samuel Goldwyn Company, 1985).
Penny Dreadful, creator, John Logan (Showtime, 2014–16).
Perfect Creature, dir. Glenn Standring (Magna Pacific, 2006).
Pulse [Kairo], dir. Kurosawa (Tojo, 2001).
Red Dragon, dir. Brett Ratner (Universal Pictures, 2002).
The Return of the Vampire, dir. Lew Landers (Columbia Pictures, 1943).
Ring [Ringu], dir. Hideo Nakata (Toho, 1998).
Rings [The Ring: Rebirth], dir. F. Javier Gutiérrez (Paramount Pictures, 2017).
Rise: Blood Hunter, dir. Sebastian Gutierrez (Samuel Goldwyn Films, 2007).
Sanctuary, creator, Damian Kindler (Entertainment One, 2008–11).
The Satanic Rites of Dracula, dir. Alan Gibson (Hammer Film Productions, 1973)
Scream Blacula Scream, dir. Bob Kelljan (American International Pictures, 1973).
Species, dir. Roger Donaldson Metro-Goldwyn-Meyer, 1995).
The Strain, creators Guillermo del Toro and Chuck Hogan (20th Television, 2014–17).
Taste the Blood of Dracula, dir. Peter Sasdy (Hammer Film Productions, 1970).
Terminator 3: Rise of the Machines, dir. Jonathan Mostow (Columbia Pictures, 2003).
Thirst, dir. Rod Hardy (New Line Cinema, 1979).
300, dir. Zack Snyder (Warner Brothers Pictures, 2006).
The Tudors, creator, Michael Hirst (Working Title Television, 2007–10).
Twilight, dir. Catherine Hardwicke (Summit Entertainment, 2008).
Twilight Saga: Breaking Dawn Part 1, dir. Bill Condon (Summit Entertainment, 2011).
Twilight Saga: Breaking Dawn Part 2, dir. Bill Condon (Summit Entertainment, 2012).
Twilight Saga: Eclipse, dir. David Slade (Summit Entertainment, 2010).
Twilight Saga: New Moon, dir. Chris Weitz (Summit Entertainment, 2009).
Ultraviolet, creator Joe Ahearne (World Productions, 1998),
Ultraviolet, dir. Kurt Wimmer (Screen Gems, 2006).
Underworld, dir. Len Wiseman (Screen Gens, 2003).
Vamp, dir. Richard Wenk (New World Pictures, 1986).
Vampira [a.k.a. Old Dracula], dir. Clive Donner (Columbia-Warner, 1976).
The Vampire Bat, dir. Frank R. Strayer (Majestic Pictures, 1933).
The Vampire Diaries, created Julie Plec

and Kevin Williamson (Warner Brothers Television, 2009–17).

The Vampire Lovers, dir. Roy Ward Baker (Hammer Film Productions, 1970).

Van Helsing, dir. Stephan Sommers (Universal Pictures, 2004).

Werewolf of London, dir. Stuart Walker (Universal Pictures, 1935).

The Wolf Man, dir. George Waggner (Universal Pictures, 1941).

Chapter Notes

Introduction

1. This study concentrates on films and television series as they often provide the most popular and widely viewed/consumed adaptations of the original text.

2. One might go as far to say that "land beyond the forest" is equivalent to "once upon a time" in signaling a time and place that is separate and different to our own, and only causes problems when they intersect.

3. Certain parts of the novel suggest he might understand and have made use of some of these technologies though it is never explicitly shown—he has contacted and made arrangements with more than one solicitors office in England, arranged for travel to and from London and across Europe.

4. Florence Marryat's *Blood of the Vampire*, published the same year as *Dracula* touches on these themes with an energy vampire, created by miscegenation returning to Britain from the colonies in the Caribbean.

5. Van Helsing himself employs a level of mind-control, and his understanding of ancient knowledge often suggests that the battle between the two "foreigners" is less Old World versus New but simply a matter of conflicting personalities.

6. Lord Godalming (a.k.a. Arthur Holmwood) is an interesting case in point as although part of the aristocracy it is intimated that he is not indicative of the old order—as seen in the death of his father—and actively joins in the hunt for the vampire and effectively subsidizing the adventure with his own money.

7. "Victims" can be a problematic term to use in this context as it is possible to argue that the female characters affected by the vampire are already victimized by the patriarchal society within which they live (are enslaved).

8. Violence is inherently part of Stoker's novel and not just that performed by Count Dracula upon his victims—though this is more often than not eroticized—but by the crew of light on the female body and in particular that of the vampire. It is not an obvious marker of the vampire's otherness but the violence he performs is always evil whilst that by his hunters is "righteous."

9. The settings of the main part of *Dracula* as a "dining room drama," although taken from the original English play of Stoker's novel, encourage the audience to view both the location and the characters within it as Americans—sophisticating audiences at the time would have read the intelligent characters and their accents as more New than "Olde" England.

10. This is even more clearly seen in the slightly later film *Return of the Vampire* (Landers: 1943) also staring Bela Lugosi where his vampiric character, Armand Tesla, is revived by the bombings in World War II.

11. This last aspect is the focus of *Ganja*

& Hess (Gunn, 1973) where an ancient African knife "infects" all who are cut by it with the memories of its past.

12. The film itself is peppered with many racial/racist jokes without it being clear whether they are due to the Eastern vampires uncivilized/non-western sensibilities or otherwise.

13. In this reading Will Graham, Lecter's nemesis, makes a surprising yet well suited Mina figure.

14. As noted by my colleague Teresa Cutler-Broyles there is also a hint here of Eve inviting the serpent into the garden of Eden, playing on the correlation between Dracula and the Dark Lord used in some later narratives such as *Penny Dreadful* (Logan: 2014–15).

15. As pointed out to me by my colleague Andy Boylan the two leads share their names with the key players in Universal's *Dracula*—Edward Van Sloan and Bela Lugosi.

16. The early Universal films tend to hint at it rather than depict it, not unlike the way the vampire's fangs were never shown, so it was not until the highly graphic and sensational Hammer films that the real violence involved in killing vampires was shown on screen.

17. Richard Matheson's novel *I Am Legend* (1954), from which the film is adapted, features three species; humans, of which Nèville is the last survivor; Infected humans that are a cross between vampires and zombies as although they exhibit many traditional vampiric characteristics—aversion to sunlight and garlic—they move slowly like voodoo zombies; and Humans who have discovered medication to limit the effects of the infection but still have an aversion to garlic.

18. This is actually made more complicated than normal with Blade as his mother was already pregnant when she bitten by a vampire rather than the usual woman being impregnated by one.

19. Dragonetti is meant as something of a nod to the name Dracula. The historical figure Vlad Țepeș often linked to Stoker's character was also known as Vlad Dracula (the diminutive of Dracul), meaning "son of the devil" or "son of the dragon." Dragonetti can be seen as a playful Italianized diminutive of dragon by the addition of "etti."

20. The films imply that Blade actually does what he does not just for vengeance but to save humanity.

21. The actions here are also extremely similar to the then contemporary situation where the Western U.S./UK alliance attacked/destabilized the Middle East for oil—in *Dracula* it is the ottoman Empire that they destabilize, and they oppose the (apparently) clean energy due to their capital reliance on fossil fuels.

22. The series makes the connection between Dracula and Vlad the Impaler explicit and adds some imaginative flourishes about the historical ruler's connections to the Order of the Dragon.

Chapter One

1. See Byerly 2014.

2. In Stoker's novel Renfield has little backstory and is only an inmate at the much younger Dr. Seward's asylum who senses the approach of the vampire and comes under its thrall.

3. In Stoker's novel the young solicitor becomes the plaything of both Dracula and his wives yet seems to suffer none of the vampiric and/or deadly consequences of this confluence as did Lucy or Mina—Lucy became a vampire and Mina was telepathically/psychically linked to the Count.

4. The odd inclusion by Browning of opossums and armadillos to this signifier of decay intimates a connection to America itself—both creatures being native residents of the U.S.—suggesting that either there is an innate connection between the undead vampire and 1930s America or that maybe Transylvania is a liminal space that already exists there (the Great Depression literally sucking the life out of people).

5. Stoker named the vessel The Demeter, in regard to the goddess of the Spring, but in the film though it has become The

Vesta, goddess of hearth and home giving it the duel implication of either bringing the vampires home to the New World or being his vehicle to invade, lay claim to, the hearth of America.

6. See Leese 2002, and Showalter 2009, 167–194.

7. See Micale 2008.

8. Zeleska is a slightly more complicated character as she is named as Count Dracula's daughter, though it is her preoccupation with morbid matters that prevents her from escaping her vampiric ancestry.

9. These films, particularly, highlight the dangers of women who are given agency and are allowed to think for themselves; consequently, it is usually men who kill them to restore patriarchal order.

10. See Clover 1992.

11. In theory, Mina would need to sleep in her own native soil rather than Count Dracula's.

12. This is shown quite well in *Bram Stoker's Dracula* (Coppola: 1992).

13. This only happens after she has been accidentally, mortally wounded.

14. Mamuwalde originally opposed slavery, but his later actions align him with similar methods of violence and murder.

15. The brief mention of the dinner party that took place at Castle Dracula is rather odd as it suggests that those invited were either ignorant of the Count's vampirism or are complicit in his deception of the African visitors. The latter interpretation emphasizes Dracula's construction of being representative of white, capitalist society in general.

16. At the end of the 18th century slavery was legal in Transylvania—at that point it was under the auspices of the Hapsburg Empire—but it almost exclusively involved the enslavement of the Roma peoples.

17. Heather L. Duda identifies Blacula as the first film featuring a love-struck vampire, though one could argue this case for Murnau's *Nosferatu* where Orlock only decides to go to Wisborg after seeing an image of Hutters wife Ellen.

18. *Ganja & Hess* is often grouped within the category of Blaxploitation—the studio produced a cut of the film released as *The Black Vampire* which more easily fits that—however, the original cut won the critics' choice prize at the Cannes Festival.

19. Paul R. Lehman and John Edgar Browning offer a more positive reading of the mixed race, gay couple in the film in that their very inclusion offers the possibility of it being seen acceptable—they run a profitable business together and are shown as having a very good relationship before the vampire appears. See Browning and Picart 2009, 29.

20. The African nation that Mamuwalde supposedly comes from.

21. Apparently, Marshall himself came up with the idea of this ending in which Blacula chooses his own demise. See Scivally 2015.

22. Interestingly once the African American victims have become vampires their skin gets noticeably whiter, as often does their hair, reflecting a similar transformation that occurred in the slightly earlier vampire film *The Omega Man* (Sagal: 1971). Here all those infected with vampirism go extremely pale and become part of a pre-industrial cult called the Brothers led by Mathias. As such vampirism in the film is also a trauma from the past returning its victims to a time before technology and everyone is united in their "whiteness." *Blacula* does not explicitly suggest such an extreme but it does infer that the undead have not necessarily been linked back to their African heritage in the same way that Mamuwalde has and becoming a vampire separates them from both the past and the present, and black and white communities.

23. Contrarily one can also read the doctor's exploration of vampire lore as uncovering a white European cultural past that is based on sucking the life out of others and should serve as a warning to save himself rather than use it as a resource to destroy a connection to his own cultural history.

24. The film portrays Nadja as a child

of Count Dracula and of a human mother, though it does not explain whether this is through sexual intercourse or whether the mother was bitten during pregnancy, as in *Blade* (Norrington, 1998).

25. Zeleska invites the girl back to her apartment so that she can paint her—an attempt to possess her but not kill her—to prove to herself that she is not like her father, but this inevitably fails.

26. A very similar scene/feel is created by the skate-boarding vampire in *A Girl Walks Home Alone at Night* (Amirpour, 2014).

27. Abbott further relates this relationship of the female vampire to New York in the films *The Hunger* (Scott, 1983) and *The Addiction* (Ferrara, 1995), though only the latter also examples a similar kind of possession of the city space as seen in *Nadja*.

28. This is a bad trait that often seems to be leveled at female vampiric characters in that they are too "morbid," "obsessed," or "distant."

29. Van Helsing later notes that particular rites were not performed by his daughter to ensure that Dracula was truly dead, meaning that something of him might still be alive in some form.

30. Van Helsing himself is not immortal and there is little mention of a family tradition in vampire hunting, so why he does so is left largely unexplained.

31. There is also a sense here that as in *Carmilla* the unknown narrator (the eye of the camera) in *Let the Right One In* could be Oskar looking back on his past.

32. Eli's sexuality is purposely complicated in the film and whilst she looks like a girl, she has no sex organs—the novel from which the film was adapted shows her as a castrated boy. Alfredson uses this ambiguity to suggest a love story beyond sex, and indeed the novel's author, John Ajvide Lindqvist, affirms this in the sequel, "Let the Old Dreams Die," where both "children" are now vampires.

33. This idea was prevalent in many teen-vampire films of the 1980s where adolescent sexual angst was manifested and conquered through the figure of the vampire: see *Once Bitten* (Kendall, 1984), *Fright Night* (Holland, 1985), *The Lost Boys* (Schu-macher, 1987), *Vamp* (Wenk, 1986), and *Near Dark* (Bigelow, 1987).

34. There is a point when Eli kisses Oskar with her bloodied mouth, but arguably he is already under her spell by then.

35. Lindqvist's novel makes it clear that Håkan only remains with Eli for the occasional sexual favors she allows him as "payment" for his services.

36. Reeves' film *Let Me In* (2010) more explicitly shows that Abby (Eli here) grooms her assistants from a young age and replaces them when they are no longer useful.

37. In the novel she fails to break his neck after feeding and he returns as a zombified creature that is trapped in the basement of Oskar's building.

38. For statistics on the sudden increase of immigrants into Sweden during the 1980s see Hosseini-Kaladjahi and Kelly 2012.

39. Interestingly, a colleague from Sweden related that the majority of the immigrants were well received as they were largely of the secular and professional classes fleeing the new regime.

40. The sequel story shows this to be Spain.

41. This is sometimes changed to be unconsecrated earth or soil from the graves of suicides.

42. In the novel at least one of these items is of great value, and she offers it to Oskar.

43. Interestingly Blackeberg also has no churches, although it is never suggested in the book or film that religious artifacts have any effect on Eli.

44. Something of the results of the vampire's influence on the area are spoken of in "Let the Old Dreams Die."

45. The narratives in all three formats share much of the same storyline, it is only the television series that makes significant changes.

46. The Master does not require soil from his homeland or grave as seen in Stoker but with earth that is infected with the contaminated worms that carry the vampiric infection. The novels further complicate this situation as it transpires that North America is actually the Master's place of birth, so he is in fact traveling back to his homeland, not to virgin territory requiring an invitation.

47. Nora dies quite quickly in the television series as compared to the novels, where she survives throughout, but is replaced in the team of vampire slayers by Dutch.

48. In the original novel, Lindqvist explains that Eli (Elijah) was abused, castrated and vampirized by the historical Blue Beard, Gilles de Rais from 15th century Brittany. Eli's subsequent victims can be read as a repetition of this original trauma.

49. This aspect constantly rears its head in the series both in the attraction of the Master to Ephraim's teenage son Zack, but also in the conversion of a school bus full of blind children into a pack of vampire tracker dogs.

50. This is a device used somewhat more ironically in the film *The Omega Man* (Sagal, 1971).

51. "White" is a more extreme version of "V," vampire blood, that was used as a recreational drug in *True Blood*. Setrakian himself takes white to stay alive long enough to kill the Master. He is 94 years old in the series though looks considerably younger—and a similar idea is used in *Dracula 2001* (Lussier, 2000). Of course, it also suggests that "whiteness" offers a firm of immortality itself.

52. Many thanks to David Skal to pointing me to the script of the play in his book *Dracula: The Ultimate Edition of the World-Famous Vampire Play* (1993).

53. The creates something of the "eternal," or "immortal" moment that Wittgenstein discusses in *Tractatus Logico-Philosophicus*.

54. Which might partly answer why they go to loved ones, as the loved ones are seen as a comfort from that trauma—however the vampire then infects them with the traumatic past.

55. In the novels and comics, the destruction of The Master destroys the vampiric infection completely.

Chapter Two

1. Murnau seemed to favor the addition of incongruous animals as much as Browning would nine years later, and the trip to Transylvania features hyenas as "werewolves," and just as in the later film they serve to add a surreal quality to the landscape, marking it as "other" and more imaginary than simply foreign.

2. Stoker took the most extreme characteristics of the Counts appearance from Sabine Baring-Gould's *Book of Were-Wolves* (1865), though this still allowed for obvious racial prejudices.

3. Stoker was influenced by the figure of Svengali from du Maurier's *Trilby* (1894).

4. "*Die Jüdischen Gefallenen*" (The Jewish War Dead) A roll of honor commemorating the 12,000 German Jews who died for their fatherland in World War I.

5. There is a sense that this forms the inevitable punishment for sympathizers, who think they will gain power from such a connection but are rewarded only with corruption and madness.

6. As noted by Erik Butler, premodern European societies often saw the Jews as the "guilty" party during outbreaks of plague and other diseases (Butler 2010, 160).

7. This strengthens the idea of Knock already being a sympathizer and that he found the weak spot/perfect victims for the vampire to penetrate Wisborg (Germany).

8. Albin Grau, the film's co-producer and art-director was deeply involved in the occult and a student of Eastern philosophy, so a reading of the film as creation myth might not be so farfetched.

9. Deborah Christie explains this in

terms of Romantic desire that the vampire cannot resist and where Ellen embodies a concentrated form of life force (Christie 2015, 279).

10. Werner Herzog's remake of *Nosferatu* came out in the same year, as did John Badham's *Dracula* which mixes Browning's *Dracula* with a more faithful adherence to the Balderston, Deane play. Interestingly Badham went very a very romantic view of the vampire using Frank Langella to play the vampire, not unlike Dragoti's choice of Hamilton, though with less irony.

11. A similar scenario where the Count loses his castle to the communist regime in Romania is used in the comedy *Dracula and Son* [Dracula père et fils] (Molinaro: 1976).

12. Renfield here is played by Arte Johnson who very much models his character on Dwight Frye's portrayal in Browning's *Dracula*.

13. The Socialist Republic of Romania existed between 1947 and 1989 and was a Soviet-aligned, Eastern Bloc country largely run by the Romanian Communist Party that was led, notoriously, by Nicolae Ceaușescu from 1965. He was president from 1974 until the fall of his totalitarian government in 1989.

14. Something of this "out-of-placeness" is also seen in the short film *Dracula Bites the Big Apple* from the same year by Richard Wenk, who later directed Vamp starring Grace Jones.

15. This preceded Almereyder's use of Van Helsing ancestral links in his plot for *Nadja*.

16. Brainwashing seemed to be a favorite trope of Cold War conflicts, though often more linked to communist countries in Asia, as controversially seen in the earlier film *The Manchurian Candidate* (Frankenheimer, 1962).

17. This plays a curious counterpoint to *Nosferatu* as here Cindy's fiancé Dr. Rosenberg is Jewish, so when Hamilton's Dracula steals her away, he reverses the earlier symbolic role of the vampire.

18. Curiously Jamaica was also the destination of Dracula in the earlier film *Vampira* [a.k.a. Old Dracula] (Donner: 1976).

19. Vampires and communism are not an uncommon pairing, in *Dracula and Son*, mentioned above, the hammer and sickle are used as a cross. In *Karmina* (Pelletier: 1996) a communist vampire uses a hammer and sickle to defeat the Christian cross, and in *Back to the USSR* [takaisin Rysslin] (Halonen: 1992) it is insinuated that Lenin is (was) a vampire.

20. See Alec 2016.

21. Cindy's last comment, and indeed her lifestyle, is something of a forebear to the more famous line from *The Lost Boys* (Schumacher, 1987) "Sleep all day. Party all night. Never grow old. Never die. It's fun to be a vampire."

22. Interestingly in John Badham's *Dracula*, which was released 4 months after Dragoti's film, the Count is "crucified" on a ship's mast in the sunlight whilst trying to escape his pursuers with his vampire bride (Mina), but his cape, which is the only part of him left, flies off into the sky rather like a large bat, oddly copying Hamilton's vampire.

23. See Jones 1931.

24. See 'What was the Second Wave Feminist Movement?' 2016.

25. See Lindquist 2012.

26. The fact that the film is set in L.A. throws up some interesting comparisons and contrasts with *Blacula*, particularly in terms of how the African-American community is portrayed in each.

27. In the rather confused racial politics within the film the Count does not approve of African Americans being made into vampires.

28. Not unlike Stacey Abbott's description of "Road Movie" vampires seen in films such as *Near Dark*, *The Forsaken* (Cordone: 2001), etc. See Abbott 2007, 163–76.

29. Though there has been some pushback against this idea as being over simplistic.

30. Erik Butler suggests that Quincey Morris in *Dracula* is a vampire and so would predate Dallas's claim. See Butler 2013, 92.

Chapter Notes—Three

31. Something of this idea was also used by Stephen King and Scott Snyder in the comic book series *American Vampire* (Vertigo, 2010-present, though King only co-scripted on issues 1–5) where Skinner Sweet, as an American vampire, usurps the European vampires that are exploiting the Wild West in the 19th century.

32. For Count Dracula's predilection for middle-class female victims see Winthrop-Young 1994.

33. One might speculate that if Lucy had been allowed to survive as a vampire, she might have re-befriended Mina in the way that Nico becomes friends with Rachel.

34. In the inherently transgressive and contrary nature of vampires, Dallas can also be seen to be her (vampire) father, and indeed even though she tries to kill him, they end up as lovers.

35. Fuller's series begins when Hannibal Lecter is still accepted as a doctor and a psychoanalyst, before it is discovered he is a cannibalistic mass murderer.

36. This study also only references the first two seasons of the series, which act as a prequel to the more well-known narrative of *Manhunter* (Mann, 1986) and its remake *Red Dragon* (Ratner, 2002) and which are used in season 3.

37. Meehan 2014, 252.

38. The film made popular the notion of such prisoners wearing hockey masks for safety and being kept in a cage in a larger room for extra security.

39. For fan opinion about the accent see https://obsessingaboutinterestingpeople.wordpress.com/2013/04/12/hannibal-foreign-actors-to-americans-accent-and-xenophobia/.

40. See Porteous 203.

41. See Shapira 2015.

42. See McGuire 2013.

43. See McGuire 2013.

44. There was much online speculation regarding the nature of the relationship between Hannibal and Will, see Miller, Nguyen, Travers, and Greene 2017.

45. See Oxford Dictionaries, https://en.oxforddictionaries.com/definition/hysteria.

46. See King 1993.

47. Two of the main ones being that Dracula is killed in a way not detailed earlier in the tale as capable of destroying the vampire; and there is and inference that the undead Count's blood has passed through Mina into her child Quincey.

48. Badham's *Dracula* avoids the eternal love motif as seen in the earlier *Blacula* and later *Bram Stoker's Dracula* (Coppola, 1992), and sees the Count as besotted with a rather modern Mina (not unlike Count Orlok) and wanting to escape with her back to Transylvania.

49. Stoker himself had read Emily Gerard's *The Land Beyond the Forest*, in which she says: "He must, however, be careful to keep within the circle traced until the devil, who may very likely have chosen to appear in the shape of a goat, crow, toad, or serpent, has completely disappeared." (Gerard 1888, 204)

50. In similar vein Dracula in *The Satanic Rites of Dracula* (Gibson: 1973) is shown as the Antichrist when killed in a hawthorn bush at the film's end, mirroring the crown of thorns worn by Jesus.

51. In the catholic medieval bestiary, which can be seen to inform much Satanic imagery, the bear and the wolf are both equated to the devil whereas the goat is allied to Christ, both having a love of high mountains. However, Isidore of Seville [7th century] sees them as hot-tempered, lustful creatures whose blood can dissolve diamonds (The Medieval Bestiary n.p.).

52. As touched on in Chapter One in regard to *Let the Right One In*.

53. See Dearden 2017.

54. The later parts of the film can be blamed on ergot, or corn mold, which has hallucinogenic properties, and indeed has been cited as a factor in regard to the later Salem witch trials. See Wickham, 2016.

Chapter Three

1. Women were given the right to vote in the United States in 1919 due in part to

the role women played on the home front during WWI.

2. The film uses the conceit of calling the vampire Count Alucard, which is Dracula in reverse, a point which is labored upon during the movie. It was the first movie to use this anagram of Dracula, which has since become a cliché. In part it is also an attempt to justify the title of the film even though it is obvious the vampire is not the son of the Count, but Dracula himself.

3. One of the most well-known examples of this recurring cultural trope at the turn of the 20th century is seen in the film *A Fool There Was* (Powell, 1915) starring Theda Bara, an extremely famous actress of the time whose publicity explicitly promoted her as being a vamp. Indeed, one can read the film as Bara's character not only being a Vamp, but an energy vampire as well sucking the life out of her victim.

4. It is never made clear why Frank has not been called up for the army as he is of an age to be enlisted, a point made more obvious as nearly all the other men in the film are quite aged.

5. Lon Chaney is the only actor to have played all the major monster roles for Universal: Dracula, Wolf Man, Frankenstein's Monster, and the Mummy.

6. The film boasts being the first to show on screen Dracula transforming into a bat—a rather cartoonish piece of animation when compared to later movies.

7. Reference to Carol A. Senf's work on Mina and Lucy as exampling the idea of the "New Woman" at the end of the 19th century. See Senf, 1982.

8. The film never explicitly correlates Alucard to Nazi-Germany, only as an outside enemy wishing to ruin America as they have their former homeland. Many American corporations and their affiliates were happy to deal with the regimes in Germany and Italy before and even during the war, and it is possible to read this into the non-specific Europeanness of the vampire.

9. Rather curiously the plot of the film stipulates that Dracula can only sleep in his coffin and nowhere else, otherwise he could have eluded capture quite easily.

10. My colleague Andy Boylan has suggested that on some level Frank might symbolize the former isolationism of America (it's younger self) that refuses to engage with Europe (Dracula), and symbolically destroys it at film's end.

11. See Goodwin 1992, and Soule 1946.

12. An interesting one of note here is the 2-part Italian mini-series *Dracula* [a.k.a. Dracula's Curse] (Young: 2002), where Jonathan, an American lawyer, Arthur, a debt-ridden British diplomat, and Quincey, a businessman and swindler, try to con Dracula (Count Vladislav Tepes) out of money raised on the aristocrats sale of artworks and antiques from his castle in Budapest.

13. As seen in *Taste the Blood of Dracula* (Sasdy, 1970) and *Dracula A.D. 1972* (Gibson, 1972).

14. In an odd plot explanation, Van Helsing hypothesizes that Dracula is actually seeking his own death by destroying his only source of food.

15. Whether meant or not, Chin Yang links *The Satanic Rites* to the final installment of Hammer's Dracula films *The Legend of the Seven Golden Vampires* by Roy Ward Baker released the following year— The Count was played by John Forbes-Robertson. Although set in 1804, the action moves the Count to China and links him to a supposed Chinese legend about the titular undead. This film is mainly of interest for its linking of vampires and martial arts, which is something of a stalwart of the genre now but highly unusual in the 1970s in Anglo-American films.

16. See The Biological Weapons Convention, *UNODA*, https://www.un.org/disarmament/wmd/bio/.

17. Which she further notes is an idea used in later films such as "*Ultraviolet* (Ahearne, 1998), *Kindred: The Embraced* (Conway, 1996), the Blade trilogy (1998/2002/2004), and *Underworld* (Wiseman, 2003)."

18. See Dyer 2016.
19. "On This Day" 1974.
20. Maybe more understandable as Lorimmar had killed the Count in the previous film in the series.
21. The camera position makes it appear as if Dracula is hanging upside down with a crown of thorns as he dies purposely referencing the Antichrist as an inversion of Jesus being crucified.
22. Human farming seems a popular motif in Australian vampire films as seen in *Thirst* (Hardy, 1979) and *The Matrix* (The Wachowskis, 1999).
23. A similar scenario is seen in *Netherbeast Incorporated* [a.k.a. Vampire Office] (Ronalds: 2007), and *Bloodsucking Bastards* (O'Connell: 2015).
24. Whilst the film suggests that companies face competition from abroad, there appears to be only one blood-synthesizing plant shown in the story.
25. There is also a fleeting shot at the start of the film blaming bats for the plague.
26. The Subsiders then embody both the poor, who cannot partake of consumerist society, and those ideologically against it (socialists) who will not be part of it.
27. It is worth noting that *The Omega Man* critiques such a view of American society being naturally white, though rather complicated it by making Charlton Heston, as Neville, a white savior for the reborn multicultural society.
28. This is usually seen in regard to their desire to suck the blood of Jonathan Harker. *Dracula* (Fisher, 1958) is a good example of this and even more so *The Living Corpse* [Dracula in Pakistan aka Zinda Laash] (Sarfraz, 1967) where Dracula (Prof. Tabini) has to literally wrestle with his "bride" to fend her off from Dr. Aqil, the Harker character.
29. In this reading she kills herself as she cannot bear the thought of a never-ending existence of continual consumerism.
30. They manage to do this via medication and drugs, imagining a rather cyborgian vision of the future.
31. Somewhat equatable to the spread of ideological and/or revolutionary fervor.
32. *Twilight* (Hardwicke, 2008) attempts at some level of plot exposition not requiring foreknowledge of characters and motivations, etc., but the later films, and the two-part finale of *Breaking Dawn Part I* and *Part II* in particular, cater very much to the faithful.
33. Bethan Jones sees an equivalence between the two characters if not a direct correlation. See Jones, 2012.
34. The official sequel to Stoker's novel, and written by his descendent Dacre Stoker, *Dracula: The Undead* (2009) makes this specialness of Quincey explicit.
35. Jim Steinmeyer also does this, if rather perfunctorily, in *Who Was Dracula?: Bram Stoker's Trail of Blood* (New York: Penguin, 2013).
36. Dan Curtis used the same idea of a reincarnated love in his *Dracula* (1974) and which he had used earlier in his television series *Dark Shadows* (Curtis: 1966–71).
37. There is no suggestion in *The Twilight Saga* that Edward and Bella have met before or that one of them is a reincarnation of an earlier self.
38. This sculptural, stone-like quality of vampire flesh/skin is mentioned a few times in the novels, though less in the films. The most obvious reference to this is when the undead's heads are twisted off they break as if they were made of marble.
39. None of the Cullens but Edward worries about his "soul," and that is more as an aspect of the angst-ridden modern vampire than a true fear of biblical damnation.
40. This is also much of what troubles the local werewolf population—that simultaneously embody the land, the indigenous community, and the poor and disadvantaged—and causes them to make more of their kind as a form of defense against the wealthy white undead consumerists.
41. Thus, making it the perfect location for the Cullens.

42. To put it into perspective, the tabloid Press in the UK listed the two big weddings of 2011 as the one between Prince William and the Duchess of Cambridge and that between Edward and Bella.

43. See McConnell 2011.

44. See Mitzeliotis 2011.

45. See "Twilight Wedding Songs," *Wedding Music Help*, http://www.weddingmusic-help.com/twilightweddingsongs.html.

46. This author has attended at least one wedding in 2017 that used both pieces of music.

47. in theory the film explains this as Jupiter having the exact same DNA profile as the vampire Matriarch, but is not actually her—which is enough to satisfy the intergalactic courts that she is the rightful owner of the Earth. However, in light of narratives within the vampire genre that see a female vampires soul/spirit transfer to another body or are reincarnated this is arguably the more likely scenario.

48. This reading sees the plot of the film as driven by infanticide, whereas in contrast Paul Johnson reads *Jupiter Ascending* as an Oedipal tale but revising matricide for patricide. See Johnson 2017.

49. Something of the same occurs in the film *The Host* (Niccol, 2013) a more oblique vampire narrative by Stephenie Meyer where the "souls" of space vampires take residence in human bodies.

50. Erzsébet Báthory, 1560–1614, who allegedly tortured and killed hundreds of girls before being walled up in solitary confinement for the final 4 years of her life. She is often compared to Vlad the Impaler—a possible ancestor—and has been called The Blood Countess and Countess Dracula.

51. It is worth noting again that much of Stoker's description of the vampire comes from Sabine Baring-Gould's *Book of the Werewolf* and indeed when the Demeter lands at Whitby Dracula is in the shape of a wolf as he jumps off the ship. Stoker also states in *Lady of the Shroud* that "The Wehr-Wolf is but a variant of the Vampire" (Stoker 1909, 67).

52. It has been suggested the odd chemistry between the two leading actors was due to the uncomfortable prosthetic jaw that Channing Tatum (Caine) was forced to wear to make him look more dog-like.

Chapter Four

1. These are quite often Dhamphirs (see McClellend 2006, 12) who are born of vampire and human parents, meaning violence is not unfamiliar to them either.

2. Van Helsing burns Mina with a symbol of patriarchy (the host). Similarly, the Professor reads the funeral rites as he encourages Arthur to violently stake Lucy in an over-the-top fashion when simply firing a bullet would have been sufficient before decapitating her.

3. As seen in John Polidori's *The Vampyre* (1819) where the undead Lord Ruthven is restored to full vigor by moonlight. This is also a feature also used in many of the ensuing plays inspired by the work.

4. As mentioned by Andy Boylan Stoker's novel Lucy is a mirror of Dracula. He has three wives/brides (we can assume he has fed from) and Mina. In mirror fashion Lucy has three suitors/husbands and Van Helsing—all of whom she fed from through transfusions (Van Helsing confesses as much when calling Lucy a polyandrist and himself a bigamist [Stoker 1996, 189]). See Boylan 2012.

5. A good spoof of this aspect Van Helsing leadership is made in Mel Brooks' *Dracula: Dead and Loving It* (1995).

6. Matheson's book more explicitly examples post–WWII, post–Hiroshima fears around radiation and science out of control whilst Ragona and Salkow's movie hints more toward anxieties caused by the ongoing Cold War.

7. They also supposedly want Morgan's blood, but such sanguinary thirst is never shown.

8. This aspect is particularly brought to the fore in *Omega Man* (Segal, 1971) and *I Am Legend* (Lawrence, 2007).

9. The novel makes Neville/Morgan

even more monstrous by having him perform experiments on the vampires in his attempt to find a cure, dragging them out into the daylight to test his latest vaccine only to dispassionately watch them all die in agony.

10. Alive vampires here indicates the new breed, the humans that carry the vampire infection but medicate to not become one of the undead. Cortman is an interesting point in the narrative hinting at both homosexual and racial readings of the vampires. As such Morgan's willful killing, "penetration" of the vampires and the attraction between him and Cortman, can be read as repressed homosexuality or queerness (See Ransom 2018), or as overt racism and antagonism to the end of racial segregation in America—at one point he calls the vampires "black bastards." (See Pulliam and Fonseca 2016, 117–36.)

11. Though oddly no other vampire animals are seen in the film.

12. Something very similar is seen at the end of *The Omega Man* with Charlton Heston (Neville) being impaled and falling into a fountain in a Christ-like position turning the water blood-red, and the later *I Am Legend* with Will Smith as the hero similarly sees Neville giving his blood to save humanity. It should be noted that Matheson's novel is almost anti-religious and bereft of such symbolism.

13. See Bishop 2010, 106, Golub 2017, 99, and Ransom 2018, 116.

14. Of course, both here in *Last Man* and in Matheson's novel Ruth is now the last human—Roger Corman released *Last Woman on Earth* in 1960 though not to explore such unsensational ideas—but what might become of her having blood that might lead to a cure is never examined or explored

15. In folklore, dhamphirs have a vampire parent, in a more conventional sense, and are often vampire hunters (see McClellend).

16. In *Blade* the vampire Deacon uses technology to research and resurrect the ancient blood god; in *Blade II* (del Toro, 2002) the vampires use it to produce a degenerated version of themselves, and in *Blade Trinity* (Goyer, 2004) it is used to unearth the past in the firm of Dracula, the original vampire.

17. My colleague Andy Boylan pointed out that in the earlier comic books Blade, though always wearing sunglasses, wore more period specific ones in the 1970s (i.e. more disco-like). Whereas by the time of the film's starting in the late 90s they were far more wrap-around and like those worn by Arnold Schwarzenegger in the Terminator films.

18. Similar constructions of dhamphir/ vampire slayers, though less-weaponized ones, are seen in *BloodRayne* (Boll, 2005) and *Rise: Blood Hunter* (Gutierrez, 2007). In being part human, part vampire, Blade is also oddly like Mina Harker in belonging to two worlds yet able to navigate the borders between them.

19. The idea forms the basis of Del Toro and Hogan's *The Strain*.

20. Whilst "yuppies" was coined in the 1980s the term has been continued and modified since to categorize the young, well paid, urban, professional classes. As Paul Graham observes, the term came about as the generation of the 1980s was the first to be well paid for their work and since then it has become a norm amongst young professionals working in the city, so the term no longer has much relevance. See Graham, 2016, http://paulgraham.com/re.html.

21. This knowingly points to and exceeds the excess of the vampires in *The Lost Boys* (Schumacher, 1987) who had the tag line of partying all night and sleeping all day.

22. This last is mainly due to Dr. Johnson, who Blade saved from one of Frost's henchmen, and who is trying to synthesize a replacement serum for her rescuer, though even this becomes weaponized at the end of the film.

23. This is not to say that all the Count's victims are "courted" in the same manner as Lucy and Mina, as seen in Browning's

film. The flower girl he encounters in London is summarily drained and killed with no further mention of her coming back as a vampire.

24. Curiously Dr. Johnson actually creates a cure for Blade, but not only does he refuse to take it himself he does not allow it to be administered to any other turned vampires either. In contrast in the animated film *Batman vs Dracula* (Goguen, 2005), Bruce Wayne/Batman—something of a vampire-like character himself—perfects a cure and saves all the Gothamites infected by the vampire.

25. The films imply that Blade does not seek vengeance or gain pleasure from what he does but only does it to save humanity.

26. To a degree, there is almost a Marxist reading that sees the working/laboring classes (manual labor nominally embodied by Blade) reasserting their importance over those who live off their labors and exploit them (as seen in Frost).

27. We also find out not long before this that Frost was the vampire that bit Eric's mother whilst she was pregnant so that in some way, he is Blade's father. This would suggest an Oedipal reading of the story, not least as Blade also penetrates his mother with a large bone (one suspects Norrington was aware of the play on words) but his further actions tend to play this down somewhat.

28. It is not until the third film in the franchise that Blade mistakenly kills a human, but we are clearly told that it was a trap set by the vampires and that the victim is a "familiar"—more often than not a human who wants to become a vampire—and so deserving of such a fate.

29. Western society in particular at the start of the 21st century makes much of the importance of children, and what it terms as "childhood" and the "rights of the child" and arguably more so than at any other point in history (See Bacon forthcoming). However, contemporary consumer culture simultaneously sexualizes and commodifies those same children (see Faulkner 2010) somewhat complicating their true cultural value and notions such as "innocence." (See Giroux 1998)

30. Something of the same is seen in *30 Days of Night* (Slade, 2007) where the town's sheriff sacrifices himself to become a vampire as the only way to defeat the army of undead that are killing everyone in Barrow.

31. This is quite an interesting scene in the film as when Vlad's people fear and shun him because he is now an unholy monster, he turns on them shouting "Do you think you are alive because you can fight? You are alive because of what I did to save you!" Obviously, this is not befitting a self-sacrificing father and he is roundly scolded by his wife, effectively reintegrating him into the nation family.

32. In Greek mythology, Atlas was a titan condemned to hold up the heavens. He attempted to trick Heracles into taking over his burden, as anyone willingly offering to do so must continue for all time.

33. We never see who or what this demon is but it is potentially the same one that created the mummy, in the film of the same name by Alex Kurtzman (2017), that was intended to be part of the same Dark Universe franchise created around the classic Monsters (Dracula, Frankenstein's Monster, The Wolf Man, and The Mummy, etc.) from Universal Pictures in the 1930s and 40s.

34. This does throw up an odd comparison of Vlad to Jesus in that the latter sacrificed himself for his people, just as Vlad will do for his own.

35. Mirena is played by Sarah Gadon who also played Lucy, the focus of vampire attention, in the film *The Moth Diaries* (Harron, 2011). Her fate equally decided the ultimate outcome between the two monsters in both narratives.

36. *Dracula Untold* touches upon the ecological link between Vlad and his homeland, which is seen in many Dracula adaptations.

37. Historical reports, however, suggest that Vlad was a little more creative in his approach to combat, even using biological

weapons—he would send those suffering from deadly diseases into the Ottoman camps, and would also disguise himself and his men as Turks to trick the enemy.

38. See Holmes 2018.

39. Though *The Vampire Diaries* novels (originally published 1979 and republished 1991–2) were written before both Meyers *Twilight* (2005–8) and Harris's *Southern Vampire Mysteries* [True Blood] (2001–13) the television series very much came out of the huge popularity of the two later texts.

40. This is except for Matt Donovan who often appears to be the only human left in the town of Mystic Falls.

41. In *Dracula*, the Count appears as a wolf (werewolf), bat, "moonlight rays" and "elemental dust" (Stoker 1996, 258), he casts no reflection, can change his appearance and can "come out from anything or into anything, no matter how close it be bound or even fused up with fire." (Stoker 1996, 258) As such his human appearance, which can also change between young and old, is just a fleeting coagulation of the matter or energy that constitutes the King Vampire in the narrative.

42. It is never explained how they knew what vampires were if they are the first of their kind. In Norse mythology the "Draugr" is possibly the closest entity to a vampire (and translated as such by Sabine Baring-Gould) in being one who walks again after death. This is usually to guard their burial mound or take revenge on one who has wronged them. They can have insatiable appetites and eat flesh and blood and can be killed by decapitation, burning the body and spreading the ash over the ocean. See Blutwölfen 2005.

43. *The Vampire Diaries*, and indeed the spin-off series *The Originals*, has a very complicated relationship with indigenous peoples and other ethnic backgrounds, and has often been accused of "white-washing." See Shannonjeana, 2015.

44. A common stereotype for werewolf packs, See also *True Blood*.

45. In all these narratives the vampire was invariably human once and not an evolutionary different species.

46. When Stefan is in his "Ripper" phase his conscious mind is largely unaware of what he is doing, not unlike that of the doctor and his alter ego in Stevenson's *Strange Case of Dr. Jekyll and Mr. Hyde* (1886).

47. Series such as *The Vampire Diaries* quite often seem to construct their protagonists as having multiple characters or as susceptible to being controlled by others, making the idea of a true identity almost impossible to define, not least of which because this authentic self is one that those around them construct—Elena believes in an ultimately good Stefan, just as Stefan believes in an ultimately good Damon no matter how much of their lives they have spent harming or killing others.

Chapter Five

1. Curiously Quincey Morris is equally excluded from adding his own voice to the narrative and there is much conjecture on him being a vampire himself. See Moretti 1988, 96.

2. This idea forms the basis of the Wolf Man films where Larry Talbot often goes in search of a medical cure for his "affliction."

3. Mad scientists in film are as old as cinema itself, being frequent characters in the movies of Georges Méliès from the end of the 19th century (Frayling 2013, 49), but its intersection with the vampire did not really occur until *The Vampire Bat* (Strayer, 1933). The mad scientist here, Dr. Otto von Niemann, has created a "sponge-like mass of "living, growing tissue" that feeds on blood" (Meehan 93, 2014) and to fill its needs he is forced to kill many local inhabitants, covering his nefarious deeds by blaming them on a nearby nest of vampire bats. This film in particular can be seen to prefigure such vampire films as *Blood of the Vampire* (Cass, 1958), *Atom Age Vampire* (Majano, 1960), *Rabid* (Cronenberg, 1977)—examined above—and even *Frost-*

bite (Banke, 2006) which all feature scientists who go beyond the limits of rational behavior.

4. Lugosi also starred in *Mother Riley Meets the Vampire* (Gilling, 1952) where he plays another mad scientist but this time in control of a robot with which he plans to conquer the world.

5. Lon Chaney Jnr. was more well known for portraying the Wolf Man, a role he reprises in Barton's film.

6. See Gaia Staff 2017. Potentially one could read the film as a commentary on this operation and the inevitable "monsters" it would create/let free.

7. *Blood of Dracula* (Strock, 1957) does something very similar where a brilliant female science teacher proposes a more feminine approach to technology and innovation that would not have created nuclear weapons. Her teachings, when passed on to one of her female students, turns the young girl into an aggressive, uncontrollable monster (a woman with her own mind).

8. In *Blood of Dracula* a similar scenario occurs when the teacher/scientist, Miss Branding, is killed by her "creation" Nancy, who in a struggle pushes her onto a piece of broken furniture, impaling her.

9. Curiously Chaney and Lugosi had starred together in the 1943 film *Frankenstein Meets the Wolf Man* (Neill) but whilst the former was the Wolf Man, the later was actually the Monster.

10. Richard Matheson's *The Shrinking Man* (1956) is a good example where its protagonist Scott Carey is affected by radiation and begins to shrink. This continues until he disappears from human sight and moves into a fantastic world on the molecular lever (something of this is seen toward the end of *Ant-Man* Reed, 2015).

11. Something of *The Invisible Man* is seen in the earlier *Strange Case of Dr. Jekyll and Mr. Hyde* (Stevenson, 1886) where science causes the mad scientist to split into two personalities, arguably both as monstrous as the other.

12. As pointed out by my colleague Teresa Cutler-Broyles the name of the clinic as interesting as keloid is also the name given to a raised scar that sometimes grows larger than the area of the original injury.

13. Adult stem cells are regularly used in curing various forms of cancer though the potential for embryonic ones, which can now be synthetically produced, is much wider.

14. Something of this idea is used later in *Terminator 3: Rise of the Machines* (Mostow, 2003) where a liquid metal robot from the future can change its shape to look like anything but needs to sample (taste) the object first, and in relation to humans this usually requires killing them.

15. This last is rather reminiscent of *Blood of the Vampire* by Florence Marryat that was published the same year as *Dracula*. The story tells of a young mixed-race girl from the Caribbean after the death of her parents—her father was a vivisectionist whose brutality against his slaves is responsible for the young girl's affliction—who travels to Europe but who, unbeknownst to herself, drains the energy from those around her, particularly those she loves. Once she realizes her effect on people, she decides to end her life.

16. Particularly *The Omega Man* (Sagal, 1971) and *I Am Legend* (Lawrence, 2007).

17. One can read that the Bloofer Lady's prey is chosen to highlight her monstrosity whereas Rose's reveals the monstrous nature of the culture around her. As such, the former is containable whereas the latter requires the destruction of society.

18. Curiously, not unlike Peter Pan that preceded Orlok by 14 years. For an interesting reading of Peter Pan's teeth as [possible vampire] potency, see Kincaid 1992, 282–3.

19. The technology here is not really in the same mold as the ubiquitous steampunk variety usually employed in such films but is more organic and supernatural in its workings whilst still producing the same effects as cutting edge machines.

20. Not unlike Sauron's all seeing "eye" in the Lord of the Rings films (Jackson, 2001–3).

21. The fluidity of the vampire is rein-

forced throughout the series of films as different actors play Dracula in each installment; Gerard Butler in *Dracula 2001*; Stephen Billington in *Dracula II: Ascension*; and Hauer in *Dracula III: Legacy*.

22. There is also the intimation here that if Dracula exists as a cloud of flying bats that he can equally be transmitted as a wave or signal.

23. The film never names other forms of media, but it bears obvious connection to the *Ring* series of films that began in 1998 (*Ringu*, Nakata) and have continued up to the present, seeing a curse traveling across all forms of information technology from video tapes to computer viruses (*Rings*, Gutiérrez, 2017).

24. The book of course owes much to the 1991 Koki Suzuki novel *Ring* and its later cinematic adaption of the same name by Hideo Nakata from 1998, where a cursed videotape kills all who watch it, and *Pulse* (Kurosawa, 2001) where spirits try to enter reality vis the Internet.

25. Not unlike that seen in *Daughters of Darkness* (Kümel, 1971), *The Hunger* (Scott, 1983), *Nadja* (Almereyda, 1994), and *The Last Sect* (Dueck, 2006).

26. Unlike many 21st century horror films, the terror does not begin when there is no signal but when it is at its strongest.

27. These ideas play a large part in the sprawling narrative of *The Vampire Diaries* and which in turn connects to similar anxieties in relation to the ongoing War on Terror, religious extremism, and online grooming and propaganda.

28. *The Lawnmower Man* (Leonard, 1992) was an early example of cultural anxieties around the idea of being able to upload one's identity into cyberspace.

29. The series makes the connection between Dracula and Vlad the Impaler explicit and adds some imaginative flourishes about the historical ruler's connections to the Order of the Dragon.

30. In this reading, President Trump's policies toward environmental issues and oil consumption would place him firmly within the Order of the Dragon.

31. Part of the inherent structure of steampunk is the way it inherently views the 19th century from the perspective of the 21st, so that whilst the story is visually set in the Late Victorian period it is more of an otherworldly space that is as much about contemporary times as it is the past. This is also reinforced by the curiously clean streets of London seen in the series which is supposedly being poisoned by the use of fossil fuels. This contrasts quite sharply with *Penny Dreadful*, that started the same year which creates London as a dark, sinister, and Gothic space.

32. Interestingly Tesla is portrayed as a vampire in the earlier series *Sanctuary* (Kindler, 2008–11).

33. The scenes of Dracula's revival owe much to the beginning of *Blade Trinity* (Goyer, 2004) where the body of the "original" Dracula is found and revived in the desert of the Middle East. Haddon and Knauff's story locates this burial site at an unknown location in Eastern Europe but both narratives contain the death of one of the finders of the tomb with their blood facilitating the reawakening of the vampire, and the subsequent uncontrollability of the undead once brought to civilization.

34. Mention is made by Nathan of Robert Oppenheimer's "I am become death" speech, and the song "Enola Gay" by OMD, about one of the bombers who dropped the nuclear device on the Japanese city, is played just before Ava takes control of the underground facility.

35. This of course does not necessarily apply to vampires that are constructed as a different evolutionary species and are biologically born rather than "made," as in *Perfect Creature* (Standring, 2006), *The Hunger* (Scott, 1983), or *Vampire Diary* (James and O'Shea, 2006).

36. Theoretically Rachel, Pris, and Zhora from *Blade Runner* (Scott, 1982) would also fit into this framework, though their wholly biological construction slightly alters this as they really are gendered when being "built."

Bibliography

Abbott, Stacey. *Celluloid Vampires: Life After Death in the Modern World.* Austin: University of Texas Press, 2007.

_____. "Embracing the Metropolis: Urban Vampires in American Cinema of the 1980s and 90s," in Peter Day, ed., *Vampires: Myths and Metaphores of Enduring Evil.* Amsterdam: Rodopi, 2006, 125–43.

Agamben, Georgio. *State of Exception,* trans. Kevin Attell. Chicago: University of Chicago Press, 2005.

Alec. "Death, Destruction, and Debt: Photos of Life in 1970s New York," *Allthatsinteresting,* 16 April 2016, https://allthatsinteresting.com/1970s-new-york-photos, accessed 28 October 2018.

Arata, Stephen. *Fictions of Loss in the Victorian Fin De Siecle.* Cambridge: Cambridge University Press, 1996.

Bacon, Simon. "Alex Garland's *Ex Machina* (2015)—Vampire Gothic," in Simon Bacon, ed., *The Gothic: A Reader.* Bern: Peter Lang, 2018, 225–33.

_____. *Becoming Vampire: Difference and the Vampire in Popular Culture.* Bern: Peter Lang, 2016.

_____. "Children for Ever! Monsters of Eternal Youth and the Reification of Childhood," in Simon Bacon and Leo Ruickbie, eds, *Little Horrors: Interdisciplinary Perspectives on Anomalous Children and the Construction of Monstrosity.* Lanham, MD: Rowman & Littlefield, forthcoming, 117–34.

_____. "The Expectational Body: the Becoming of the Tortured Vampire Horde in Daybreakers," in Mark de Valk, ed., *Screening the Tortured Body: The Cinema as Scaffold.* London: Palgrave Macmillan, 2016, 71–88.

Baring-Gould, Sabine. *Book of Were-Wolves.* London: Smith, Elder & Co., 1865.

Baudrillard, Jean. *Simulacra and Simulation* [1981], trans. Sheila Faria Glazer. Ann Arbor: University of Michigan Press, 1994.

Baumann, Zygmunt. *Liquid Modernity.* Cambridge: Polity Press, 2000.

Beard, William. *The Artist as Monster: The Cinema of David Cronenberg.* Toronto: University of Toronto Press, 2006.

Berger, Arthur Asa. *The Art of the Seductress: Techniques of the Great Seductresses from Biblical Times to the Postmodern Era.* San Jose: Writers Club Press, 2002.

Billson, Anne. *Let the Right One In: Devils Advocates.* Leighton Buzzard: Auteur, 2011.

"The Biological Weapons Convention," *UNODA,* 2017, https://www.un.org/disarmament/wmd/bio/, accessed 28 October 2018.

Bird, Steve. "Treachery of Cold War Spy Anthony Blunt Was Kept from Tory Prime Minister," *The Telegragh*, 24 July 2018, https://www.telegraph.co.uk/news/2018/07/23/treachery-cold-war-spy-anthony-blunt-kept-tory-prime-minister/, accessed 28 October 2018.

Bishop, Kyle William. *American Zombie Gothic: The Rise and Fall (and Rise) of the Walking Dead in Popular Culture.* Jefferson, NC: McFarland, 2010.

Blutwölfen. "The Walking Dead: Draugr and Aptrgangr in Old Norse Literature," *Skadi Forum: Germanic Community Online*, 7 November 2005, https://forums.skadi.net/threads/76010-The-Walking-Dead-Draugr-and-Aptrgangr-in-Old-Norse-Literature?s=87517f007f48b78a4f28eabf7fe8228d, accessed 28 October 2018.

Boylan, Andrew M. *The Media Vampire: A Study of Vampires in Fictional Media.* Morrisville: Lulu.com, 2012.

Browning, John Edgar. "The *Dracula* and *Blacula* (1972) Cultural Revolution," in John Edgar Browning and Caroline Joan (Kay) Picart eds., *Draculas, Vampires and Undead Forms: Essays on Gender, Race, and Culture.* Jefferson, NC: McFarland, 2009, 19–36.

Burnham Bloom, Abigail. *The Literary Monster on Film: Five Nineteenth Century British Novels and Their Cinematic Adaptations.* Jefferson, NC: McFarland, 2010.

Butler, Erik. *Metamorphoses of the Vampire in Literature and Film: Cultural Transformations in Europe, 1732–1933.* Rochester: Camden House, 2010.

_____. *The Rise of the Vampire.* London: Reaktion Books, 2013.

Butler, Octavia. *Fledgling: A Novel.* New York: Seven Stories Press, 2005.

Byerly, Carol R. "War Losses (USA)," *International Encyclopedia of the First World War*, 8 October 2014, https://encyclopedia.1914-1918-online.net/article/war_losses_usa, accessed 28 October 2018.

Cain, Jimmie E., Jr. *Bram Stoker and Russophobia: Evidence of the British Fear of Russia in Dracula and Lady of the Shroud.* Jefferson, NC: McFarland, 2006.

Case, Sue Ellen. "Tracking the Vampire," in Ken Gelder, ed., *The Horror Reader.* London: Routledge, 2000, 198–209.

Christie, Deborah G. "Flickering Nitrate: the Cinematic Vampire as Social Other in *Nosferatu*," in Nadine Farghaly, ed., *Beyond the Night: Creatures of Life, Death and the In-Between.* Newcastle upon Tyne: Cambridge Scholars Publishing, 2015), 265–82.

Clover, Carol J. *Men, Women and Chain Saws: Gender in the Modern Horror Film.* Princeton: Princeton University Press, 1992.

Colman, Penny. *Rosie the Riveter: Women Working on the Homefront in World War II.* New York: Crown Publishers, 1998.

Craft, Christopher. *Another Kind of Love: Male Homosexual Desire in English Discourse 1850–1920.* Berkeley: University of California Press, 1994.

Crandall, Nadia. "Cyberfiction and the Gothic Novel," in Anna Jackson, Karen Coats, and Roderick McGillis, eds, *The Gothic in Children's Literature: Haunting the Borders.* London: Routledge, 2013.

Crow, David. "Explaining The Witch Ending," *Den of Geek*, 1 October 2016, http://www.denofgeek.com/us/movies/the-witch/253108/explaining-the-witch-ending, accessed, 14 July 2017.

Dearden, Lizzie. "How Isis Attracts Women and Girls from Europe with False Offer of "empowerment," *The Independent*, 5 August 2017, http://www.independent.co.uk/news/world/europe/isis-jihadi-brides-islamic-state-women-girls-europe-british-radicalisation-recruitment-report-a7878681.html, accessed 28 October 2018.

Del Toro, Guillermo, and Chuck Hogan. *The Fall.* London: Harper, 2010.

_____. *The Night Eternal.* London: Harper, 2011.

_____. *The Strain.* London: Harper, 2009.

Dick, Bernard F. *The Star-Spangled Screen: The American World War II Film*. Lexington: the University Press of Kentucky, 1985.

Donald, Ralph. "America's 'Great Satan' Then and Now," *American Studues Resources Centre*, 20 Feb 2014, http://www.americansc.org.uk/Online/Great_Satan.htm, accessed 28 October 2014.

Duda, Heather. *The Monster Hunter in Modern Popular Culture*. Jefferson, NC: McFarland, 2008.

Du Maurier, George. *Trilby* [1894]. Oxford: Oxford World's Classics, 2009.

Dyer, Colin. "Mind the Gap: the Boom and Bust of the London Office Market, 1970–1976," *JLL*, 2016, https://www.jll.com/cities-research/Documents/WEF-case-study/WEF_JLL_London_Case_Study_Jan16.pdf, accessed 28 October 2018.

Eighteen-Bisang, Robert and Elizabeth Miller. *Bram Stoker's Notes for Dracula: A Facsimile Edition*. Jefferson, NC: McFarland, 2008.

Faulkner, Joanne. *The Importance of Being Innocent: Why We Worry About Children*. Cambridge: Cambridge University Press, 2010.

Foucault, Michel. *The Spectacle of the Scaffold*. London: Penguin, 2006.

Frayling, Christopher. *Mad, Bad and Dangerous? The Scientist and Cinema*. London: Reaktion Books, 2013.

Freeland, Cynthia A. *The Naked and the Undead: Evil and the Appeal of Horror* [2000]. New York: Routledge, 2009.

Gaia Staff. "The CIA's Operation Paperclip Hired Nazi Party Scientists During the Cold War," *Gaia*, 15 August 2017, https://www.gaia.com/lp/content/operation-paperclip/, accessed 28 October 2018.

Gelder, Ken. *New Vampire Cinema*. London: Palgrave Macmillan, 2012.

Gerard, Emily. *The Land Beyond the Forest: Facts, Figures and Fancies from Transylvania*. New York: Harper and Brothers, 1888.

Gibson, Matthew. *Dracula and the Eastern Question: British and French Vampire Narratives of the Nineteenth Century Near East*. London: Palgrave Macmillan, 2006.

Giroux, Henry A. "Stealing Innocence: the Oolitics of Child Brauty Pageants," in Henry Jenkins, ed., *The Children's Culture Reader*. New York: New York University Press, 1998, 265–82.

Golub, Adam. "Locating Monsters: Space, Place and Geographies," in Adam Golub and Heather Richardson-Hayton, eds, *Monsters in the Classroom: Essays on Teaching What Scares Us*. Jefferson, NC: McFarland, 2017.

Goodwin, Doris. "The Way We Won: America's Economic Breakthrough During World War II," *The American Prospect*, Fall 1992, http://prospect.org/article/way-we-won-americas-economic-breakthrough-during-world-war-ii, accessed 28 October 2018.

Graham, Paul. "The Refragmentation," *paulgraham.com*, January 2016, http://paulgraham.com/re.html, accessed 28 October 2018.

Halberstam, Judith. 'Technologies of Monstrosity: Bram Stoker's Dracula,' *Victorian Studies*, 36/3 Victorian Sexualities, 1993, 333–52.

Hallub, Mary Y. *Vampire God: The Allure of the Undead in Western Culture*. Albany: State University of New York Press, 2009.

"Hannibal, Foreign Actors (to Americans), Accent and Xenophobia," *About*, 12 March 2013, https://obsessingaboutinterestingpeople.wordpress.com/2013/04/12/hannibal-foreign-actors-to-americans-accent-and-xenophobia/, accessed 28 October 2018.

Hassan Hosseini-Kaladjahi and Melissa Kelly. "SWEDEN Iv. Iranian Community," *Encyclopedia Iranica*, 8 March 2012, http://www.iranicaonline.org/articles/sweden-iv, accessed 29 October 2018.

Höglund, Johan. "Militarizing the Vampire: Underworld and the Desire of the Military

Entertainment Complex," in Takish Khair and Johan Höglund, eds, *Transnational and Postcolonial Vampires: Dark Blood*. New York: Palgrave Macmillan, 2012, 173–88.

Holmes, Adam. "It's Been One Year Since the Dark Universe Was Announced, So What Happened?" *Cinemablend*, June 2018, https://www.cinemablend.com/news/2423971/its-been-one-year-since-the-dark-universe-was-announced-so-what-happened, accessed 28 October 2018.

Holte, James Craig. *Dracula in the Dark: The Dracula Film Adaptations*. Westport, CT: Greenwood Press, 1997.

Horace, Jan-Christopher. "Tough Enough: Blaxploitation and the L.A. Rebellion," in Allyson Fielding, Jan-Christopher Horak and Jacqueline Najuma Stewart eds., *Rebellion: Creating a New Black Cinema*. Berkeley: University of California Press, 2015, 119–55.

Jackson, Kevin. *Nosferatu (1922): Eine Symphonie Des Grauens*. London: BFI Film Classics, 2017.

Janzen, Janet. *Media, Modernity and Dynamic Plants in Early 20th Century German Culture*. Boston: Brill, 2016.

Jensen, Gary. *The Path of the Devil: Early Modern Witch Hunts*. Lanham, MD: Rowman & Littlefield, 2007.

Jódar, Andrés Romero. "Bram Stoker's Dracula. a Study on the Human Mind and Paranoid Behaviour," *ATLANTIS, Journal of the Spanish Association of Anglo-American Studies*, 31.2 (December 2009), 23–39.

Johnson, Paul. "Adapting to New Spaces: Swords and Planets and the Neo-Peplum," in Nicholas Diak, ed., *The New Peplum: Essays on Sword and Sandal Films and Television Programs Since the 1990s*. Jefferson, NC: McFarland, 2017, 21–43.

Jones, Bethan. "Buffy Vs. Bella: Gender, Relationships and the Modern Vampire," in Deborah Mutch, ed., *The Modern Vampire and Human Identity*. London: Palgrave Macmillan, 2012, 37–54.

Jones, Ernest. *On the Nightmare*. London: Hogarth Press, 1931.

Kaes, Anton. *Shell Shock Cinema: Weimar Culture and the Wounds of War*. Princeton: Princeton University Press, 2011

Khair, Tabish. *The Gothic, Postcolonislism and Otherness: Ghosts from Elsewhere*. London: Palgrave Macmillan, 2009.

Kincaid, James R. *Child-Loving: The Erotic Child and Victorian Culture*. New York: Routledge, 1992.

King, Helen. "Once Upon a Text: Hysteria from Hippocrates," in Sander L. Gilman, Helen King, Roy Porter, G. S. Rousseau, and Elaine Showalter eds., *Hysteria Beyond Freud*. Berkeley: University of California Press, 1993, 3–90.

Kirkland, Ewan. "Racial Whiteness and *Twilight*," in Wickham Clayton and Sarah Harman, eds., *Screening Twilight: Critical Approaches to a Cinematic Phenomenon*. London: I. B. Tauris, 2012, 151–63.

Kurtlander, Eric. *Hitler's Monsters: A Supernatural History of the Third Reich*. New Haven, CT: Yale University Press, 2017.

Lapham, David, Guillero del Toro, Chuck Hogan. *The Strain Trilogy*. Milwaukee: Dark Horse Comics, 2011–15.

Le Fanu, Sheridan. *Carmilla* [1872]. Maryland: Wildside Press, 2005.

Ledger, Sally, and Scott McCracken. *Cultural Politics at the Fin de Siècle*. Cambridge: Cambridge University Press, 1995.

Leese, Peter. *Shell Shock: Traumatic Neurosis and the British Soldiers of the First World War*. London: Palgrave Macmillan, 2002.

Lennig, Arthur. *The Immortal Count: The Life and Films of Bela Lugosi*. Lexington: University Press of Kentucky, 2003.

Lindquist, Malinda Alaine. *Race, Social Science and the Crisis of Manhood, 1890–1970: We Are the Supermen*. London: Routledge, 2012.

Lindqvist, John Ajvide. *Let the Right One in (Låt Den Rätte Komma In)* [2005], trans. Ebba Segerberg. New York: St. Martins Giffen, 2008.

_____. *Let the Old Dreams Die and Other Stories* [2011], trans. Marlene Delargy. London: Quercus, 2012.

Malchow, Harold L. *Gothic Images of Race in Nineteenth-Century Britain*. Stanford: Stanford University Press, 1996.

Marryat, Florence. *Blood of the Vampire* [1897]. Brighton: Victorian Secrets, 2010.

Matheson, Richard. *I Am Legend* [1954]. London: Gollanz, 2007.

_____. *The Shrinking Man,* [1956]. London: Gollanz, 2002.

McClellend, Bruce. *Slayers and Their Vampires: A Cultural History of Killing the Undead*. Ann Arbor: University of Michigan Press, 2006.

McConnell, Donna. "Revealed: Bella Swan's Stunning $35,000 Twilight Wedding Dress Unveiled (and Doesn't It Look Familiar)," *Mailonline*, 28 November 2011, http://www.dailymail.co.uk/tvshowbiz/article-2067211/Twilight-Breaking-Dawn-Bella-Swans-stunning-Twilight-wedding-dress-doesnt-look-familiar.html, accessed 28 October 2018.

McGuire, London. "Fashion and Food According to Dr. Hannibal Lecter," *Criminalelement.com*, 25 October 2013, http://www.criminalelement.com/blogs/2013/10/fashion-and-food-according-to-dr-hannibal-lecter, 28 October 2018.

McMahon-Coleman, Kimberley, and Roslyn Weaver. *Werewolves and Other Shapeshifters in Popular Culture*. Jefferson, NC: McFarland, 2014, 101.

McNally, Raymond T., and Radu Florescu. *In Search of Dracula: The History of Dracula and Vampires*. Boston: Houghton Mifflin Company, 1994.

Means Coleman, Robin R. *Horror Noire: Blacks in American Horror Films from the 1890s to Present*. New York: Routledge, 2011.

The Medieval Bestiary. "Beast Index," 1 February 2012, http://bestiary.ca/beasts/beastalphashort.htm, accessed 14 July 2017.

Medovoi, Leerom. "Theorizing Historicity, or the Many Meanings of Blacula," *Screen*, Volume 39, Issue 1 (March 1998), 1–21.

Meehan, Paul. *The Vampire in Science Fiction a Film and Literature*. Jefferson, NC: McFarland, 2014.

Meyer, Stephenie. *Breaking Dawn*. London: Atom Books, 2008.

_____. *Eclipse*. London: Atom, 2007.

_____. *New Moon*. London: Atom Books, 2006.

_____. *Twilight*. London: Atom Books, 2005.

Micale, Mark S. *Hysterical Men: The Hidden History of Male Nervous Illness*. Cambridge, MA: Harvard University Press, 2008.

Miller, Cynthia J., and A. Bowdain Van Ripper. "Introduction," in Cynthia J. Miller and A. Bowdain Van Ripper, eds., *Undead in the West: Vampires, Mummies, Zombies, and Ghosts on the Cinematic Frontier* [2012]. Lanham, MD: Rowman & Littlefield, 2013, xi–xxvi.

Miller, Liz Shannon, Zack Sharf, Hanh Nguyen, Ben Travers, and Steve Greene. "The 25 Best TV Love Stories of the Last 25 Years," *IndieWire*, 17 October 2017, https://www.indiewire.com/2017/10/best-tv-love-stories-x-files-buffy-friends-1201888069/2/, accessed 28 October 2018.

Mitzeliotis, Katrina. "You Can Now Buy Bella's Breaking Dawn Wedding Shoes: Here's How," *Hollywood Life*, 13 December 2011, http://hollywoodlife.com/2011/12/13/bellas-breaking-dawn-wedding-shoes-manolo-blahnik-where-to-buy, accessed 28 October 2018.

Moretti, Franco. *Signs Taken for Wonders: Essays in the Sociology of Literary Forms,* trans. by Susan Fiscer, David Forgacs and David Miller. London: Verso, 1988.
Neely, Clare Thomas. *Distracted Subjects: Madness and Gender in Shakespeare and Early Modern Theatre.* Ithaca, NY: Cornell University Press, 2004.
Newitz, Annalee. "Dracula Gets a Makeover for the ISIS Age in *Dracula Untold,*" *Gizmodo,* 10 October 2014, https://io9.gizmodo.com/dracula-gets-a-makeover-for-the-isis-age-in-dracula-unt-1644837610, accessed 28 October 2018.
O'Brien, Daniel. *Black Masculinity on Film: Native Sons and White Lies.* New York: Springer, 2017.
"On This Day: March," *BBC,* 15 March 1974, http://news.bbc.co.uk/onthisday/hi/dates/stories/march/15/newsid_4223000/4223045.stm, accessed 28 October 2018.
Poole, W. Scott. *Vampira: Dark Goddess of Horror.* Berkeley: Soft Skull Press, 2014.
Porteous, Jordan. "How the New Hannibal Lector Became the Best-Dressed Man on TV," *Esquire,* 15 May 2013, http://www.esquire.co.uk/culture/film/news/a3899/hannibals-style-mads-mikkelsen/, accessed 28 October 2018.
Porter, Roy. *Mind-Forg'd Manacles: A History of Madness in England from the Restoration to the Regency.* London: Athlone Press, 1987.
Pulliam, June M., and Anthony J. Fonseca. *Richard Matheson's Monsters: Gender in the Stories, Scripts, Novels, and Twilight Zone Episodes.* Lanham, MD: Rowman & Littlefield, 2016.
Ransom, Amy J. *I Am Legend as American Myth: Race and Masculinity in the Novel and Its Film Adaptations.* Jefferson, NC: McFarland, 2018.
Schneider, Franziska. "From Bullerby to Blackeberg: Gothic Thenes and National Settings in the Writings of John Ajvide Lindqvist," in Ellen Reading and Christian Schneider, eds., *Gothic Transgressions: Extension and Commercialization of a Cultural Mode.* Vienna: Lit Verlang, 2015, 103–18.
Scivally, Bruce. *Dracula FAQ: All That's Left to Know About the Count from Transylvania.* Milwaukee: Backbeat Books, 2015.
Senf, Carol, A. "*Dracula*: Stoker's Response to the New Woman," *Victorian Studies,* Vol. 26, No. 1 (Autumn, 1982), 33–49.
_____. *The Vampire in Nineteenth Century English Literature.* Madison: University of Wisconsin Press, 1988.
Shannonjeanna. "The Problematic Treatment of People of Color on the Vampire Diaries," *Rebel with a Cause,* 17 July 2015, https://shannonjeanna.wordpress.com/2015/07/17/the-problematic-treatment-of-people-of-color-on-the-vampire-diaries/, accessed 28 October 2018.
Shapira, A.J. "Stylishly Executed—The Clothes of Hannibal & How to Dress Like Lector," *Gentlemen's Gazette,* 15 September 2015, https://www.gentlemansgazette.com/suits-hannibal-lecter-how-to-style/, accessed 28 October 2018.
Sharrett, Christopher. "The Horror Film in Nonconservative Culture," in Barry Keith Grant, ed., *The Dread of Difference: Gender and the Horror Film* [1996]. Austin: University of Texas Press, 2015.
Showalter, Elaine. "Male Hysteria," in *The Female Malady: Women, Madness and English Culture 1830–1980.* London: Virago, 2009, 167–194.
_____. *Sexual Anarchy: Gender and Culture at the Fin de Siècle.* London: Virago, 1992.
Simmons, Dan. *The Children of the Night* [1992]. New York: St. Martin's Press, 2012.
Skal, David. *Dracula: The Ultimate Edition of the World-Famous Vampire Play.* New York: St. Martin's Press, 1993.
Snyder, Scott, and Stephen King. *American Vampire* [issues 1–5]. New York: Vertigo, 2010.
Soule, George. "Profits by the Billion," *The New Republic,* 7 January 1946., https://newrepublic.com/article/93520/profits-the-billion, accessed 28 October 2018.

Spadoni, Robert. *Uncanny Bodies: The Coming of Sound Film and the Origins of the Horror Genre*. Berkeley: University of California Press, 2007.

Steinmeyer, Jim. *Who Was Dracula? Bram Stoker's Trail of Blood*. New York: Penguin, 2013.

Stevenson, Robert Louis. *Strange Case of Dr. Jekyll and Mr. Hyde*. New York: Charles Scribner's Sons, 1886.

Stoker, Bram. *Dracula* [1897]. London: Signet Classics, 1996.

_____. *The Lady of the Shroud*, from *The Journal of Occultism* (Mid-January 1907), Bramstoker.org, http://www.bramstoker.org/pdf/novels/11shroud.pdf, accessed 28 October 2018.

Stoker, Dacre, and Ian Holt. *Dracula: The Undead*. New York: Berkeley, 2009.

Suzuki, Kôji. *Ring*. Tokyo: Kadokawa Shoten, Vertical, 1991.

Treptow, Kurt W. *Vlad III Dracula: The Life and Times of the Historical Dracula*. Iasi: Center for Romanian Studies, 2000.

"Twilight Wedding Songs," *Wedding Music Help.*, http://www.wedding-music-help.com/twilightweddingsongs.html, accessed 28 October 2018.

Valente, Joseph. *Dracula's Crypt: Bram Stoker, Irishness, and the Question of Blood*. Urbana: University of Illinois Press, 2002.

Waller, Gregory A. *The Living and the Undead: Slaying Vampires, Exterminating Zombies*. Urbana: University of Illinois Press, 2010.

Weinstock, Jeffrey. *The Vampire Film: Undead Cinema*. London: Wallflower, 2012.

Wells, H G. *The Invisible Man* [1897]. New York: Oxford University Press, 1996.

_____, *War of the Worlds* [1897]. London: Penguin, 2018.

"What Was the Second Wave Feminist Movement?," *Daily History*, 7 November 2016, https://dailyhistory.org/What_was_the_Second_Wave_Feminist_Movement%3F, accessed 28 October 2018.

Wicke, Jennifer. "Vampiric Typewriting: Dracula and Its Media," *ELH* 59/2 (Summer, 1992), 467–493.

Wickman, Forrest. "All the Witch's Most WTF Moments, Explained: a Spoiler-Filled Interview with the Director." *Slate*, Slate.com. 23 February 2016, http://www.slate.com/blogs/browbeat/2017/07/18/george_romero_s_movies_were_about_more_than_zombies.html, accessed 28 October 2018.

Wilson, Paige A., Melissa Goldsmith, and Anthony J. Fonseca. "Alienation, Essentialism, and Existentialism Through Technique: an Analysis of Set Design, Lighting, Costume, and Music in *Dracula's Daughter* and *Nadja*," in Douglas Brode and Leah Deyneka eds., *Dracula's Daughters: The Female Vampire on Film*. Lanham, MD: Scarecrow Press, 2014, 45–68.

Winthrop-Young, Geoffrey. "Undead Networks: Information Processing and Media Boundary Conflicts in Dracula," in Donald Bruce and Anthony George Purdy, eds., *Literature and Science*. Amsterdam: Rodopi, 1994) 107–30.

Wittgenstein, Ludwig. *Tractatus Logico-Philosophicus*. London: Routledge & Kegan Paul, 1922.

Index

Numbers in **_bold italics_** indicate pages with illustrations.

Abbot and Costello Meet Frankenstein **147**
abject 1, 29, 30, 34, 36, 49, 84, 132, 133
absolute other 1, 2, 4, 15, 17, 22, 24, 29, 35, 42, 43, 47, 49, 62, 65, 66, 68, 72, 74, 76, 77, 88, 98–9, 101, 112–3, 114, 115, 116, 118, 121–2, 126, 128, 131–2, 136–7, 141, 142, 143, 145, 148–9, 150, 158, 161, 165, 166, 168, 171, 172
Africa 6, 22–6, 28, 181
African-American 6, 22, 25, 27, 63, 65–6, 81, 181, 184
Alfredson, Tomas **39**
Allbritton, Louise **83**
Almereyda, Michael **31**
America 1, 6, 7–9, 15–6, 18, 20–1, 22, 24, 29, 41, 43–4, 55–6, 59, 61–7, 75, 76, 77, 80–6, 100, 131, 137, 139, 146, 148, 162, 166, 172
anti-Semitism 7, 18, 42, 43, 48–9, 51
aristocracy 3, 6, 9, 16, 17, 28, 55, 56, 61, 60, 86, 99, 117, 126, 179, 186
Aubert, Lenore **147**

Bara, Theda **156**
Barton, Charles **147**
bat 17, 18, 43, 49, 56, 58, 61, 74, 81, 84, 85, 92, 97, 109, 121, 134, 135, 144, 146, 148, 159; bat-like 29, 92
Bathory, Elizabeth 108
battle 19, 53, 72, 84, 86, 109, 117, 123, 127, 131, 132, 133, 134, 135, 148, 179
Benjamin, Richard **60**
birth 24, 30, 56, 98, 102, 147, 159, 160, 167; *see also* rebirth
Blacula 6, 22–8, **26**, 56, 58, 65, 76, 99
Blade **127**
blood 8, 9, 12, 17, 18, 20, 23, 24, 27, 33–5, 36, 38, 42, 43–4, 49, 50, 52, 53, 55, 56, 70, 75, 76, 77, 78, 89, 91, 92, 93, 95, 97–8, 99, 102, 107–8, 112, 121, 127, 128, 129, 131, 132, 134, 138, 139, 140, 144, 145, 148, 151–2, 155, 157, 158–9, 167, 168; abstain 98, 99, 101, 165;
menstrual 32, 33, 113; transfusion 12, 33, 68, 120, 188
bloodthirsty 3, 31, 62, 84, 123–6, 137, 161, 165
Bram Stoker's Dracula (Coppola, 1994) 74, 76, 99
bride 1, 8, 10, 17, 18, 20, 22, 56, 69, 75, 77, 84, 101, 105, 106, 109, 113, 117, 120, 121, 132, 133, 139, 152, 159, 168, 169, 172, 184, 187, 188
Browning, Tod **19**

Caldwell, Kay 9, 20, 80, 86, 99, 115
capitalism 2, 69, 81, 86, 88, 94, 144, 163, 168
Carmilla 30, 34, 182
castle (Dracula) 8, 10, 16, 17, 22–3, 25, 29, 33, 38, 50, 54–5, 81, 82, 86, 93, 94, 95, 99, 112–4, 115, 116, 126, 130, 133–4, 139, 143, 145, 148, 149, 158–60, 161, 168, 169, 181, 184, 186
Chaney, Lon, Jr. **83**
children 7, 8, 33, 34, 36, 38, 40, 42, 44, 63, 64, 73, 75, 76, 102, 109, 115, 119, 131, 133, 135, 154, 167, 168, 190; monstrous 35, 36, 37, 39, 182, 183
city 9, 29–30, 32, 33, 40, 42–3, 45–6, 57, 93–4, 95, 97, 119, 120, 125–6, 152, 154, 156, 172, 182, 189, 193
Cold War 8, 54, 55, 87, 162, 184, 188
colonialism 1, 6, 21, 104; postcolonialism 21, 89, 104; reverse 2, 7
consume 8, 9, 18, 44, 53, 67, 69, 73, 88, 90, 92, 104, 106, 109–110, 144, 151, 155, 163, 172
consumerism 6, 7, 9–10, 43, 47, 56, 80, 88–9, 90, 91, 93–8, 100, 101–4, 105–7, 108, 110, 144, 153, 155, 158, 166, 187, 190, 193
contagion 37, 43, 45, 54, 57, 126, 140, 152–3, 155, 156, 157, 159, 160, 166
Cooper, Dominic **135**
corruption 17, 20, 27, 36, 37, 42, 43, 44, 46, 49–50, 53, 54, 57, 69, 77, 88, 134, 157, 183
Crain, William **26**
curse 23–4, 130, 137–8, 148, 166, 193

203

Index

Dancy, Hugh **71**
Dawson, Lucas **75**
Daybreakers **93**
decadence 3, 56, 77, 83, 106, 126
De Gouw, Jessica **164**
del Toro, Guillermo **44**
demon 2, 49, 132, 133, 190
devil 55, 74, 75, 86, 89, 130, 180, 185, 190
distracted/distracting 1, 3–5, 7, 8, 10–3, 20, 21, 25, 27–8, 32, 33–4, 37–8, 40, 43, 52, 57, 72, 73, 76, 85, 89, 95, 109, 110, 111, 114, 116, 118, 122, 135, 137, 153, 160, 170, 172, 173
Dracula (Badham, 1979) 10, 72, 98, 155, 167
Dracula (Balderston/Deane stage play) 17, 45, 184
Dracula (Browning, 1931) 6, 15–22, **19**, 30, 37, 61, 68, 69, 131, 132–3, 144, 148, 155, 172
Dracula (Fisher, 1958) **116**
Dracula (Haddon/Knauff, 2014) **164**
Dracula (novel) 1, 3, 6, 7, 11, 13, 31, 34–5, 41, 45, 49, 50, 59, 61, 63, 67, 71, 72, 74, 75, 84, 92, 94, 95, 96, 98, 99, 101, 105, 108, 109, 112, 113, 120, 121, 122, 123, 130, 137, 143, 151–2, 159, 161, 168, 170, 172
Dracula Untold (Shore, 2014) 99, 129–36, **135**, 141
Dracula's Daughter 20, 28, 30, 83, 105, 144, 181
Dragotti, Stan **60**

economics 39, 86, 91, 101, 125, 150
ecosystem 101, 106, 191
Eggers, Robert **75**
election 41, 46
electricity 12, 145, 149, 160, 163, 164, 165
elements 49, 53, 74, 146, 151, 191
eroticism 12, 89, 127, 140, 155, 179
Europe 3, 6, 11, 16, 20, 21, 22, 37, 49, 58, 61, 62, 66–7, 76, 80–2, 84, 86, 100, 129, 132–3, 135, 136, 145, 146, 162, 179, 181, 185, 186, 192; Eastern 8, 15, 41, 55, 67, 112, 130, 157
evil 2, 41, 54, 55, 65, 74, 76, 82, 84, 88, 105, 118, 132, 136, 141, 173, 179
Ex Machina **171**
extremism 7, 8, 11, 48, 61, 73, 76–9, 133, 134, 136, 193
exploitation 9, 23, 36, 55, 92, 106, 150, 162, 166, 170, 185, 190

femininity 33, 34, 72, 100, 116, 152, 172, 173, 192
feminism 29, 30, 60, 167, 184
feminization 10, 20, 70, 71, 113, 114, 116, 117, 119, 133
Fonda, Peter **31**
A Fool There Was **156**
forest 2, 7, 13, 17, 39, 48, 73, 77, 78, 105, 113, 141, 168, 179, 185
Frankenstein's monster 12, 54, 144, 145, 148, 149, 163, 186, 190
Frye, Dwight **19**
Fuller, Bryan **71**
future 8, 9, 13, 23, 25, 26, 36, 37, 40, 46, 49, 50, 56, 59, 77, 82, 84, 85, 86, 96, 104, 106, 121, 122, 132–3, 135, 136, 142, 149, 157, 168, 174, 187, 192

Garland, Alex **171**
gender 10, 30, 71, 81, 126, 156, 172, 173, 174, 194
glamor 5, 139, 148, 167
gothic 17, 23, 117, 149, 169, 193
Grainger, Ellie **75**
grooming 8, 76–7, 134, 170, 182, 193

Haddon, Cole **164**
Hannibal **71**
Hardwicke, Katherine **99**
Harker, Jonathan 2, 3, 4, 10, 16–7, 18, 20, 21, 35, 48, 49, 58, 59, 62, 70, 85, 87, 95–6, 98, 99, 101, 113–4, 117, 121, 133, 143, 153, 161, 167, 169, 172, 187
Harker, Quincey 96, 98, 108, 112, 122, 185, 187
haunt 3, 29, 154
Hedebrant, Kåre **39**
heteronormative 10, 24, 125
history 2, 3, 5, 6, 7, 15, 16, 30–4, 40, 43, 45–6, 59, 65, 86, 89, 121, 181, 190
Hogan, Chuck **44**
Holmwood, Arthur 5, 10, 16, 41, 95, 117, 133, 152, 179
Holt, Claire **141**
home 5, 8, 16, 30, 31, 32, 35, 37, 38, 40, 42, 54, 55, 62, 66, 72, 77–8, 81–2, 92, 93, 94, 100, 113, 114, 117, 120, 122, 143, 144, 146, 157, 158, 181, 186; land 22, 50, 62, 73, 86, 183, 186, 191
homosexuality 3, 24, 116, 119, 189
hybrid 37, 59, 68, 95–7, 109, 119, 120–2, 123–4, 127, 128, 136, 137–8
hypnotism 5, 49, 70, 89
hysteria 19, 20, 70–1

identity 3, 4–6, 10, 11, 13, 32, 34, 60, 61, 62, 66, 72, 79, 81, 102, 105, 106, 109, 120, 124, 151, 160, 164, 191, 193; divided 21, 73
immigrant 2, 7, 8, 16, 36, 37, 44, 112, 182
immigration 2, 36
imperialism 2, 23, 66
industrialization 2, 94, 181
innocence 36, 42, 43, 50, 76, 90, 131, 152, 190

Jewish 2, 8, 16, 49–52, 59, 62, 65–6, 183, 184
Jones, Doug **44**
José, Edward **156**
Jupiter Ascending **107**

killers 36, 63, 66, 67, 70, 72, 84, 113, 118, 119; serial 8, 11, 68–9
Knauff, Daniel **164**

The Last Man on Earth **123**
Let the Right One In **39**
London 2, 4, 7, 9, 12, 29, 31, 45, 48, 58, 63, 86, 87–8, 90, 112, 135, 154, 162–3, 168, 179, 190

Index

Los Angeles 6, 22, 24, 27, 61, 62, 63, 65, 125
Love at First Bite 60
Lugosi, Bela 6, 8, 12, 15–6, 22, 23, 33, 55, 67, 68, 74, 82, 144, 146, 148, 163, 179, 180, 192

Marsh, Carol 116
Marshall, William 26
Matheson, Richard 91, 92, 96, 118–20, 122, 145, 149, 150, 151, 174, 180, 188, 189, 192
McGee, Vonetta 26
media 12, 41, 76, 144, 154, 160, 193
medical 12, 65, 70, 90, 96, 129, 144, 146–7, 148, 150, 153–6, 159, 166–7, 180, 187, 189, 191
memory 9, 20, 24, 27, 31, 39, 64, 81, 108, 122, 144, 169; undead 10, 18, 56
Meyers, Jonathan Rhys 164
Mikkelsen, Mads 71
Mina (Wilhelmina Harker) 3, 10, 11, 17, 20–1, 25, 31, 35, 41, 52, 56, 57, 59, 64, 68, 69–71, 73, 76, 96, 98, 105, 108, 112, 114, 120, 126, 133, 138, 144, 151, 152, 153, 155, 161, 163, 164, 166–7, 170, 180, 181, 184, 185, 186, 189
miscegenation 24, 126, 179
mist 20, 74, 84
modernity 2, 5, 39–40, 143, 144
money 3, 6, 9–10, 18, 22, 44, 50–1, 55, 65, 80, 81–2, 84, 86–8, 91, 99, 100, 102, 125, 135, 162, 179, 186
monstrous 2, 11, 22, 26, 35, 43, 50, 54, 80, 94, 96, 99, 105, 115, 120, 125, 128, 129, 131, 134, 140, 144, 146, 147, 149, 150, 154, 189, 192
Moretti, Franco 3, 9, 69, 81, 100, 113, 144, 163, 191
Morris, Quincey 16, 21, 112, 133, 141, 161, 184, 186, 191
Murnau, F.W. 51

Nadja (Almereyder, 1994) 6, 29–34, *31*, 57, 59, 85, 104–5, 180–1, 182, 184, 193
Nazism 7, 43, 62, 65, 84, 144, 146, 186
neo-liberalism 88, 101
New Woman 10, 59, 84, 155, 161, 66, 186
New York 6, 7, 8, 16, 28–9, 42, 43, 44, 55–8, 59, 63, 160, 182
Norrington, Stephan 127
Nosferatu 1, 7, 8, 10, 48–54, *51*, 143, 153–4, 181, 184

occult 20, 51, 82, 89, 165, 166, 183
oppression 23, 167
Orlok, Count 8, 43, 48–54, 75, 99, 153, 154, 185, 192
otherness 1–3, 5–7, 8, 10, 11, 15, 16–7, 21, 22–4, 27, 29, 30, 32, 35–6, 42, 43, 47, 48, 49, 50, 51, 54, 65–6, 68, 73–4, 76, 88, 94, 98–9, 101, 111, 118, 121–2, 126, 131, 136, 141–2, 148, 150, 158, 161, 163, 166, 168, 170, 174, 179
otherworldly 17, 48, 113, 114, 158, 163, 193

patriarchy 20, 23, 24, 25, 30, 35, 63, 73, 74, 80–2, 85–6, 112, 114–5, 117, 119, 121–2, 132, 138, 147, 152, 154, 155, 179, 181, 188

Pattinson, Robert 99
pedophilia 36, 43
plague 3, 8, 9, 22, 49–50, 52, 87–8, 90–2, 96, 118–9, 122, 127, 152, 183, 187
Plec, Julie 141
Polidori, John 188
politics 41, 44, 49, 56, 125, 170, 184
possess 3–5, 30, 32–4, 81, 89–90, 109, 125, 128, 145, 172, 182
possession 29, 31, 68, 182
Powell, Frank 156
Price, Vincent 123
privilege 3, 89, 101
Probets, Bryan 93

queen 108, 109
queer 3, 173, 189

Rabid 12, 150–6, 157, 165, 168, 169, 192
racism 27, 43, 54, 65, 66, 189
Ragona, Ubaldo 123
railway 37, 40, 88, 93, 143, 144, 145
rats 50, 74, 109, 153
rebirth 33, 53, 160
Redmayne, Eddie 107
Renfield 7, 11, 17–21, 23, 29, 35, 37, 41, 43–4, 48, 50, 55, 58, 89, 90, 95, 96, 105, 109, 138, 153, 166, 172, 180, 184
resurrection 6, 34, 84, 91, 117, 124, 125, 148, 189
Romania 8, 54–6, 74, 157, 160, 184
Russia 2, 16, 49, 55, 130

Salkow, Sidney 123
Satan 8, 9, 55, 74, 76, 78, 87–8, 92, 133, 185
Schreck, Max 51
science 2, 11, 12, 28, 89, 90, 123, 125, 143–6, 148–50, 153–6, 159, 161, 163, 165–7, 188, 192
Seward, John 5, 17, 20, 35, 41, 72, 90, 95, 133, 143, 144, 149, 180,
sexuality 3, 10, 12, 17, 22, 35, 43, 56, 64, 79, 113, 116, 119, 127, 133, 137, 140, 151–6, 172–3, 182, 190
Shore, Gary 135
Siodmak, Robert 83
slayer 45, 62, 92, 111, 117, 119, 123, 126, 128, 183, 189
Snipes, Wesley 127
soil 38, 41, 81, 83, 84, 181, 182, 183
Somerhalder, Ian 141
The Son of Dracula 83
sparkly 41, 99, 100
specter 27, 122, 148
the Spierig Brothers 93
spiritual 49, 52, 53, 100, 121, 124
Stoker, Bram 1–5, 7–8, 10–3, 16, 18, 21, 29, 31, 34, 38, 41, 45, 48–50, 52, 57, 59, 61, 63–5, 67, 70–5, 79, 82, 84, 86–7, 90, 92, 95, 98–101, 104, 107–9, 111–2, 117–8, 121–3, 126, 129, 130, 132–3, 136–9, 143–4, 149–51, 154–

5, 158–9, 161, 163, 166, 167–70, 172, 179, 180, 181, 183, 185, 187, 188, 191
The Strain **44**
supernatural 2, 8, 12–3, 52, 73, 79, 87, 111–2, 114–6, 122, 129, 136, 138–40, 145–50, 153, 155, 157, 160, 163–6, 193

technology 2, 6, 11–3, 45–6, 91–2, 123–6, 128–9, 142, 143–5, 150, 154–9, 161–74, 181, 189, 192, 193
television 12, 40, 42, 45–6, 67, 142, 158–61, 164, 179, 182, 183, 187, 191
terror 7, 8, 43, 101, 136, 138, 193
terrorism 43, 69, 73, 78
torture 11, 20, 43, 110, 129, 137–42, 188
transgressive 1, 3, 10, 17, 36, 79, 80, 82, 113, 116, 119, 122, 132, 172, 185
Transylvania 22, 29, 32, 34, 49, 50, 54, 56–7, 61, 67, 80, 86, 105, 107, 130, 143, 158, 180, 181, 183, 185
trauma 3, 6–7, 15, 16, 18–28, 30–4, 39–43, 46, 64, 102, 111, 118–9, 124, 135, 142, 181, 183
trouble 1, 3–7, 9, 17–21, 25–6, 30, 32, 34, 37, 40, 43–6, 48, 50, 52, 54, 57–8, 60–1, 63, 65–6, 69–73, 77, 79–80, 82, 84, 89–90, 92, 93–7, 101, 103–4, 105, 109–10, 116–8, 120–1, 124–5, 128–9, 135, 137–41, 146–9, 153–4, 151, 158, 160, 165–7, 170, 172, 187
Trump, Donald 8, 41, 44, 64, 66, 193
Twilight **99**

undead 5, 6, 7, 8, 9, 10, 12, 15, 16, 18, 20, 22–3, 27, 28, 30, 33, 36, 39, 40, 42–3, 58, 61, 62, 64–5, 68, 75, 80–1, 84, 86, 88, 90–3, 96–8, 99, 101–2, 111, 118, 120, 124, 128, 130, 142, 144, 146, 150, 155, 163, 166, 173, 180, 181, 185, 187, 189, 193
urban 29, 189

The Vampire Diaries **141**
Van Helsing, Abraham 2, 7, 11, 15, 20–1, 25–7, 29–34, 38, 41, 52, 56, 58–9, 61–3, 65–6, 69, 71, 75, 84, 87, 89–91, 98, 111, 114–5, 117–8, 121, 124, 129, 132, 149, 155, 161–3, 165–8, 170, 179, 182, 184, 186, 188
Van Sloan, Edward **19**
vegetarian 41, 97, 100, 125
Vikander, Alicia **171**
violence 8, 9–11, 23–4, 25, 30, 32, 43, 45–6, 79, 102, 110, 111–22, 124, 126–9, 132–3, 135–42, 154, 160, 171, 179, 180, 181, 188
virus 91, 96, 121, 151, 192
Vlad Țepeș 2, 11, 74, 130, 162, 180, 186, 188, 191
voice 6, 15–6, 29, 32, 67–8, 76, 108, 117, 119, 144, 149, 160, 191

the Wachowskis **107**
war on terror 7, 43, 48, 193
wealth 3, 9, 12, 18, 39, 40, 49, 50, 51, 55, 59, 69, 81–2, 86, 88–90, 98–103, 109, 110, 125, 135, 157, 163, 187
werewolf 59, 98, 100, 136–8, 149, 187, 188, 191
Westnra, Lucy 4, 35, 57, 79, 80, 98, 136
whiteness 6, 20, 23–4, 27–8, 39, 43–4, 63, 65–6, 89, 94, 100, 121, 127, 181, 183, 187, 191
Williamson, Kevin **141**
witch 8, 68, 73–9, 111, 136, 137, 147, 185
The Witch **75**
wolf 42, 74, 76, 109, 146, 185, 186, 190, 191, 192
World War I 6, 8, 16, 18, 19, 21, 49, 50–1, 54, 71, 183
World War II 9, 12, 42, 61–2, 65, 80, 86, 144, 146, 148, 153, 179

zombie 11, 81, 91, 118, 150, 152, 158, 180